CROSSING THE GREAT DIVIDE

Crossing the Great Divide

Worker Risk and Opportunity in the New Economy

Vicki Smith

ILR Press
an imprint of
Cornell University Press
Ithaca and London

First published 2001 by Cornell University Press

Printed in the United States of America

Library of Congress Cataloging-in-Publication Data

Smith, Vicki, 1951–
   Crossing the great divide : worker risk and opportunity in the new economy / Vicki Smith.
      p. cm.
Includes bibliographical references and index.
   ISBN 0-8014-3737-7
   1. Labor market—United States. 2. Working class—United States. I. Title.
   HD5724 .S6143 2001
   331.12'0973—dc21

                              00-011936

Cornell University Press strives to use environmentally responsible suppliers and materials to the fullest extent possible in the publishing of its books. Such materials include vegetable-based, low-VOC inks and acid-free papers that are recycled, totally chlorine-free, or partly composed of nonwood fibers. Books that bear the logo of the FSC (Forest Stewardship Council) use paper taken from forests that have been inspected and certified as meeting the highest standards for environmental and social responsibility. For further information, visit our website at www.cornellpress.cornell.edu.

Cloth printing   10   9   8   7   6   5   4   3   2   1

FSC FSC Trademark © 1996 Forest Stewardship Council A.C.
      SW-COC-098

For Steve and Molly

Contents

Acknowledgments

In many respects a tenured academic in a major research university is not ideally positioned to comprehend and interpret employment instability, tenuousness, and personal risk. To the extent that I am able to convey a compelling account of how these conditions have become a routine part of work and employment for many people, I am deeply indebted to the individuals who gave their time to be interviewed, who allowed me to watch and talk with them as they worked, and who gave me permission to enter their plants and offices. This book exists only because of their time, graciousness, curiosity, and ability to articulate their personal understanding of work and employment in ways that reveal larger institutional changes and sociological themes. Their comments eloquently capture the contradictory crosscurrents of economic and organizational change.

Doing this study has made me all the more appreciative of the conditions and the resources that have allowed me to direct my work and pursue my intellectual interests, methodological persuasions, and personal passions. I did the bulk of the research and wrote the manuscript after joining the Department of Sociology at the University of California, Davis. Colleagues in this department and throughout the university have provided a supportive environment for conducting qualitative field research and writing a book. I have benefited from grants from the UCD Committee on Research, as well as from the University of Pennsylvania Research Foundation and the American Sociological Association/National Science Foundation for the Advancement of the Discipline. All were vital to the completion of this book.

The labor of a number of individuals enabled me to search for and review relevant literature and gather archival material. I thank the following people for this assistance: Laura Carpenter, Suzanne Cole, and Raquel Kennedy-Bergen, all at the University of Pennsylvania; Pamela Forman, Jonathan Isler, Anna Muraco, Ellen Scott, and Eva Skuratowicz, all at the University of California, Davis; and Christina Friberg in Montana. I relied on the transcribing skills of Nichole Bennett and Jeni Cross at UC Davis, Bernice Fishman in Georgia, and Deborah Putnam-Thomas in Philadelphia.

Many colleagues, friends, and associates read and commented on the material that ultimately found its way into this book. Taking time to read the in-progress work of fellow scholars is the invisible and usually unrewarded labor behind the creation of a good manuscript. In this case Fred Block, Chuck Bosk, Michael Burawoy, Dan Cornfield, Linda Fuller, Heidi Gottfried, Kevin Henson, Randy Hodson, Carole Joffe, Arne Kalleberg, Demie Kurz, Annette Lareau, Robin Leidner, June McMahon, Mark McMahon, Steve McMahon, Ruth Milkman, Sean O'Riain, Brian Powers, Jackie Krasas Rogers, Chris Tilly, Mike Useem, and Steve Vallas have my great gratitude for posing criticisms and suggesting changes. With any luck, I have managed to use their advice to best effect.

Fran Benson is an editor with a strong vision, and she has helped me move toward that vision with the highest of expectations and with much-appreciated support and humor. Every author should be so lucky as to have an editor like Fran.

Audiences attending my presentations at Rutgers University, Brown University, the University of Pennsylvania, the Sloan Foundation Conference on Workplace Research, the University of California at Berkeley, Northwestern University, Stanford University, and the annual meetings of the American Sociological Association, the Society for the Study of Social Problems, the Society for the Advancement of Socio-Economics, the Eastern Sociological Society, and the Pacific Sociological Association gave me critical feedback which helped me sharpen my ultimate conclusions.

As always, friends and family members patiently endured as I talked about this project over the years, complained about obstacles I ran into in the field, and refused to believe that there was a light at the end of the tunnel. They encouraged me even when I am certain they wondered what I was *really* doing all this time. They include Allison Berry, Cynthia Brantley, Carole Joffe, Anna Kuhn, Ming-cheng Lo, Kari Lokke, Beth

McMahon, Brian McMahon, June McMahon, Mark McMahon, Francesca Miller, Poh Ngau, Brian Powers, Diana Smith, Chris Wee, and Diane Wolf.

I dedicate this book to Molly McMahon, my daughter, but her cousins Brenna McMahon and Erin McMahon, and her surrogate brothers and our neighbors Gregory Wee and Kean Wee, all have lessened much of the dryness of academic life and have connected me to a lively world quite apart from academic schedules, rhythms, and pressures. Brenna, Erin, Greg, Kean, Molly and my nephew Griffin make urgent, for me, the project of striving for work with dignity, as well as humanizing our work institutions and our employment relations, and I wish them the highest level of well-being and integrity in their lives and work in the future.

Anything that I say about Steve McMahon, my husband, for his part in my academic and our family life barely touches my gratitude to him. He has been the anchor in our lives during various stages of my own employment insecurity. When I have despaired about whether I had anything meaningful or important to say he has always reminded me, right or wrong, that there were few other sociological topics more worthy of study. His extraordinary involvement in raising Molly has made it possible for me to devote the time I needed to do research and to write. These were never simply tasks that he *had* to accept as circumstances have demanded. Rather, his care stems from his ongoing commitment to make family, work, and community the best they can possibly be for all of us. This stance on the world informs his personal relationships, his moral beliefs, and his political activism. For these things, I thank him.

CROSSING THE GREAT DIVIDE

1

Work and Employment
at the Turn of the Century

After meeting Mike Daly at a job search workshop for unemployed professional and managerial workers, I interviewed him over lunch at a busy Thai restaurant in Sacramento. Mike was a white man in his early forties who had worked in temporary and contract positions for several years as a computer programmer and data-base manager. Unemployed and searching for "permanent" employment at the time of our interview, he articulated his bafflement about what he was encountering in this urban labor market.

> I have to really search my soul, do whatever I can to make sure that unemployment doesn't happen again. We all hear like it's hard to find a job, but I think if a person looks at what the, um, pundits—or whatever the market researchers are called—I think you'll get conflicting information. I was reading in the paper...about how companies now are looking for employees. They can't find the people they want, and it's so bad that they won't even build plants 'cause they can't find any workers they want. So, this is really weird. And unemployment is supposed to be at an all-time low right now. But then you turn around and you read all these articles about how it's impossible to find work. *The upshot is if you manage your career well it probably won't be a problem if you get downsized. But if you get downsized out, haven't managed your career, it's probably gonna be a real problem.*

Madeline Cox, whom I met at the same workshop, was a forty-six-year-old white woman with a bachelor's degree in environmental science. She had served time in the military and worked in the field of environmen-

1

tal planning, and she had been laid off when the hazardous-waste management company where she worked was bought out by another firm six months earlier. She was immersed in what was becoming an agonizing search for a job in her field when I interviewed her in my university office. After thoughtfully noting that I had something that was increasingly unavailable to most American workers—a private office, with a door that locked, and filled with my private possessions—she said:

> Most of us are facing the prospect we're not gonna make the salary we made before, not gonna have the promotability, we're not gonna have the opportunity. We're on the decline. Age discrimination is real. People are gonna view our experience as a threat. So maybe this is a time…to make radical changes, *but how can you treat this period as a period of opportunity when you don't know where to go?* I mean the buzz word is "change"; everybody knows "change." But what do I change into? Even if I can go back, what do I go to school *for?* Everybody tells me computers are the way to go. Catch a clue. There are a hell of a lot of computer people at (our job search club) unemployed.

Brent Haven, too, expressed his understanding of *his* current job search with an anxiety that mirrored Mike's and Madeline's. Years earlier, Brent, a white man in his forties, had been an officer in the Marine Corps. This was followed by a stint as a fast-food restaurant manager and eight years as a civilian employee at an air-force base which had recently been decommissioned. At the time of our interview he held a temporary position at Packard Bell as a materials procurer and was, perhaps continually, seeking a stable job:

> I'm never going to be able to stop looking for a job. My father worked for his company for over thirty years and retired from there with a pension. I don't think that's going to happen with me. I just don't think that with our generation, so to speak…people who are working now are not going to be able to rely on that kind of employment. *The term "permanent" has become open to quite a bit of interpretation.*

As we enter the twenty-first century, American workers, social scientists, and policy makers are confronted by a bewildering set of changes in the world of work and employment. Downsizing, restructuring, the increased use of contingent labor, together with economic prosperity, progressive work reform, and job creation—all amply documented in the media and in academic studies—have created a wholly new playing field for those who work for wages in the United States.[1]

The uneasy and surprising marriage of prosperity, continual change, business shrinkage, and increasing tenuousness of employment makes it difficult to decipher what is going on in the workplace and in employment relations. Whether in our private conversations with friends and family members about the "facts" of jobs and careers today, or in our readings of academic studies or articles in the press, we find ourselves unable to decode changes that are simultaneously ambiguous, contradictory, and often patently mystifying. Few would dispute the observation that fundamental and complex transformations in the world of work are underway, or that our economy is turbulent, marked by change and unpredictability (Frenkel et al. 1999; Herzenberg, Alic, and Wial 1998; Osterman 1999; Sennett 1998). But although it is clear that what lies ahead will diverge significantly from the experiences and arrangements of the past, our vision of the future is blurry and partial, complicated by overlapping cultural, organizational, and employment innovations.

Accordingly, answers to questions that are central to social scientists who study work, employment, stratification, and mobility are murky and indeterminate. What is happening to our opportunity structure, to authority and power relations? Who benefits from work reform? How do workers perceive change and uncertainty? What risks are they willing to take to get jobs and to position themselves in the restructured economy? Similarly, answers to questions that in retrospect appear to have been comparatively clear and obvious to the general population—How does one get a foothold in the door of a "good" company? How can I know what a good job is? What are the rules for and rewards of "succeeding" in the workplace?—are ambiguous and open-ended. It sometimes appears that the only certainty is uncertainty, that the only trend we can predict is continued unpredictability, and that the only way we can preserve our economic and social well-being is to take a leap of faith onto career ladders that might have missing rungs, on which definitions of opportunity and reward are being contested.

Crossing the Great Divide addresses these issues by untangling the contradictory strands present in the contemporary transformation of jobs and work organizations and weaving them back together into a coherent but variegated whole. Academic studies that rely on surveys to analyze workplaces, interviews with managers only, single organizational case studies, or statistical reports compiled by labor, employment, or polling organizations have yet to break through the surface to discover patterns in the ways our major business institutions are stirring up work and employment. This book journeys to the core—examining people at their jobs in three different companies, as well as people who are looking for work—to explore the complex, subtle, and obvious ways in which uncertainty, risk, and opportunity are playing out in diverse settings and locales.

In part, I am concerned with exploration and discovery because I am convinced that one of the challenges facing social scientists at this point in time is to systematically describe the array of strategies and innovations that are transfiguring workplaces and hiring practices in a postindustrial and shifting economy. Analytically, it is important to examine common and dissimilar threads running across white-collar service occupations and blue-collar industrial or assembly settings, particularly given the ascendance of service jobs and nonunionized production jobs in the U.S. economy. These organizational and cultural changes underwrite our current employment culture, and it is within this context that workers' responses to corporate transformation can be explained. For this reason, it is critical to look at these changes and arrangements through the eyes of the workers participating in them.

Like others, I view contemporary production practices and employment conditions as a distinctive new terrain that differs from the practices, norms, and relationships of the industrial era. What constitutes the new era and ways in which it diverges from the postwar regime of industrial production processes, control systems, and social relations is the subject of this book. But although one of my central objectives is to provide a meaningful *descriptive* narrative, I also strive to offer some tentative *explanations* about why the new industrial era is taking hold despite tremendous ambiguity about its rewards and its future. Social scientists need to resist taking current practices and organizational arrangements for granted or assuming that they emerge full-blown in an overly deterministic or mechanical way.

Crossing the Great Divide explores the journey that many workers are taking to acquire the skills, the know-how, the cultural and human capital, and the mental aptitudes that might enable them to reap some of the benefits of the new economy. Learning how to map the divide, making it comprehensible, learning the new job and employment rules, identifying emergent opportunities—all are tasks workers must master to cross the divide to the new era. To not do what they can to make the trek entails risks and costs of which workers are keenly aware.

Using three case studies of diverse work settings and a case study of a job search organization, I explore how different groups of people have tried to make the trek. By showing how contradictory dynamics coexist and reinforce one another in a range of postindustrial, turn-of-the-century work sites and occupations, I explain why they undertake the trek across the divide, and why work reform has taken hold, persisted, and elicited the compliance and often the commitments of a range of American workers.

I derive the concept of the divide—its distinctive features, its depth, its implications for American workers—from three streams of social science, industrial relations, and policy literature. The first stream analyzes workplace flexibility, an internationally debated topic that was sparked by Piore and Sabel's immensely influential book, *The Second Industrial Divide* (1984). To cross an economic and industrial divide into the postindustrial world, Piore and Sabel argued, corporate businesses needed to move away from traditional, rigid, mass-production industrial methods and toward novel, more varied, and ever-changing production techniques. This new system, which they termed flexible specialization, would be based on committed, involved workers who would be able to skillfully adjust to different production processes and products in variance with changing market conditions.

Furthermore, decentralized, less hierarchical organizational structures would require that workers retool themselves for this task. Piore and Sabel embraced an idealized conceptualization of the flexible workplace and its possibilities, both for capital and labor, although they also acknowledged the potential stumbling blocks to getting there, in the employers who were unwilling to let go of traditional management and organizational strategies, and state policy makers who had not adapted to the exigencies of the emergent international economy.

Critics of flexible systems argued that these arrangements constituted little more than a new permutation of work that disadvantaged workers but offered employers significant dividends (Shaiken, Herzenberg, and Kuhn 1986). The flexible model, in this view, might specify alternative production techniques or novel work-group formations, but wouldn't necessarily entail a substantive break with traditional hierarchical modes of control and authority relations. It might well embody and even deepen those traditional arrangements by obscuring power behind participatory language (Pollert 1988). New models of work calling for greater involvement and responsibility could conceal structural sources of power and inequality and lead to the intensification and acceleration of work. Some feared as well that flexible work systems, and the collaborative work relations on which such systems are based, would erode the power of the already-weakened organized labor movement (Fantasia, Clawson, and Graham 1988).

A second stream flowing into the imagery of the divide is the "good job/bad job" debate, one that similarly has been framed in polarized terms. Good jobs characteristic of the postindustrial economy, it is argued, encompass skilled blue-collar jobs, in which workers are located in the flexible-specialization production model, or in well-paid, white-collar jobs requiring highly educated workers. The latter perform the information- and knowledge-intensive labor called forth by new technologies, communication systems, and the globalization of the economy (Frenkel et al. 1999; Reich 1992). Stably employed, those holding good jobs have opportunities for mobility, professional growth, and ongoing training and are engaged and satisfied with their jobs. Other workers, it is argued— those excluded from core firms and from cutting-edge sectors and jobs— have "bad," peripheral-sector jobs. Workers in these jobs earn low wages, have few or no structural mobility opportunities or prospects for stable employment, are assumed to be marginalized from and peripheral to the privileged workers, are unskilled, and are excluded from training or other company benefits (Harrison and Bluestone 1988; Mishel, Bernstein, and Schmitt 1999). For people lacking the requisite education and skills, the divide between good jobs and bad ones seems to be untraversable.[2] Although some have brought a more nuanced tone to this discussion (e.g., Newman 1999) the debate largely continues in polarized terms (Harrison 1994, chap. 9).

Yet a third stream of literature depicts a distressing division between a contingent and stable workforce. Contingent, often temporary workers are positioned on one side of the divide, experiencing insecurity, risk, even poverty, while "permanently" employed workers are positioned on the other, with guaranteed jobs and living wages. Workers in the core were assumed to be relatively immune to the "dark" side of the new economy (Harrison 1994).

These varied perspectives on the nature of the current divide, the dichotomizing assumptions about privilege on one side and disadvantage on the other, fail to capture the complexity of work and employment at the turn of the century. Experts on both sides of the debate have captured an important element of truth about current changes. But it is time to consider the possibility that these elements are planted side-by-side in dissimilar cases, not separated off with unquestionably "good" jobs and work settings on one side and unquestionably "bad" job and work settings on the other.

The central argument of this book is that uncertainty and unpredictability, and to varying degrees personal risk, have diffused into a broad range of postindustrial workplaces, service and production alike. Tenuousness and uncertainty have become "normal" facts of work and employment across the occupational spectrum in the United States, and they thrive in concert with past opportunity structures in a restructuring economy. This concert is played off a unique postindustrial composition, a score on which aspiration and consent are inscribed at the turn of the century. Thus, opportunity and advancement are intertwined with temporariness and risk. This dual, mutually reinforcing relationship has shaped surprising, hopeful aspirations, as well as pervasive anxiety about occupational and economic fates.[3]

When I refer to risk and risk taking I am speaking of different chances that workers take, whether in workplaces or in relation to their employment contracts, that may or may not lead to a tangible payoff. Examples of the former might include agreeing to experiment with new ways of interacting, collaborating, and brainstorming with coworkers or clients, while retreating from traditional interactions that may have allowed workers to maintain one-upmanship vis-à-vis others but also perpetuated hierarchical and less productive ways of getting work done.

Examples of risk taking in relation to the employment contract might include agreeing to learn new skills and accepting responsibility for new tasks or increasing work loads even when working as a temporary and marginal worker. An even broader set of risks for workers occurs when they must absorb costs that corporations have been sloughing off to a greater degree: employment security or guarantees, health care and other benefits packages, and the protection of workforces from economic volatility (Capelli et al. 1997). When corporations no longer buffer their workers from the uncertainty of production and employment, workers must take risks and expend greater personal and group resources to control that uncertainty themselves.

Uncertainty, temporariness, and risk obviously mean very different things to different groups, depending on organizational/industrial context, labor market and regional variations, class, race, gender, education, and age, and I chart out this variability in the following chapters. Yet, to a very real degree, all three are pervasive and consistent factors shaping how people view their jobs, what they experience when working, the goals they strive to attain, and the ways in which they are willing to accommodate to, or motivated to resist, new work arrangements. Analyzing data collected from three diverse firms, and from a sample of individuals who were looking for jobs, I map out and evaluate a continuum, the degrees differentiating work sites and workers from one another, as well as the unique configurations in which uncertainty, temporariness, and risk combine.

By doing this, I hope to take a step toward resolving a core paradox about the new economy. As Paul Osterman notes with some surprise in his assessment of the recent discrepant trends in work and economy, "Despite tremendous insecurity caused by downsizing and restructuring, employees have been willing to implement high-performance work systems that draw on their ideas and commitment to the enterprise" (1999:181). His data suggest that workers have become engaged with new flexible and participative types of work reform even when faced by glaring reminders that secure employment has become elusive or uncertain. This observation goes right to the heart of industrial relations theory, industrial sociology, critical studies of work, power, and inequality, and political sociology. Why don't workers, in the face of unsettling and sometimes transparently detrimental circumstances, collectively band together to campaign against or sabotage their employers' agendas when such agendas don't appear to advance workers' interests or goals? My preliminary answer, which I develop in the following chapters, is that the dynamics identified by Osterman are less enigmatic when one looks closer at changes in jobs and work, at the character of new opportunities, and at the embedded lives of the people confronting transformed business institutions.

When I began this research, I, too, was puzzled by the lack of discernible, widespread outcry about the sweeping changes, initiated roughly in the 1980s, that were reconfiguring production processes and employment relationships. Upon first entering the firms analyzed in this book, I would have predicted that in all three, the new work arrangements I found there would nullify or at the very least minimize workers' cooperation and consent. A service-delivery organization that placed its modestly paid employees in diverse, challenging, often stressful work settings; a blue-collar timber-products plant where local management had introduced participative management but corporate management was trying to sell the plant; a high-tech assembly division that employed significant numbers of temporary workers and where managers used policies that clearly signaled the temps' marginal status—all these cases seemed to put flexible work and employment practices, based on workers' efforts and commitments, to severe test.

Yet many of the people whose stories I tell in this book were willing to adapt to uncertainty because they felt they were gaining skills and insights that would allow them to maintain a solid footing in the new economy. Their calculations about the cost of shouldering more responsibilities and being held more accountable were weighted by individual work histories and perceptions of current and future opportunities. They desired and valued attachment to their employing organization and often organized their efforts to remain attached to them. Thus, in addition to exploring flexibility in different workplaces, I strive to make a case for the fundamental importance of having enduring connections to employment institutions in contemporary society.

Obviously, in an era when job tenure is declining, contingent work is rising, layoffs are pervasive, and the culture and language of permanency are eroding, stressing the importance of building sustained relations to employment organizations seems naive, perhaps quaint. It is my hope, however, that this research highlights the urgent need *not* to blindly accept a currently popular version of reform and flexibility that makes it seem as though lack of connection and attachment is in the interests of workers. Rather, I remain faithful to, and hope the research will be used toward the goal of, constructing an employment framework, albeit a flexible one, that is characterized at its core by attachment, reward, protection, commitment, and dignity for American workers.

What Social Scientists Know about Workers' Efforts to Cross the Great Divide

A number of insightful studies have examined the implications of corporate restructuring and downsizing for various aspects of work, business structure, culture, loyalty, commitment, and identity.[4] Workplace reforms, changes in staffing arrangements, unemployment and displacement numbers, growth of the temporary workforce, the confusion and anxiety that people feel outside and about their jobs, have all been well documented.[5] Yet, with a few exceptions, we lack knowledge about how these changes are playing out in different worksites. We lack a textured understanding of how workers of different categories perceive the workplace changes described above—whether they see themselves as empowered or marginalized, whether or not they see any benefits or advantages attached to the demands and changes of restructured workplaces, and what makes them decide whether or not to comply with or participate in new work and staffing reforms.[6] When do workers view change and risk as a cost and when do they consider it an opportunity?

This book traces the linkages between the contemporary, destabilized conditions of work and changes in the opportunity structure and in our employment culture. It builds on but attempts to push beyond a growing field of literature that looks at the tensions, ambiguities, and ambivalences generated by forces that are both opening up new opportunities and contracting them. Researchers in this field have focused on workers located in the interstices between two eras: one, an era of institutional stability, growth, and security; and the other, an era of occupational and industrial transformation, economic volatility, global competition, and job and career insecurity. In short, these studies explore the dynamics characterizing the transformation from the industrial to the postindustrial economy, from one side to the other of the great divide.

Some of the best research studies illustrate the turbulence and undertow of the transformation and the difficulties of crossing over to the new economic and institutional era. Kathryn Newman (1988), for example, analyzed how workers viewed corporate restructuring and whom they blamed when their jobs and their income disappeared. Newman interviewed displaced male middle managers, male air traffic controllers, male and female factory workers, and middle-class divorced women, looking at the ways in which their views of downward mobility were shaped by the causes of their displacement. Middle managers, to take one case, who had lost their jobs when company leaders engaged in widespread layoffs, individualized the blame for the destabilization of the traditional male career. For many, demoralization and inertia followed.

In contrast, when top management of the Singer Sewing Machine Company closed their factory in Elizabeth, New Jersey, blue-collar workers refused to take the blame. They instead directed their collective ire at the top managers who had allowed what had once been the flagship factory for Singer to deteriorate because of corporate diversification and disinvestment. In its comparative view of the employment experiences and subjective impressions of workers in a restructuring economy, Newman's work was pathbreaking. She was one of the first to examine the deep swath that corporate restructuring was cutting through stable employment institutions and to explain how and why U.S. workers differentially perceived this destabilization. Yet interviewing workers about job loss retrospectively gave Newman little purchase on the contradictory terms of jobs once held, or on the unlikely marriage of, for example, progressive work reform and temporary or nonstandard hiring arrangements.

Milkman (1997) examined the rocky transition to a new era through the lens of the experiences of auto workers in a restructuring GM plant. Comparing two groups of primarily male workers—one that accepted a buyout package from GM-Linden (New Jersey), while the other opted to stay at the plant and participate in new, purportedly progressive work programs—Milkman identified several fracture lines around which workers in the current transitional era became tenuously positioned. One was the divide within the Linden auto plant between the old, autocratic and stressful mass-production system and the new participative system, formally built around concepts of increased worker engagement and responsibility. By interviewing workers and collecting data about changes in jobs, skill levels, and production arrangements, Milkman was able to document how workers became immobilized between the two systems.

The new, participative model of work had intractable continuities with the old, authoritarian Fordist model. Plant-level management never fully committed itself to or threw the necessary resources behind the new program, thus constraining workers from realizing the benefits of participative principles. Employed auto workers were left cynical and frustrated, contemptuous of the organization of the industrial era, desirous of what they felt they could learn from new, participative arrangements, but ultimately held back by traditional approaches to control and efficiency on the part of management. Here, it was managers who blocked workers from successfully crossing the divide.

The second divide was between the plant and its environment, the leap that the newly unemployed workers took to reposition themselves in alternative jobs and careers outside GM. By interviewing the latter group, Milkman was able to sketch out the crosscurrents of postindustrial labor markets. Many of the individuals had difficulty resettling into stable jobs, and many were self-employed, a notoriously precarious basis of employment. Few were earning a living or family wage comparable to their earnings at GM. Yet these workers felt liberated from the shackles of authoritarian management and modes of work at GM. Few regretted that they no longer held "stable" jobs, and most were highly critical of the mass production organization of work. The bought-out workers, then, experienced some downward mobility with respect to wages, security, and benefits, but experienced upward mobility with respect to dignity, self-respect, and self-esteem. Milkman's work highlights the uncertainty that workers experience as they navigate the terrain of the industrial divide, the line separating mass production from participative work systems, and the one separating workers employed by a core company from those with more tenuous entrepreneurial jobs.

Dudley (1994) investigated the same set of social and economic changes but explored a different divide within them. *The End of the Line* is a superb exploration of the chasm between industrial factory workers— whose traditions of work, social relations, and community organization faced extinction when their plant was shut down—and the professional, white-collar strata of that community—who not only blamed male and female factory workers for the uncompetitiveness of the American economy but rejoiced in the disappearance of their traditions. In Kenosha, the currents of industrial organization crashed up against the currents of postindustrial economic and labor-market change, isolating different classes of people. The auto workers were stranded, stripped of their jobs, faced with the demise of strongly held moral traditions, and left without adequate or appropriate resources for navigating the streams feeding into the reconfigured, white-collar and service-sector labor market. The rising professional class, in contrast, well positioned in the postindustrial economic order, blamed factory workers for inflated wages, the stifling of innovation, and the rigidity of the economic system itself, and felt little obligation to extend a hand to enable blue-collar workers to join them. This study, perhaps more than any other, profoundly illustrates the shifting, complex cultural and institutional conditions characterizing the contemporary divide and workers' dilemmas in crossing it.

These studies tilled the ground for broader and comparative research on industrial, labor-process, and cultural transformations in work and employment. *Crossing the Great Divide* strives to break new ground by retheorizing four issues in the contemporary employment context. First, like authors such as Newman, Milkman, and Dudley, I extend the analysis of changes in work and employment beyond the narrow confines of the immediate labor process or business organization. Early work and labor-process studies tended to focus primarily on relationships and conditions experienced at the point of production—the material and social arrangements in which labor was carried out—to explain cooperation, resistance, and commitment.[7] I argue that looking only at the moment and point of work is insufficient for understanding motivation to work and the meanings generated in and by work. I focus especially on the ways that constraints placed by local, regional factors (community, broadly defined; geography, industry, labor market) and individual factors (embeddedness in a class-, race-, and gender-stratified opportunity structure) shape workers' participation, aspirations, and calculations about the trade-off of risk and uncertainty for opportunity.

On this issue my thinking has been influenced strongly by research in the last decade that has focused on personal aspirations and the way they are shaped by social-structural circumstances. MacLeod's book (1995), for example, is an exemplar in this field, a powerful study of the processes through which disadvantaged youth attempt to take control over their mobility and employment prospects, or through which they are discouraged from doing so. Aspirations refer to "an individual's view of his or her own chances for getting ahead and are an internalization of objective probabilities" (15). For MacLeod, these aspirations constitute our subjective views about the world that we develop in relation to class, race, and gender location. This insight—that micro-, individual-level perspectives and actions shape and are shaped by social structures that sustain or disrupt opportunities—is a core premise in *Crossing the Great Divide* and indeed in sociology as a discipline. MacLeod and others (Fine 1991; Ford 1996; Powers forthcoming; Willis 1977) have all emphasized the need to view individuals as creative agents negotiating through the often-disadvantaging structures within which they find themselves.

Second, *Crossing the Great Divide* moves the analysis of control, participation, and organizational structure beyond the bureaucracy-centered framework that has prevailed in the sociology of work, labor-process, and industrial relations theory since the late 1970s. This framework, formulated in the image of large, stable, industrial corporations with internal labor markets, has focused principally on control and consent in bureaucratically organized, hierarchical, rationalized, and centralized work systems. Best captured in the widely cited work of Richard Edwards (1979), the framework developed in his *Contested Terrain* has failed to incorporate the empirical changes of the last two decades: the growth of decentralized work systems, the diffusion rather than centralization of power and decision making, the relaxation of formerly rigid rule-based procedures of production, the proliferation of cultural rather than structural tactics for gaining consent, and the widespread use of workers on a temporary basis. In this book I consider these changes to develop a more historically sensitive model of control and cooperation.

Third, I suggest that while it is easy to romanticize the past era of stability and prosperity for American workers—the era of the social contract and implicit guarantees of employment and mobility in core-sector corporations—this is a partial view that fails to capture the experiences and perceptions of many who were excluded from the privileges bestowed by the contract. For many of the employed workers I studied, their previous jobs held no more, and usually less, employment stability or dignity than their present ones. Few of them wax nostalgic for the past, while many are cautiously optimistic about the future. To grasp their reasoning, it is necessary to closely examine contemporary organizational and cultural features of work and employment, and the meaning that people acquired from and attached to these features. Only in this way is it possible to understand willingness, commitment, and desire for attachment in the new economy.

Finally, though, it is important to step back from this micro-level view of commitment, meaning, and experience and place workers' commitments and aspirations in the macro context of corporate power and the future of the larger economy. For while workers may have reason to feel challenged and enabled in ways that empower them, such impressions ultimately are held together by a very slender thread. I argue that, although it is true that in the 1990s and on into the twenty-first century employers have had many reasons to create conditions that appear promising to the workers they employ, these conditions are fragile, by their very design collapsible and retractable.

One of the ironic beauties of new work and employment relationships, it seems to me, is that turbulence, decentralization, variation, and unpredictability, now driven by dynamic and prosperous economic circumstances, are construed by many workers as enabling. These conditions encourage workers to invest themselves in their work, take risks they may previously have been reluctant to take, live with ambiguity and uncertainty without collective resistance or demands for additional compensation, and strive to take advantage of opportunity. Yet a reversal of economic prosperity can so easily turn turbulence and unpredictability into the raison d'être for massive layoffs of workers at all levels; closure of offices, plants, or divisions; and elimination of training and mobility opportunities. Resolving this tenuous character of jobs and business institutions and addressing the implications of this tenuousness for the very social fabric of American society is a pressing problem for social scientists and public policy makers.

Crossing the Great Divide: The Research

Crossing the Great Divide examines occupational, industrial, and labor-market reform from workers' perspective, uncovering the obstacles many workers have faced approaching the divide and explaining how workers' preferences about how to cross it, or about the consequences of not making the effort to cross, develop in particular contexts. Comparing workers in different work organizations and in different locales enables us to develop a more complex and accurate understanding of the institutional divide and of contemporary transformation, to specify factors that condition new work arrangements, to sift through what seem to be contradictory and mutually undermining aspects of change, and to show how they fit together. In the chapters that follow I examine closely the dynamics of uncertainty, risk, and opportunity as they combine and play off one another.

Conducting the Case Studies. Gaining access to American corporations to conduct research on work and employment relations has become a tricky enterprise. Particularly given the nature of my research—I was investigating company innovations and strategies, such as employee involvement programs and the use of temporary workers, on which companies often stake significant financial resources as well as their public reputation—many corporate organizational gatekeepers were strongly opposed to admitting me into their fold. I approached, and was turned down by, four major corporations in the course of carrying out this research. This is not an unprecedented number: other organizational researchers have reported many more rejections (cf., Jackall 1988; Thomas 1994; see Smith forthcoming/A, for expanded discussion of this problem). Nevertheless, each rejection was a major blow, a resounding and depressing reminder of time and effort lost.

In several of these cases, I had invested extensive personal, temporal, and administrative resources struggling to get access: negotiating to schedule my teaching load so as to maximize the time I could spend in the field (were I to be granted access), contacting key individuals, waiting for them to return my phone calls, waiting for appointments, preparing cover letters—carefully worded, neutral statements of purpose about what I was seeking to understand and how I would protect the confidentiality of everyone involved—presenting my case in person, waiting for a response, and then, finally, being turned down.

In one case, my negotiations with a site manager at a computer-manufacturing plant had reached a point where I was feeling confident and optimistic about the tone of the discussions, about his interest in my project, and about the conditions of research. We made an appointment to discuss his final decision (the fourth visit I was to make to the plant); I drove forty miles for our appointment, only to be taken to a private office and told by his assistant that I was being denied permission to do the research. In consulting with the company's corporate lawyer, she informed me in flat terms, the site manager had been told he would be "crazy" to let me study flexible manufacturing and temporary workers. My meeting with her, the denouement of several months of legwork, lasted less than five minutes. Thus is the story of workplace research: its precariousness, uncertainty, and potential for abrupt termination mirrors the conditions of work that I eventually uncovered.

However, between 1992 and 1997 I did manage to gain access to the offices and factory settings of three well-known U.S. corporations. My entrance into these research sites was primarily the result of personal connections. At Reproco, I was invited to give a presentation to a group of professional women whose male manager, in the interest of advancing the company's employee involvement program, had "empowered" them to convene to talk about problems women faced in their jobs. We had a lively and, for me, very instructive session. Later, when I approached one of the key women in that group about studying employee involvement at Reproco, she cleared the path for me to obtain permission, setting up an appointment with her aforementioned manager, volunteering to serve as a liaison, and making herself available to me on numerous occasions for interviews and informal fact checking.

Getting into WoodWorks at a time of deep uncertainty and turbulence was greatly facilitated by the fact that my parents-in-law personally knew the plant manager and were able to assure him that I wasn't out to write a sensationalist expose of the plant. Finally, and serendipitously, at exactly the time I was gathering secondary information on a state-sponsored job search club called Experience Unlimited (EU) and scheming as to the best way to study it, a student in my organizations class informed me that her father was the statewide administrator for this organization. After corresponding with him and receiving his approval for my research—lubricated no doubt by the fact that I was his daughter's professor—it was a straight and narrow path to the daily life of EU.

The one exception to these personal means of entering corporations was in my research at CompTech. While I had the name of the personnel director there, I didn't know her personally; I approached her via formal letters and phone messages. To my great surprise and appreciation, she returned my communications and thus began a working relationship that was very constructive and on which I was wholly dependent. I believe that her enthusiasm and support were predicated on two factors. First, as a long-term member of a firm with an open and progressive culture, she seemed to believe that the company would always benefit from a scholarly study of its practices. But as important, she had a genuine interest in gaining a better understanding of what was going on with their temporary employment system. For reasons revealed in Chapter 4, many high-ranking managers had made it clear to her that they were unhappy with the mandate to use temporary workers, and she was interested in hearing what a sociologist had to say about the matter. Thus, I happened upon the right place at the right time to gain access to a firm where I had no prior connections.

I studied photocopy workers who had temporarily secure employment contracts with Reproco, a company that leads its industry in high-quality photocopy and related technologies; timber-supply workers with historically secure employment contracts who were on the verge of losing them at WoodWorks, a timber-processing plant; and assembly and office workers with temporary employment contracts at CompTech, a high-technology company that specializes in hardware and software products. I cannot make a claim that these work settings represent the "typical" work settings of a restructuring, postindustrial economy, and I am certain that no one could actually make such a claim. To be sure, I chose each company carefully because they had undertaken one or more of the reforms I was interested in, such as an employee involvement, quality, or participative management program, or temporary hiring practices.[8]

But when I began the research, I was working with a manual of standard operating assumptions, drawn from my reading of social science literature, about contemporary work. Reflecting the dichotomy I found in the literature on the great divide, I assumed I would find companies where empowerment, involvement, and good employment conditions would exist on one side and marginalization, degradation, and bad jobs on the other. Influenced by reading critical studies of industrial settings where employee involvement and flexibility had been introduced, I expected to find clear-cut cases of collective—read "genuine"—empowerment and equally clear-cut cases of individualized—read "false" or "superficial"—empowerment, with sharp lines between the two. Instead of polarization, I found that work experiences were comparatively fluid and open-ended, and the lines demarcating the advantaged and the disadvantaged more blurred than I would or could have predicted. Each case represents a paradigmatic way in which the uncertainty/risk/opportunity equation is configured. Each case stands apart from the others by degrees: it is not a matter of whether or not each element of the equation exists, but how it exists, its precise form. I explored this equation in a fourth case study, in a job search club called the Sacramento Professional Network (SPN, or, Experience Unlimited), which was organized and funded by the California Employment Development Department.[9]

In these settings I explored the worlds of work from a variety of vantage points. In the three companies, I formally interviewed trainers, managers, and workers—eighty individuals—using semi-structured, in-depth interview schedules.[10] I informally interviewed countless others in the three firms when the opportunity presented itself. I observed many of those workers on the job, in eighteen different work sites scattered across three distinct regions around the nation. I attended team meetings where groups of workers and sometimes supervisors discussed work problems and solutions. I studied an array of company and organizational documents: glossy manuals spelling out the guidelines for employee involvement programs and quality teams; worksheets that groups used to run their meetings and solve problems; meeting agendas; mission statements; in-house reports assessing the progress of particular organizational innovations; and company and facilitator newsletters.

Under the tutelage of an amused and crusty logyard worker, I learned how to drive a thirty-three-ton wagner, a gargantuan vehicle used to pick up batches of logs, drive them about, and dump them on log piles or in holding ponds. (I was genuinely terrified while doing it but proud when it was over, having managed not to drown us by driving it into a pond. I also managed to avoid a clumsy or untoward manipulation of the machine's giant pincers that might have overturned and crushed us to death. Although this sounds melodramatic, these were real possibilities.) But despite that accomplishment, a major one in my private estimation, I laughed along at the countless jokes, made over the course of my research, about inept sociologists/academics who could not possibly be mechanically minded or know how to work with their hands. (At CompTech, as a temporary assembly worker led me away from his manager to show me his line and introduce me to his coworkers, the manager nervously shouted across the factory floor, "Don't let her make anything!"—a comment that was repeated with much laughter to many others that day. I'm sure its comic value had as much to do with the manager's awkwardness with the situation as with the novelty of having a sociologist in their midst.) I presented a talk on my research findings to an audience at CompTech that included low-level temporary workers, permanent assembly and office workers, and their managers and supervisors.

During the summer of 1996 I attended weekly member meetings and observed at the SPN facility at the Employment Development Department. In this job search organization I interviewed sixteen club members and two administrators, one responsible for this particular SPN site and one responsible for statewide SPN operations. I participated in SPN's mandatory weeklong orientation, partaking of the received wisdom on how job searches should be carried out and how labor markets and career structures had changed, as well as pointers on how to package myself: polish my resume, prepare for the job interview, and brace myself to negotiate for the best compensation.

Although four organizational case studies do not allow me to make definitive generalizations about the organizational conditions or political consciousness of all American workers, each does open a window into the mechanisms of a wide variety of workplaces where work reform is coupled with uncertainty and flexibility.

The Organization of the Book

The organization of this book is as follows. In Chapter 2, I analyze the circumstances of the nonunionized entry-level, white-collar workers who were contracted out to provide photocopy services to a variety of clients in the larger Philadelphia metropolitan area. Viewed from one perspective, the employment conditions of the photocopiers who worked for Reproco were a harbinger for the model of work that American policy makers and social scientists most fear. These jobs, on the surface, appeared to require little skill. The wages Reproco photocopiers earned, even though above minimum, were low. The flexible model of work within which the photocopiers labored every day was defined by continual uncertainty and risk. Yet these jobs proffered meaningful opportunity, in the form of an employee involvement program, semi-autonomous work conditions, and limited mobility opportunities within the firm. Thus, in Reproco opportunity was permeated with uncertainty, but it was a positive or enabling uncertainty.

This division of Reproco was growing, and its primary purpose was to exploit other firms' downsizing processes. Employment was, for the time being, secure in this division—it was what I call temporarily permanent—but in other, more volatile divisions of the company workers had been laid off and positions cut back. The Reproco workers, I argue, had just made it to the positive side of the industrial divide. Although they worked in a context in which their entry-level jobs were considered of marginal skill, their work was ever-changing (both in the location of their jobs and in the tasks they performed); their wages were not high, and their social status was low, but their risks were few. They were employed by a "good," core employer; and they labored inside companies where they were able to gain new interpersonal skills and insights, had access to training opportunities, worked semi-autonomously, and had temporary job security that led them to embrace their jobs and deepen their identification with the company's goals. Their case illustrates the contradictory swirls of uncertainty, risk, and opportunity, showing how the three dynamics play out, and stands as a partially promising template for one flexible path that American employers and workers might follow—an uncertain but enabling path—in the flexible economy. It is a template, I will show, that is conditioned by local labor-market dynamics and by personal work and educational histories.

At WoodWorks International, the subject of Chapter 3, long-term, unionized, blue-collar workers processed timber and manufactured plywood, studs, and other timber byproducts. WoodWorks was a decades-old timber plant in the Pacific Northwest that had been bought, had merged, and was, in fact, on the auction block at the time of my research, about to fall victim to corporate management's decision to disinvest in its timber-products division. The parent company had, over the years, cut back the size of the workforce from several thousand to about five hundred, and workers' futures were tremendously uncertain. Like the auto workers Milkman (1997) studied, WoodWorks' employees were willing to try to struggle across the divide by actively engaging in a new participative management program. But here, opportunity was infused with negative risk and uncertainty: participative management, which placed new challenges before workers, was about plant survival, not individual empowerment, and workers took all the risks in agreeing to participate. Workers were being reconstructed as "pseudo-managers" who were to absorb the risks involved in decision making without additional reward and despite the fact that the organizational power structure was fundamentally unaltered. And, by sidestepping the formal grievance process and resolving problems on the shop floor, they ran the very real risk of undercutting the power of their union, their primary source of institutional power.

Top management's commitment to divest the company of timber products meant that the purported opportunity that would result from participative management was actually a cruel and coercive plan, held out as a carrot to workers. If their plant were sold, the woodworkers faced chronic unemployment and underemployment or migration to other regions of the country. Their experiences stand as another template, an all-too-familiar depiction of the more disadvantaging uses to which participative programs are deployed in American workplaces and of the bottom-line insecurity in the final instance that is the hallmark of employment in the United States. Although workers agreed to experiment with participative management, it is difficult to avoid the conclusion that companies on this path seem merely to exploit the concept of participation and flexibility.

CompTech was a social and employment system divided. In Chapter 4 I argue that this company embodied both sides of the divide, creating a peculiar mixture of control and cooperation, of uncertainty and opportunity. I explore that mixture by focusing on temporary assembly workers working inside a highly participative work setting. The company's commitment to avoid layoffs if possible, its generous employee benefits, its emphasis on management/employee partnership, and seemingly limitless opportunities for learning, training, and mobility (both lateral and vertical) made CompTech an extremely desirable place to work. As a CompTech employee, one shouldered the risks of personal and professional change, of being held accountable for the company's health, but not the risk of employment itself.

Yet CompTech, in recent years, has experimented with a strategy more typical of what Harrison (1994) calls the dark side of the postindustrial economy: it has utilized temporary workers to the point that long-term temporaries constitute one-fourth of its several thousand workers. The case of temporary workers, like that of the low-skilled photocopy staff, similarly exemplifies a scenario that scholars and policy makers would prefer to avoid. But here, too, a fine-grained investigation reveals that this scenario is far more complicated than one would expect.

Many of these temps had spent all their working careers in unstable jobs in the secondary labor market. As temporary workers, the risk of unstable employment was their burden, but in CompTech's work culture, that burden was mitigated by their desire to become members of the permanent workforce and their desire to gain the *privilege* of absorbing the risk of personal change, unpredictability of production, and accountability. Their active participation in a work system with questionable opportunities for permanent employment was embedded in their work biographies and labor-market constraints. The collision of the two systems of work created tensions and paradoxes in CompTech's work culture and was the basis for a high level of participation on the part of temporaries, typically considered to be the least attached, least committed workers in the economy. Evidence from the study of CompTech, like the study of Reproco and WoodWorks, underscores how much context conditions control and consent. Working as a temporary in a *progressive* company held forth more unexpected status attainment, skill acquisition, and mobility opportunities than would be expected from a one-sided view that sees all temporary work as detrimental.

In the Sacramento Professional Network, a job search club organized by the California Employment Development Department, I looked at uncertainty, risk, and opportunity from the other side of the coin: the situations of unemployed managerial, technical, and professional workers. In Chapter 5 I explore what it meant in the 1990s to have had many years of experience at one job or with one employer, to be looking for work in a dramatically reconfigured job market, and to have to obscure previous stability from the eyes of future employers. These workers assumed all the risks, and their experience of uncertainty was possibly permanent and consequently personally devastating. However, much effort was made, in this club and in the popular job search literature that they were encouraged to read, to turn risk and uncertainty into opportunity, to push them to exploit what to many were discouraging and even frightening circumstances as a chance to engage in self-reconstruction. The contradictory dynamics of the postindustrial economy and of restructuring labor markets thus crystallized in the experiences and perspectives of the unemployed who had decent jobs in the past.

Throughout this book I document the ways in which different groups of workers struggled to contain uncertainty—in their lives, in their current jobs, and in their prospective jobs. To an increasing degree, firms refuse to buffer workers from the turbulence of the restructuring economy. Responsibility for controlling uncertainty and gaining certainty more and more rests on the shoulders of workers of different occupations, in differing industrial settings, and of varying employment status. In the case studies that follow I trace the way that many individuals accept the rules of the new economy but endeavor to do so on their own terms and for their own goals. In the concluding chapter, I weave together the promised whole cloth. I link the comparisons of these particular case studies back to work and employment culture more broadly, sketch out some of the implications of the findings reported here for the future of work and employment, the flexible economy in the United States, and identity itself.

2

Reproco:
Creating Flexibly Specialized
Service Workers

The white-collar, service-providing division of Reproco where I conducted the first stage of my research embodied both the optimistic vision and the pessimistic apprehension about workplaces and jobs of the postindustrial, restructured economy. Reproco had fashioned a service-delivery workplace that in key respects matched an ideal blueprint for a less hierarchical, decentralized organizational structure, one designed to enable workers to self-manage and to coordinate their efforts. The company had designed a nationally renowned employee involvement program to train workers in procedures and problem-solving skills that would enable them to work autonomously. At the same time, certain features of the jobs, such as wages, status, and mobility opportunities, conformed to prophesies that most new service jobs, even in restructuring workplaces, will be primarily dead-end and low-wage. In this chapter I explore how the experiences of machine operators—prototypical service workers in the postindustrial economy—as well as their commitments to and participation in new forms of work organization were shaped by these apparently contradictory features.

The central office of the document management services division that I studied was located in the congested streets of downtown Philadelphia. But, emblematic of one of the key features of new flexible workplaces—the decentralized organizational structure—nearly all the services of this division were delivered in multiple, changing, near and far-flung locations on the premises of other firms. Indeed, an organizational chart of this division was suggestive of a gigantic, organizational octopus. Reproco was the beneficiary of the corporate downsizing trends of the 1990s, and its service workers were riding on the concomitant wave of growth in the business services sector.[1] Specifically, companies that had eliminated their own permanent mail-room and photocopy employees subcontracted Reproco's equipment and workers. Reproco leased its state-of-the-art reprographics technology, the company's administrative expertise, and specialized workers—*machine operators*—who copied, sorted, and filed documents and maintained machines. The company sent groups of workers who were prepared to conduct their work autonomously and with only minimal coordination from management. Ironically, then, what was profitable for other firms—to outsource some functions—and thus bad for employees who had been downsized at those firms was good for the employment outcomes of the Reproco machine operators.

These industry trends shaped my research experience in unequivocal ways. In the course of observing and interviewing mail-room and photocopy workers, as well as their supervisors and managers, I drove several hundred miles to reach ten different work sites, ranging from the divisional office in downtown Philadelphia to satellite offices (mini-versions of the downtown office) in two different states and to seven different facilities, the name given to the small, subcontracted, off-site units.[2] The facilities, scattered around three states, included a variety of business and industrial settings, such as a high-powered corporate law firm housed in one of the sleek postmodern buildings downtown; a large but more relaxed, urban architectural office; a nuclear power plant located in an isolated area on the Eastern seaboard; and a sprawling mortgage services company in suburban New Jersey. The proliferation of facilities and satellites faraway from their employer greatly diluted the sense of an organizational center and facilitated the experiential sense, for workers, of wearing multiple hats and serving multiple bosses. Indeed, being part of this current of change required the machine operators to adjust to significant and continual variability in the location of their jobs, in the type of organizational setting in which they delivered their services, and in the types of services and products they rendered. How do these multiple dimensions of variability play out in particular jobs, and what do they look like to these entry-level, white-collar workers?

The Law Offices of Black, Moore, and MacIntire

One Monday morning I take an elevator up to a large law office in one of the newest postmodern office towers in downtown Philadelphia.

Environments like this have always made me feel small, anonymous, inconsequential, but, inexplicably, like a conspicuous imposter. The scale of everything is huge; every fixture, every banister, every door handle glistens and seems untouchable and impersonal. All space is controlled and marked, protected against outsiders like myself. My clothes, professional but not entirely "corporate," signal that I only marginally fit in. A security guard inquires as to my destination, making sure that I have a legitimate purpose here, and I ascend in an elevator that, although silent, is packed with the "truly corporate," who not-so-subtly eye my attire.[3]

On the forty-eighth floor I finally exit into a luxuriously carpeted lobby where my immediate impulse is to walk over to the ceiling-to-floor windows to drink in the panoramic view of Philadelphia. An authoritative receptionist thwarts this desire, however, pleasantly but firmly directing me to sign in, sit down, and stay put. She gives me a visitor's pass to affix to my jacket. The point has been impressed upon me; I know my place. As a visitor, I am being carefully classified and monitored. Spatial barriers and human gatekeepers keep anyone from passing unless they are authorized, eliminating any possibility that a stranger's gaze will observe the overt exercise of power, office politics, organizational imperfections, or workplace conflict. Knowing, as I do in advance, that most of the machine operators I am about to talk to have worked primarily in working-class white- and blue-collar jobs prior to their employment with Reproco, I wonder how they feel about such a polished and foreboding corporate environment. I suspect that their feeling of place and membership in this setting is highly circumscribed.

The law office I am visiting—a large firm with over one hundred associates and partners and countless numbers of paralegals, secretaries, and other office staff (see Pierce 1995, chap. 2, for a lengthier discussion of "large" law firms)—has contracted Reproco's mail-room and photocopy services. I have come to interview the workers providing these services, to observe their routines and the way they interact with law-firm employees. Yet, as I wait in a tasteful, overstuffed chair, I am hard pressed to find evidence of their work and labor: they are invisible. The deep carpet and the walls, paneled in walnut, absorb any sound or evidence of activity and interaction. Finally, Anna, an Hispanic woman who works for Reproco, emerges from what I only now see are heavy doors, the grain of their wood matched to blend with the richly paneled walls. She introduces herself as the lead operator or team operator—as she self-mockingly notes, a "manager without the pay"—and leads me into the bowels of the forty-eighth floor.

In a windowless room I am greeted by the sight of large, state-of-the-art, humming machines that are Reproco's trademark. Here, work is revealed: several older men, ties loosened and shirt sleeves rolled up, are busy sorting and preparing to deliver mail to individuals within the law firm, as well as to work as couriers, delivering documents to other firms and offices scattered about the city. An African American and a Hispanic man are negotiating, in irritated tones, how they will divide up their routes: neither is very happy about having to walk down city streets that they consider dangerous. Everyone, men and women, copiers and mail deliverers, at one time or another pulls a copy off the fax machine and files it in a set of stacking trays. These workers are dressed in professional garb, but their attire lacks the polish, the hint of significant amounts of money spent, the seamless stylishness: ultimately, the conformity of the "truly corporate" mold.

An African American and a white woman interact with "clients," employees of the law firm who bring a steady stream of demands; when not talking to clients, the women are stationed at the copiers. They work on one order at a time, pulling orders from a box piled high with them. Each order varies: the size (8.5″ × 11″ and 8.5″ × 14″ are but two of various sizes that can be produced) and the number of copies, the binding, the format, the method of collation, and other specifications (such as insert and paper color) are rarely the same. Orders may require the reproduction of tens of thousands of pages for particularly complex trial preparation. The photocopiers also make transparencies for lawyers and customized pads of paper for the firm's employees. The women I observe are intimately familiar with the law firm's standards, with normative modes of information and document packaging. When discussing orders with clients, the operators routinely present various alternatives, suggesting ways of improving the appearance of a document or ways of doing a job more efficiently. Shirley, the African American woman, corrects a paralegal's job request, advising him that the lawyer whose order he is arranging is notoriously picky about how his contracts are reproduced. Sensitive to the lawyer's expectations and hoping to save the paralegal from conflict with his boss, she fills him in on the "correct" specifications.[4]

Here, employee involvement has a decidedly informal character, yet this informality can't conceal the fact that copy-room workers are coordinating their tasks and are both self- and peer-managing. Periodically, several Reproco employees convene to discuss and resolve any problems that arise. These "huddles" take shape spontaneously and dissolve quickly, rarely evidencing tension or acrimony. Although they would direct any major problem—such as how to complete an unanticipated and crushing work order—to management in Reproco's central office, facility workers resolve minor and immediate problems themselves—requeuing the work orders, improvising when short of a particular type of paper, dealing with an unreasonable client, or helping a lawyer figure out the best way to send a package to another city. On some days, when the work load is heavy, a Black, Moore, and MacIntire employee steps in to help out; on other occasions, the facility gets a temporary worker, hired by Reproco, to come in to assist. Particularly large jobs are sent to the divisional center.

Reproco owns and maintains seven additional copy machines—"convenience copiers"—that are sprinkled throughout the four floors of law offices.[5] Peggy, a white woman who works in the copy room and oversees all the convenience copiers, pores over a check list containing information about where photocopy paper needs to be replenished, which machines require rudimentary mechanical tinkering (which she has learned through experimentation, attending a machine maintenance workshop, and talking with technicians), whether or not she needs to order and replace toner cartridges, and, finally—an option she is loathe to pursue since it means having to wait and possibly bear the wrath of law-firm employees—whether she needs to call in one of Reproco's technicians, at their convenience but undoubtedly not hers. Calling a "tech rep" is sometimes unavoidable, but it is also undesirable for facility workers: in particular, it is a mark against the lead operator when it comes time for his or her evaluation.[6]

Peggy maps out a plan to visit all the machines and tend to these myriad problems, large and small. As she travels about, she will tally the number of "clicks"—copies—registered on each copy machine. If she encounters a frustrated, sometimes cursing machine user (and, on some occasions, cursing at *her* as the human stand-in for the malfunctioning machine) she will troubleshoot—do a little detective work to figure out why the machine is chewing up copies, help them track down jammed paper in the countless mysterious compartments inside the machine, or get the right size of paper for their document, all the while cognizant of having to placate the user.

Because of the intense, relentless, and fast-paced business that is the heart and soul of this corporate law firm, there is a palpable sense of urgency, deepened by the constant, rapid flow of information and deadlines. The volume and texture of the machine operators' work load shifts and yields to the imperatives of the business of law. The demands of important corporate clients, the complexity of data collection and reproduction entailed in assembling cases, and the pressure of upcoming trials underlie this urgency, shaping and reshaping the machine operators' job tasks, day in and day out. Anna, who both coordinates the efforts of others in the unit and performs copy work herself, uses the term "jack of all trades" to describe these workers, and adds:

> In the copy room there's always a process, and the process is that as the work comes in it has a slip and we look at it and put it in line and finally we fulfill that copy order. There's faxes coming in all the time and we have to make sure that they are called in to the secretaries of the attorneys right away. There is mail that has to be postmarked with the date and there are large mailings sometimes involving two hundred, three hundred envelopes that have to go out in today's mail. The men do the floors—they pick up interoffice mail and they pick up post-office mail. They pick up Federal Express packages and packages that go UPS. We handle calls from "Can you give me a zip code?" to "I need to find out how I can get this to Mexico past customs by 10:30 the next day." So there's obviously a lot of work and a lot of in and out.

Many Americans would hold the copy and mailroom work that is performed here in low regard. Copy work and mail-room tasks appear to constitute no more than clerical or, in the context of this affluent and well-appointed firm, glorified gofer work. Indeed, much in the copy room telegraphs the message that the work is devalued. Unlike the front stage of the office suite, in which even receptionists and secretaries sit at expensive- and professional-looking wooden desks in their ergonomic chairs, positioned on plush carpet, behind the scenes the copy room has only linoleum on the floor, and people work in groups at large, cluttered tables rather than at individual desks. The walls are painted a flat, institutional cream color on which hang casual scribbled memos, copies of orders, and inspirational and humorous posters.

The low esteem in which many observers would hold these jobs is reflected in the way the law-firm employees treat the copy workers. Far from appreciating the tacit skills in the work and the social-relational complexities of interactions, it appears to be beyond the comprehension of most of the law firm that the Reproco photocopy workers do more than to "push buttons," or that their work entails any degree of calculation or deliberation. A lawyer or a secretary may challenge copy workers' estimates of the time it will take to complete their order; they occasionally appear irritated when a copy worker suggests that a job will be complicated; and they trivialize the machine operators' skills.

One white woman, her race and her immaculately coordinated and tailored clothes delineating her professional status in the law firm's hierarchy, impatiently snaps back at Shirley, an African American worker in the copy room. After doing some simple computations on a calculator about her standing orders, Shirley explains, in a straightforward and polite way, that there are other jobs already in the queue. Shirley names a time, the following day, when, according to her calculations, she could complete this woman's order. The client, who appears to feel that Shirley's computational work is just so much smoke and mirrors, barks out, quite startlingly, "Shirley, you always bitch about these things. You're always just pushing those little buttons, and what *are* you doing with that?" Shirley draws herself up, starts to repeat her explanation about her workload, only to be silenced as the woman takes off in a huff. Shirley breathes deeply in an attempt to compose herself, telling me that she is trying to "get over it." The problem, the visibly shaken Shirley explains, is that many of the law firm's employees have the attitude that "she's just a Reproco person, she just make copies." Soon thereafter, somewhat recovered, she returns to her work. Such instances of dismissal, of thinly veiled contempt, formed not a constant but a common thread throughout my observations of different facilities, particularly in those located in highly professional work settings.

Demographics reinforce the organizational and professional hierarchy. As is typical of many of the urban facilities that I visited, nearly half of the photocopy/mail-room workers at Black and Moore are people of color.[7] A gestalt is created that subtly suggests a link between one's subordinate status in the prevailing system of social stratification, shaped by race or ethnicity, and one's subordinate status, defined by position in the occupational hierarchy. And this gestalt does little to challenge the demeaned expectations of Reproco photocopy workers.

However, as evidenced in Shirley's response to the irate woman, and in interviews with individual workers, Reproco machine operators have a repertoire of emotion-management (Hochschild 1983) and situational-management techniques to draw on to defend themselves. As part of their communication skills and group-process skills training, employees learned how to respond to aggressive and/or hostile individuals in an "appropriate" manner, in a way that supports the adage that "the customer is always right" but that allows the worker to remain self-possessed. Machine operators used these tactics on the clients they served, to elevate clients' attitudes and behaviors to a higher level of civility (Leidner 1993). In short, by exercising their interactional skills, workers are able to maintain a sense of dignity in potentially difficult and unpredictable encounters with clients (Hodson 2000).

Eastern Seaboard Nuclear Power Plant

As I walk to the building that houses the nuclear reactor at Eastern Seaboard, I wrap my coat more tightly around me, bracing myself against the cold, brisk wind. I am accompanying Meredith, the lead operator for Reproco's account at this power plant. We are on our way to visit a copy room in the reactor building where Carlos, a Hispanic man who works as a machine operator, photocopies blueprints, maintenance forms, reports, and government documents for the engineers and technicians who oversee the reactor. To get to the building, we have to walk by the enormous cooling towers, which look quite dramatic on this clear and breezy day. The wind whips their steam around, swirling about in ways that are beautiful and seemingly benign if one forgets the underlying process generating it. I can't take my eyes off the awesome sight of the towers, but Meredith doesn't give them a second glance. The business of nuclear power is business as usual for her, as well as for the machine operators I meet at Eastern Seaboard.

The layout of the facility here at Eastern Seaboard raises the level of decentralization to new heights. In addition to being far from the main office in Philadelphia, the facility itself is scattered about the premises of the power plant, with nine employees working in four different locations. In one building, the administrative building where Meredith spends most of her time, resides a copy room that, in layout and function, resembles that at the Black, Moore, and MacIntire law firm. A small group of individuals—an African American man, a Hispanic man, an older white woman, and Meredith, herself white and in her fifties—works at three machines, photocopying material for engineers. The resemblance disappears, though, with respect to temporal and professional ambience. The work load is not as crisis-driven or as urgent as it was in the law firm. In fact, the interactional style and the clothing of the engineers in this office is markedly different from the high-pressure corporate lawyers. Here, professional workers, women and men alike, are dressed comfortably if not casually. Some of the men have long hair and many have beards. All the female engineers wear blue jeans or casual slacks. All in all, there is great congruence between the copy room and that of the surrounding organizational environment.

Various engineers crack jokes with the machine operators, and the operators themselves seem to feel fairly comfortable bantering back; occasionally they give their clients a hard time. But for Herman, the African American man, interacting comfortably with these clients represents a triumph over his own personal struggle for confidence in his interactional skills. According to him, the easy friendliness I observe is an egalitarian pose covering up a set of social relationships that seem to him to be fundamentally unequal and stratified. Herman claims that he had to learn, in his communications skills training seminar, how not to be defensive when a client pressures him or is irritated with him, and he has learned how to augment his product—copies—with high-quality service by honing his interactive skills. His defensiveness, he confesses in our interview, emerges in part from his feeling that he lacks the polish and worldly knowledge that the engineers appear to possess. Herman admits that he is battling a personal feeling of inadequacy, fighting against what he worries is the image of a "dumb operator who runs paper." Herman's comments express a fundamental discomfort with overt class and educational asymmetries, a fear that his working-class background leaves him vulnerable in this setting.

There is one other copy unit in this administration building; it serves clerical and administrative workers only. A third facility site is in a nuclear training center, where people who operate the reactors and people responsible for security go through a stringent training process. Although I ask Meredith about observing there, this center, not surprisingly, is 100 percent off-limits to me. Finally, there is the facility "behind the wire" where Carlos works: one has to go through a security checkpoint to enter this area, where the turbines and generators are located. After passing through security, Meredith and I finally reach the copy and blueprint storage area. Unlike the copy unit in the administration building, the unit in the reactor building is humming with business and has a more palpably pressing air to it. Carlos's copy room is adjacent to an enormous labyrinth of a storage area, visible to the eyes of the clients or to any visitor, in which the station's blueprints are filed. Maintenance crew members and engineers give Carlos their order slips with the precise number of the print that they need to have copied. Carlos must first track down the correct blueprint, which can range in size and shape, and then must copy it promptly. Maintenance crews take these back to their stations to use for troubleshooting and problem solving. Today, the maintenance work seems to be routine, but I am told of other times when emergencies crop up and all attention is riveted on Carlos as he retrieves the relevant plans so the crew can do their work.

Like the copy unit at Black, Moore, and MacIntire, this unit sees an ever-changing and unpredictable flow of demand which is driven by the rhythms of the surrounding work organization. I hang out here—perched on a stool in the corner trying to shrink to the smallest possible size, so as to be unobtrusive in this very busy room—and the flow of "clients" is heavy. Unlike the law firm, however, the consequences for working in an inefficient or shoddy fashion seem much more dire. At the law firm, one might incur the wrath of a high-powered attorney whose case was being held up as a result of slow work in the copy room. At the nuclear power plant, I feel constantly and nervously attuned to the potential for a more earthshaking crisis: reactor meltdown, radiation leakage, or other catastrophic outcomes, prevention of which seemed to me to be contingent on Carlos's capable work. Scenes from the movie *The China Syndrome* free-float in front of my eyes. Fortunately, during the time I conduct my observations, no alarms sound, no smoke seeps throughout the building, and no panicking engineers come charging in to demand immediate service.

The mix of the crowd pressing for Carlos's services is a variegated amalgam, distinctions among clients evidenced primarily in clothing. The engineers here are dressed professionally but as casually as professional can get, while the maintenance workers are dressed in overalls, boots, blue jeans, and denim jackets. Their clothes and often their faces are smeared with dirt and oil. Among the mechanics and maintenance men—and they are all men—race and ethnic diversity prevails; among the engineers, racial and gender homogeneity prevails, with nearly all the engineers being white, and all being men.

Carlos himself is a Hispanic man in his twenties, who, as far as I can see, keeps up with the demand in a fairly competent and professional fashion. Occasionally, he is unable to track down the requested blueprint and must return to the "customer" to confer at greater length. When Carlos returns with a print, he runs off the copies in full view of the waiting clients. For me, the pressure for performance and speed would be intolerable, and I am impressed to learn from Meredith that Carlos has been on the job here for only two months, having been transferred from a facility in downtown Philadelphia. Carlos has some strong organizational defenses against the label of being just a button pusher: those demanding his services are dependent on him, but, more to the point, they are dependent on having their orders processed thoroughly, accurately, and quickly the first time around. Simply put, if an engineer needs a copy job done swiftly and competently, it doesn't serve his interests to alienate the copy worker by treating him or her in a demeaning way. The interactions I observe today are uniformly friendly. Carlos's interactions with clients are well modulated, and he is even-keeled in his responses to the more insistent of them.

Although Carlos seems more pressured than the workers in the administration building, copy workers in the latter setting experience no greater routinization and no less complexity. Herman's discussion of the thought processes he goes through at the administration center, and the calculations he makes, illustrate the complexity of ostensibly routine work. At the beginning of each day, he and the other operators discuss the day's work load. They have to resolve any glitches in their production environment. The glitch at the center of today's group brainstorming effort is that extensive use of the copy machines keeps overheating the copy room. Herman and Meredith have had to negotiate with Eastern Seaboard managers to figure out ways to ameliorate this situation. The Reproco workers are not allowed to renovate, so they are dependent on power station managers to initiate physical improvements. The copiers' immediate goal is to upgrade the air exhaust system. As Herman notes with understatement, "it can be difficult implementing a solution [in his copy room] when it affects the facilities of the other company."

Herman usually oversees the convenience copiers in the administration building, of which he keeps a running "mental picture." He makes sure that the machines in "high-volume" areas are in tip-top shape, makes lists of machines that he knows are having problems, and searches through the limited on-site inventory to see if he has any spare parts. In addition to unpredictable work loads, machine breakdown introduces a major wild card into the machine operators' workday.

Herman also must brace himself to negotiate with a technician if he cannot fix the machine himself. The subject of technicians is especially touchy for Herman. Waiting for a tech rep to come out to the nuclear power station, remote as it is, can feel intolerable, for, as Herman notes, "if the reactor is 'out of place' the demand for copies is urgent," and they simply can't depend on company techs to get the machines up and running expeditiously. This is why Herman and his fellow workers always have backup machines in mind, alternate places in the facility where copies can be made in an emergency. In his view, the tech rep doesn't really know the "ins and outs" of the machines. On top of this, tech reps are not familiar with the particular routines in his facility and the unique sources of stress, of wear and tear on the machines. They use technical "jargon" that he doesn't always understand, and he says that he forces them to explain things to him in terms that are clear. Like the group at Black, Moore, and MacIntire, Herman sees his best fallback plan as being to confer casually with his fellow machine operators, to brainstorm about how to deal with this fault-ridden machine or with that unreasonable client.

Meredith spends most of her time circulating among the four sites, helping the machine operators prepare statistical reports about their unit and making sure they are equipped to handle the work load (one of the employees out here is a "floater" whose sole function is to travel to the unit to which Meredith directs her and help out where needed). In general, Meredith is responsible for ensuring that the Reproco machine here at Eastern Seaboard, a package of machines, of people, of expertise—in itself, a mini-octopus in the way it is spread out, located in multiple sites— is well oiled and smoothly functioning. Meredith reports to a manager in the division office in Philadelphia, but she and her fellow facility workers handle the bulk of daily business. Ironically, she started her career as a permanent worker for Reproco after having worked as a *temporary* worker for Eastern Seaboard, doing the same work that she does now.

Deconstructing Flexibility

On the face of it, the machine operator's job seems to typify the degraded and disadvantageous work characteristic of the postindustrial service economy. On one hand, machine operators were paid low wages (the typical annual income range indicated to me in interviews fell between fifteen and twenty thousand dollars); they were required only to hold a high school degree; their positions were located at the bottom of the organizational hierarchy; and the jobs offered extremely limited opportunities for upward mobility. Unpredictability and instability were built into the job, because each facility was contract-based, each was established for a delimited amount of time, and management moved workers from one facility assignment to another with little warning. Reproco didn't want customers getting too "relaxed" with the machine operators, and managers explicitly advised machine operators not to become too "situated" at the facilities, a philosophy stemming from a concern that employees would come to identify too much with the other company's interests and not enough with Reproco's.

On the other hand, if viewed in context, this occupational niche defies simple categorization or pigeonholing as a "bad" or disadvantaging job. The entry-level workers I studied had limited educational backgrounds and few experiences working in core-sector companies. To them, these jobs represented meaningful opportunity.[8] First, the machine operator job was *structurally secure*. Although they faced *positional* instability, at the time of my research they did not have to worry about *employment* instability. The company had not engaged in layoffs in this division and, since the division was growing, layoffs did not loom on the horizon. These low-level workers were hired for periods of unlimited duration, rather than on limited-time contracts, which was especially meaningful to the participants in my study because many of them began working for the company as temporary employees.

Furthermore, machine operators viewed their current employment status as a privilege compared to the unstable secondary-labor-market and temporary jobs they had held *prior* to working for Reproco.[9] In a global circuit of temporariness machine operators were, for the time being, securely positioned, with temporariness built into the particular job but not into the employment relationship. In this large, paternalistic firm, theirs was a position of relative advantage.[10] For many of the male workers I observe and interview, the labor-market conditions of the Philadelphia area look as grim as they did to the boys in MacLeod's (1995) study and the men in Bourgois' (1995) study. Specifically, Philadelphia, like Boston and New York, experienced significant deindustrialization in the years prior to my research. Many young and mature men of color must grapple with the stunning clash between traditions based on industrial factory work and the white-collar, middle-class culture in insurance, banking, business-services, and real-estate firms. Finding an industrial job is no longer even an option, and these men must carve out new employment terrain for themselves. The men in my study, obviously, have made it into these white-collar, service jobs.

Reproco workers were multivalent service workers, positioned to work for lawyers and paralegals in a polished corporate setting; for maintenance crews, administrative assistants, and engineers in a power plant; and inside a variety of other business and professional settings. The social organization of work was designed to maximize machine operators' ability to step into these different contexts with a minimum of retraining or retooling.

The organization of work seen in these two facilities—each different but each sharing elements of social organization that were common in other facilities—is an arguably positive model for the way in which flexible, decentralized service production is organized. I have elsewhere called this an *enabling model* (Smith 1993:196–98), a model in which firms pursue their profit-making goals by nurturing their workers, creating structural opportunities in which workers can use their judgment and discretion, investing in workers' skills, and encouraging worker attachment and commitment. Using various innovations, such as self-managed work groups, team work, and continual training, firms promote flexibility to enhance productivity, quality, and adaptability. The contrasting *restrictive model* downgrades the employment relationship and the quality of the work process. This approach seeks to enhance organizational adaptability and efficiency by turning labor into an easily manipulable quantity, primarily by bringing in and discarding labor according to fluctuations in demand. Rather than nurturing workers, the restrictive approach renders them disposable.

In Reproco's case, decentralized organizational arrangements opened up new domains of expertise and knowledge and provided opportunities for using judgment and exercising initiative. The company positioned workers to face the challenges of these situations by retooling workers' interpersonal and group skills. These competencies—or at least workers' preparedness—reflected the determination of Reproco top management to increase the ability of its workforce to handle the complexities of decentralized production and occupationally and demographically diverse work relations. Corporate-level management had implemented the employee involvement program in anticipation of the variability of work and of the potential problems that might occur as workers labored at the intersection of Reproco and other businesses.

Reproco was attempting to manage the unpredictable work environment and was constructing, through organizational practices and policies, flexible workers who could adjust to this unpredictability. Yet enabling flexibility so defined was not one-dimensional, seamless, or unequivocally positive for them. In fact, the opportunities posed by enabling flexibility are integrally connected to uncertainty and disadvantage for Reproco workers, and it is a juncture that has complex implications for the situation of workers across the board. Let's look at these points at close range.

The Temporary Circuit. On a spectrum of temporariness, where people experience varying degrees of attachment, permanence, and security in an economy that is continually shifting in unpredictable ways, the Reproco machine operators' position can be characterized as fairly positive, even if their jobs are limited in skill and scope. But, despite job security in the present, machine operators nevertheless continually encountered the *fact* of temporariness on many fronts. The most obvious condition of temporariness lay in *experiential temporariness*: workers' knowledge that their time at any one facility was limited, their awareness that the company had a stated policy of shifting workers from facility to facility, and their ignorance regarding their future assignments.

Most of the workers I interviewed claimed that they did not object to this type of temporariness and, indeed, a number of them "talked flexibility": that is, they spoke of constant change in ways that made it appear that they endorsed and embraced change and ambiguity in their jobs. Because they wanted to rationalize a difficult situation or to present themselves in the most positive light to me, as an outsider and researcher, or because they genuinely enjoyed turmoil and movement, workers spoke variously of being bored if they had to stay at one facility for too long; they emphasized how they were going to use their broad range of organizational experiences to their own advantage in the future (for example, to obtain better jobs or to aid them in running their own businesses). Finally, mirroring the contemporary discourse about upheaval and impermanence, a rhetoric that has so profoundly transformed our employment culture, they discussed how no one could be complacent about their work any longer, and that people had to roll with the new demands for flexibility and versatility in order to get or keep jobs in the restructuring economy.

Another dimension of temporariness rested in the transience of machine operators' social relationships with one another. By continually re-

grouping individual workers into different work sites, the machine operators were unable to build enduring relationships with fellow workers
that might provide a basis for collectively countering management's expectations for productivity, performance, and effectiveness. Repeatedly
recombining workers weakened machine operators' ability to resist the
terms on which their labor was contracted out to client companies. These
flexible work arrangements thus turned workers into individualized subjects of power and control.[11] Machine operators had no say in establishing or limiting the terms of these contracts and, in effect, were obliged
to "make do" once the facility was set up. Concretely, the facility represented a negotiated agreement struck between the hiring company and
Reproco for a set number of machines, people, and time. If a sales representative, who worked out the terms of the contract, promised too much
to the client, the machine operators were left holding the bag. They had
to handle the chaos (Juravich 1985) and scramble to meet goals that were
unrealistic (i.e., having to accomplish too much with inadequate staff and
resources).

Not only experiential temporariness shaped machine operators'
worldview. The precariousness of employment pressed in on machine operators in other reminders—some subtle, others vivid—of the possibility
of having to endure *structural temporariness* in employment. These reminders came in different shapes and degrees of intensity. I have already
mentioned that the majority of the machine operators who participated
in this study had been temporary workers in the past, and most had begun
their employment with Reproco as temporaries, later being hired into a
"permanent" position. Directly experienced temporary employment was
increasingly distant to workers: the longer they worked for Reproco, the
weaker was their identification with being a temp. The possibility that temporary employment might lie in their futures, however, worked effectively
to bind them to Reproco and temporarily permanent employment there,
cementing their willingness to work under varied and sometimes unsettling circumstances.

Structural temporariness did look machine operators in the eye when
they worked side-by-side with temporary workers hired from outside the
company. Using temporary workers was one method whereby Reproco
was able to "institutionalize flexibility" (Smith 1994): temps filled in at facilities, satellites, and the divisional center when the work flow stretched
the capacity of the permanent workforce. For some machine operators,
temps were a hassle, an unwanted factor of production that they schemed

to minimize;[12] for others, temps were a direct and living reminder of the precarious nature of employment for many workers in the 1990s. The machine operators didn't so much feel threatened by temporary workers' presence—a finding other researchers have stressed when looking at situations where temporary and permanent workers work side-by-side (Graham 1995; Rogers 2000)—as they felt grateful not to be working on such a tenuous basis themselves.

This gave rise to a final irony in the machine operators' conditions of employment. Not only were their jobs predicated on the elimination of jobs for once-permanently employed workers at the hiring companies where they worked, but the security of their current positions in work conditions that varied, shifted, and changed was predicated on the insecurity and precariousness of an entire sector of the labor force in the 1990s: the swiftly growing numbers of temporary workers. The complex and variegated condition of temporariness in their facilities; the legacy of temporariness stemming from their own work biographies; the possibility of temporariness in the future as embodied in the experiences of temps that they worked with; all charged machine operators' understanding of and appreciation for their current positions. In many ways, the Reproco workers were located dead-center in the maelstrom of the destabilized economy and, I argue in the next section, it was the tools and skills gained in training as flexibly specialized workers that allowed them to remain anchored in these currents of change and instability.

The Complexities of Boundary-spanning Work: The Importance of New Cultural Capital and Interpersonal Skills. In their daily jobs, mail-room and photocopy workers developed minor technical but significant social-relational skills, and, during their tenure with Reproco, they rotated through facilities located in different business sites. As a result, many were, for the first time, exposed to a variety of professional work settings and required to exercise new interactional skills. In the parlance of organizational theorists, machine operators' jobs required them to span organizational boundaries, to decipher congruities and incongruities between multiple organizations, negotiate between the formal and informal aspects of two business organizations at the same time, and to be accountable to both (Caldwell and O'Reilly 1982; Wharton and Erickson 1993). An inherent part of boundary-spanning work is that quite often the boundaries are fluid and interpenetrable—creating what Scott (1998) calls a "sieve" effect—even invisible, as the social relations and work tasks of one dynamically affect and spill over into the other. At Reproco the interactions that followed from this open-endedness varied from an employee of the client company stepping in to assist a machine operator in fulfilling a large and pressing order, a manager or supervisor in the client company crossing the jurisdictional borders and attempting to dictate to and control the efforts of the machine operators, and a machine operator negotiating with a client to change the terms of the contract, whether minor or major.

Learning the ropes of new and different business organizations, and learning how the expectations and ways of working of those organizations melded or did not meld with Reproco's customs and norms, was an ongoing process of insights quietly absorbed, often after painful experience (as illustrated in the case of Shirley, the law-firm worker). The professional disjuncture could be especially distressing when well-paid, highly-educated, and racially homogenous clients incorporated their class and racial biases into their treatment of entry-level, racially heterogenous facility workers.[13]

Also integral to boundary-spanning work was the fact that machine operators were subject to the imperatives of their clients' own labor processes: their own efficiency and quality imperatives, their time tables, their definitions of quality service work. This deeply intermeshed and tightly synchronized element of the job makes machine operators' work a noteworthy instance of service work. As numerous researchers have noted, contemporary service work requires that the typical frontline or interactive worker molds his or her performance to the expectations of the client (*Annals* 1999; Fuller and Smith 1990; Hochschild 1983; Leidner 1993; Macdonald and Sirianni 1996). As well, interactive service workers often try to control the emotional responses of customers (Leidner 1999). A worker's personality and the quality of the worker/customer interaction constitute a significant part of what is being purchased, and if customers consider the quality to be low, or at variance with what they prefer or want, they can buy the service elsewhere.

Reproco's service jobs were unusual in that their service clients had no choice but to "buy" the service from them. Unlike service customers who can pick and choose the company from whom they wish to purchase services, clients inside the hiring companies where Reproco facilities were located had to have their copy work done by the machine operators. This constricted aspect of the service encounter brought the machine operators, as service workers, under fire. Clients had no flexibility in choosing service providers, and the facility workers had little choice but to try to contain any ire, disrespect, and contempt if it arose.[14] The machine operators' need to control their clients' emotions may have been even greater than that of an interactive service worker, whose customers can simply walk away and take their business elsewhere if they are dissatisfied.[15] In other words, the machine operators were captive to the personalities and labor-process exigencies of this organizationally bound population of customers.

These work conditions made workers interpersonally vulnerable and heightened the stress and uncertainty related to having, over and over, to decipher unfamiliar work settings and professional styles. The personal and organizational costs entailed in boundary-spanning work were potentially numerous and complex. What is important in the Reproco case is the way in which workers drew on knowledge and interpersonal skills gained in company training to minimize these costs. With these skills, workers, positioned in settings at a remove from management, could make decisions, use their discretion, work with others as a team, and resolve disputes with clients. Photocopy workers participated in various types of training in communications, problem solving, and technical expertise. In the course of training and in cycling through different work settings, machine operators were acquiring new forms of cultural capital (Bourdieu 1977a, 1977b; Lamont and Lareau 1988), in this case a body of knowledge about and awareness of interactions in and values of the corporate world, a domain from which they had hitherto been blocked.

Swidler has noted, in her discussion of culture in action, that "To adopt a line of conduct, one needs an image of the kind of world in which one is trying to act, a sense that one can read reasonably accurately (through one's own feelings and through the responses of others) how one is doing, and a capacity to choose among alternative lines of action" (Swidler 1986:275). One of the more salient findings of this study was Reproco workers' claim that they acquired this ability to map the norms of the corporate world in their training for participation and communication. The *process* through which workers used both formal training and work experiences to enlarge their skill sets and establish a firmer footing in corporate environments emerged in one-on-one interviews. It is here that we gain some understanding of Reproco workers' readiness to at least try to accommodate the fluctuation, the change, and the high demands on the self that they experienced as business as usual.

Anita's articulation of how she had learned to map the professional environment in which she worked illuminates this process. An African

American woman who had worked for Reproco as a machine operator at various sites, Anita described her experiences and thoughts in painstaking terms that were echoed by many machine operators. Anita started working for Reproco as a temporary worker when, after a year of college, she was told that she would not be allowed to return due to poor grades. Reproco's employee involvement program (EIP) had required her to participate in meetings and problem-solving groups for the first time in her life, a process that appeared to have been personally difficult. She said she had had to become involved: "One step at a time. Its, ah, 'cause I didn't want to get out there and fall flat on my face. But people are like taking numbers. 'Oh God, there she is. She was never here before. What's she doing back there?' 'Cause you're seen, you know, you become more focused, you know, they can see it, 'Gosh, she's in view.'"

Even though major life experiences such as having children and raising them as a single parent had forced her to be a "leader" (her word) in her family, it was only recently, in the course of participating in a few problem-solving groups, that she felt other people had "brought her into focus," recognizing about her, "Oh, she *does* have a mouth, and, oh, she *does* have thought."

When I asked Anita how employee involvement might be useful to her in the way she performed her job—serving professional "clients" in a facility in a large architectural firm—she reflected that:

> There's a way that you want to be perceived. There's a way that you want people to respond to you. You don't want people snapping at you. You don't want people, ah, *just tuning you out*. You want people to try and understand what's going on with you and where you're coming from.
>
> I have to try and understand what the other person's point is. And to understand the other person's point you have to step out of your shoes for a moment and step in theirs. What they want. What they require....I come to work, put myself in the customer's position. Well, you don't want nobody snapping at you. Because if you snap at someone too much, *it's a snap back attitude*. But you have to remove yourself and think about the other person. So, yes, I've taken it and put it into everyday life.

Learning to detect and gaining the ability to deflect the "snap back attitude" of other people had been eye-opening for Anita; she spoke of becoming "voiced" (her word) and visible in her facility work group when she gained the ability to interpret the needs of clients and coworkers and to more successfully manage perceptions of herself.

Ralph was an ex-Marine and Vietnam veteran, one of ten children raised in a Hispanic family in the Bronx. He had moved through a series of working-class, white-collar jobs and had unsuccessfully tried to establish a small business before working for Reproco. He emphasized that he had never had professional role models in his family and that he ultimately aspired to run his own small business (a goal he felt he was getting closer to because of his experience with Reproco as a machine operator working at Eastern Seaboard Nuclear Power). When I asked Ralph whether the EIP assisted him in any way, he answered: "Yeah, the communicative skills impressed me. They showed me how I could get information from the customer in a clear way, *taught me how to read body language.* I used to say, 'Here's your copies, now get out of here.' Now I have to make sure I'm communicating, *to understand their needs.* The customer is important and I have to figure out what they need, and I'm trying to have more sensitivity to their needs."

Ralph believed that learning to interpret others' needs and to avoid overreacting to people had enabled him to avoid and/or manage crisis, an ability he claimed was newfound. He spoke of avoiding "chain reactions and repetition of problems" (referring to business misfortunes in the past) and of how the problem-identifying and -solving process had "organized his problem-solving" ability. In his thinking, these skills had very tangible outcomes: he saw them as necessary for eventually having his own business. He remarked: "I don't want to reach the point where I'll have multiples of problems, I don't want to make the mistakes others have made. I want to be able to identify and solve before problems turn into a big crisis. I always wanted to have my own business but I've always been insecure *about my knowledge of people,* customers."

These sentiments were echoed by Brenda, the African American woman who worked as the lead operator at Anita's facility. Many of the benefits of training were reflected in Brenda's growing understanding of professional behavior: how to act like a professional and how to evoke professional treatment from her "clients." We had been talking about her goal of becoming a small business owner at some point in the future. I asked whether the skills she had learned at Reproco would help her attain that goal.

Definitely. Mainly, it's in working with people. People are just deep. I mean, they have all kinds of attitudes! Here, I work with four or five people and all my clients, and they all have attitudes. I've learned I have to be the same way everyday. No matter what. No matter what! I mean, 'cause if I'm down or I have an attitude or if I'm nasty, then how's that going to look to the workers? And then they get an attitude 'cause you have an attitude. Or because you talk nasty to them. You know, people, they want to be treated the way you want to be treated. So I have to be the same every day. I have to come in smiling every day. Being polite. Even though you know that they're not working out or they're not doing what they're supposed to be doing. You have to still have that same niceness, attitude.

The customers, the customers...they call me on the phone. Sometimes they have attitudes. You have to calm 'em—either calm 'em down or you know, talk to 'em very nice. Sometimes it get on your nerves real bad. But...you have to really put that aside. And you have to get that professional part—keep that professional part up front at all times. We've gotten a way [in training seminars] to talk to people. I mean, there's a lot of people out there just don't. They don't know how to talk to people, especially the customer.

What quality improvement has actually taught me is, being a better person—as far as business wise it helps me to look out for anything. To look out for any type of situations, to deal with any type of situations—that's what it really taught me—to deal with any type of situation.

I heard many variations of these points in interviews. For example, James, a twenty-nine-year-old African American man who worked as lead operator in one of the satellite offices, came to Reproco via previous temporary jobs he had taken after dropping out of Howard University. James described importing the tools and insights into other realms of his life and spontaneously expressed his feeling that clear and undefensive communication enabled him to coordinate the work of the machine operators and deal with clients more authoritatively. "Like I said, what I've learned here and dealing with people, I've taken outside. And I transfer what I learned and put it into my daily life and it helped me to, I learned how to, like I said before, *how to listen and how to make sure that I understand exactly what someone is telling me*...just to listen and see if I'm able to do as someone is instructing me to do."

Using the technique of getting people to clarify their statements, confusion about which could evoke the wrath of customers (and had, on occasion), enabled him to:

> test my understanding, make sure I understand exactly what someone was telling me. [I get them] to repeat it, to clarify it. That way, you won't cause

any problems at the end, because I...if I asked you again to repeat it, to clarify, then we won't have any problems at the end. I find that it helps me to avoid conflict, helps me to resolve conflict....I find I help a lot of other people resolve conflicts and issues in their lives....It gives me a way of helping them see things from another perspective and in a nonthreatening way; it's kinda weird.

Being trained in communication and involvement and acquiring knowledge about work relations built workers' perception of greater efficacy in interaction, particularly insofar as they learned techniques to take control of situations and individuals. The formal techniques of employee involvement (EI) also provided openings for normally reticent people to take risks by verbally participating in organizational events. Gaining the confidence to talk (evidenced in Anita's comments), and thus not feeling completely at the mercy of others who could monopolize interaction, was another outcome of the EIP identified by nearly all my respondents.

Hilda's experience shows how one of the techniques followed in EI groups—the round-robin approach, which required a verbal contribution from everyone in the room—helped her overcome genuine terror over language inadequacies and to place her own insights and contributions on a par with those she perceived as being "smarter," "more impressive" (who happened to be experienced male coworkers). Hilda was a Hispanic woman for whom English was a second, extremely well-spoken language. She had undergone EIP training in preparation for her work as a facility-level machine operator, and she described her experience with her first "real" EI group in the following way:

> I remember when we were first trained in leadership through quality, that you do the meetings and we were learning the lingo—seeking information, giving information—normally in a crowd full of people I would not talk because I'd figure, I would feel—the barrier of language would come up, the barriers of, *well, these are men that have been doing this for years,* maybe they know better than I do so let me shut up and not get involved...
>
> *They were more impressive.* And then once the employee involvement makes everybody get involved and the best thing about it, which I loved, was that nobody is—when you're brainstorming, no one is allowed to criticize your idea. Even if it's weird, even if it's the worst idea you could ever make and you know it and it sorta comes out of your lips—nobody is allowed to make a comment because that's what brainstorming is. *Free ideas without an evaluation on them.*

So the facilitator was like, "No, no, no, you can't make a comment." [Her facilitator stopped people from interrupting her.—V. S.] And he makes you feel
better because you can say anything and you don't feel like, intimidated by
the boys' network.

Her insights about how public involvement and visibility rattled her vividly
equated language mastery with competency itself:

In meetings, as soon as you said a meeting—I would have a fit. My palms would
sweat. I would start sweating and I would be like, "Please God, don't let them
ask me anything." *Because my accent would automatically get very heavy and my
brain was not translating at the pace that it normally does.* So my thoughts were
coming in two languages.... You know that I had a stomachache. But it made
me say something and it made me open up a little bit more in meetings and
things like that.

These insights and experiences were seconded by others. Hillary, a
forty-eight-year-old African American machine operator, identified the
importance of understanding hidden principles of communication,
which she learned in her in-depth training session, for independently organizing cooperative relations in the course of working. She appreciated
the participative approach to problem solving because it meant that
groups had to "acknowledge that a person has made a proposal instead
of *just ignoring it and going on*," a kind of silencing process in which she
felt herself to have been on the receiving end.

Speaking especially of one communication technique (learning how
to clarify statements and requests), she pointed out the virtues of using
this technique for helping people better understand cultural complexity
and smoothing out tensions incurred in the process of accomplishing
work tasks:

These are all behaviors that this training helped us to identify, and that's part
of the first step of being able to change anybody's behavior, *is to recognize it.*
And once you are aware of it then you can begin to change it, address it. One
of the areas that they taught and I was unaware of this until this training so
this is very key for me, was the—what they call, clarifying, the clarifying behavior. To ask a clarifying question as opposed to making an assumption that
is wrong. Because our language can be very, ah, ah, *can have many meanings,*

depending on voice inflection and ah, you know, a person can say something and they can mean something totally different from what you understand.

Pondering meaning, interpreting action, and taking the perspective of others; using the communication tools and an interpretive framework to strengthen one's voice and efficacy in a complex work setting, were themes raised over and over in interviews with machine operators. The perceived benefits that service workers identified cemented their commitment to Reproco, even when it was questionable whether these benefits lent themselves to meaningful upward mobility or wage improvement. In these informants' minds, new interactional insights and skills were meaningful if intangible assets. They provided machine operators with a method for trying to control uncertainty as they shifted from location to location, clientele to clientele. Many believed also that their new skill sets were transferable to other work settings.

My belief in the importance and value of these insights and skills for low-level workers was affirmed by the unexpected reaction these data provoked when I gave a talk to a group of professional workers and researchers, many of whom had worked for Reproco. In the discussion session following my presentation, several of these middle-class professionals spoke of how much they had despised the very training that I was extolling in my talk. Several seemed furious about having been required to attend the training classes and felt that this so-called training in communicational skills was ridiculous and even a violation of their personal autonomy. My response—that perhaps they, as middle-class, highly educated professionals, experienced it as, on one hand, trivial and, on the other, as profoundly intrusive precisely because they took this understanding and interpersonal style for granted—did not appear to lessen their antagonism. I remain convinced that to look at the training as simply evidence of patronizing control or as an insult to one's intelligence is to universalize middle-class experiences inappropriately and neglect the ways in which the right class and educational credentials, cultural capital, or exposure to professional settings can profoundly privilege or disadvantage American workers.

One way of understanding this is that the entry-level workers at Reproco felt they were acquiring and were becoming more comfortable with new types of interactional and communicational capital, and they felt empowered to "activate" (Lareau and Horvat 1999) this capital under specific organizational conditions. This finding raises the possibility that the knowledge gained by workers in the course of training was knowledge that might enable them to disrupt processes of social reproduction—here, inside this large, core corporation and inside other professional settings in the future—that are important sources of social inequality. Much more research, particularly on company training and the outcomes related to training for different groups of workers, is needed, but the Reproco case is, I believe, powerfully suggestive about the potential for advancement, achievement, and expression among historically disadvantaged groups that is inherent in new work arrangements.

Finally, respondents saw these intangible benefits spilling over into their personal and family lives. Many of the machine operators spontaneously identified other domains, other types of thought processes (i.e., extra-organizational), and other types of social relationships that, for them, had been transformed by their newfound knowledge of communication, group process, and conflict resolution. I was not in a position to evaluate their claims about this spillover effect because I never interviewed or observed people in their homes or in their communities. Yet I give great weight to their comments, partly because nearly all my informants raised this issue on their own, and partly because they were able to pinpoint so explicitly where and how they used their powers of interpretation and communication. An interview with one woman, an African American who had worked with the company for nine years, nicely illustrates this topic and parallels the fashion in which it was discussed by other individuals. I asked Clarice if she wanted to add anything to our discussion of employee involvement and quality improvement and she responded:

> Right. Well, the problem-solving process, the quality-improvement process, interactive skills are all things that I think are good for *everybody* to learn, for *life.* All phases of one's life, and uh, from that standpoint, I think it's the greatest thing since sliced bread. I use it all the time. I use it with my husband, I use it with my daughter, I use it with my friends, I use it—it's becoming such a part of me I don't even realize I'm using it sometimes till sometimes I hear myself say a phrase and I say, "Hmmm, that may sound a little canned." But it's just a part of me, you know.

I then asked whether she had possessed the insights prior to working for Reproco, trying to get at whether these were new skills for her.

CLARICE: Yes, I did, but [the training] took some of the basics that I myself
knew and understood and all, and expanded it and added a lot
more than I had. I wouldn't have been able to put things in this
perspective [she's referring here to the general perspective on
communication and interaction she acquired in her seminar]. OK?
Sometimes you just need to hear something packaged a little bit
differently to make the bell go off, you know? It's an awareness-
type thing.

V. S.:   What sort of advantage has it given you, or what insights about your
life do you feel you've found?

CLARICE: Well, I find that it helps me to avoid conflict, helps me to resolve
conflict, helps me to be a happier person, helps me to—I find I help
a lot of other people resolve conflicts and issues in their lives. OK.

James, you will recall, claimed that he'd "taken his skills outside," put
them into his daily life. Other individuals claimed to use problem-solving,
conflict-resolution, and group-process techniques in their families,
churches, and community organizations.

Conclusion

The case of Reproco provides a template of an enabling, albeit imperfect
model of flexible work and organizational practices. It was a model that
exemplified, in one form, decentralized, loosely bureaucratized work settings in which line workers both internalized control and managed, in
friendly and often casual though instrumental ways, their immediate
coworkers and clients. The degree to which they felt authorized to direct
their work, on their own and with their fellow photocopiers, is an important factor in understanding their commitment to this particular version of work reform. Embedded within a strong appreciation for their
Reproco job, relative to other opportunities, and the degree to which they
were "empowered" to work autonomously, Reproco workers engaged in
this system of work with considerable intensity.

Specifically, I argue, machine operators' positive assessment of their
jobs was comprehensible in relation to their location within a flexible organizational work setting. Their definitions of a good job were circumscribed, tempered in part by historical exclusion from core-sector jobs
and in part by connections to the contemporary work world that still
seemed fragile. In the past, their positions in the temporary circuit were

structurally insecure and low in status and security; their current positions represented a comparatively secure place in an occupational world that at worst could be characterized as experientially temporary. They valued the skills they acquired in the course of becoming flexibly specialized service workers. Since their jobs entailed ongoing lateral movement, stressful social relations, and complicated demands for emotional work, workers were all too glad to adopt prevailing management wisdom about how to coopt and control the responses of the people they had to serve. In other words, management had structured a high level of experiential uncertainty into machine operators' jobs; workers used employee involvement tools to stabilize and control that uncertainty.

It should be noted that these biographical facts are nestled within another set of facts about racial prejudice in employment. Much research has documented the ways in which employers statistically discriminate against people of color, attributing to individual applicants qualities that they assume, without foundation, are held by the entire population of which that individual is a member (Holzer 1998; Kennelly 1999; Moss and Tilly 1996; Neckerman and Kirschenman 1991; Wilson 1996). Many people profiled in this chapter had made it past this screening process, laden with negative assumptions about race and class, and were struggling to survive—to do their jobs on terms acceptable to the corporation, to achieve some degree of personal and occupational efficacy in order to work with others.

I would argue that a guardedly optimistic interpretation of new work arrangements at Reproco is defensible because this division was a workplace "under construction": that is, the division was growing; its workforce was diverse; and its products were relatively new and thus open to nontraditional ways of organizing commitment and participation. Looking at different contexts—where work practices have long traditions or where power is entrenched in one group of workers, bound together by gender or racial similarity—prospects for gaining a voice and benefiting from new work arrangements might be more limited.

In the next chapter I turn to a case that on nearly every dimension differs from Reproco's situation. In the study of WoodWorks we will see an alternative scenario for the implementation of flexibility, a disheartening scenario that mirrors what has taken place in countless American workplaces over the last twenty years. Here, an employee participation program was introduced as a last-ditch effort and in a very forthright way to induce workers to do what they could to save a company. The case of

WoodWorks realizes many fears on the part of cynics who decry employee participation because it coopts workers, intensifies their work effort, and makes them do more with less. Yet even in the case of WoodWorks we find a surprising degree of qualified enthusiasm for the potential of new work arrangements. It is to this divergent, flexible path that we now turn.

3

WoodWorkers for Life?
Reconstructing Endangered Workers
as Involved Participants

However we examine it, the participative management program at WoodWorks International seemed to have little benefit for its production workers. WoodWorks, a unionized timber-products plant in Madison, Montana,[1] had been undergoing contraction and cutbacks for a full decade before I began my research in 1992. Many of the changes that had taken place mirrored the changes occurring in countless other blue-collar plants around the nation. Staffing levels at WoodWorks had been scaled down to about five hundred from a high of fourteen hundred in the early 1980s. Throughout that decade management had temporarily suspended operations in different parts of the plant because of slumping sales, episodically sending workers into unemployment. Logging operations had been contracted out to independent loggers, and road construction operations had been eliminated. Jobs had been automated by lumber sorters, plywood presses, greenchain sorters, and small-log processing systems.

All over the Pacific Northwest mills and plants just like WoodWorks had been closed, both by WoodWorks' parent company and by other companies in the timber industry.[2] Relations between these unionized workers—members of the Lumber, Production and Industrial Workers—and company management had been strained throughout the 1980s as wages and benefits were cut back, some paid holidays revoked, and jobs lost. In 1988 Madison's plant workers joined nearly one thousand other timber-industry workers in the region in a thirteen-week strike. When workers voted to ratify a contract that failed to roll back many of their concessions of recent years, they returned to the plant disgruntled and unsettled about what was to come. At first with ambivalent, and then with un-equivocal support from local union leaders, WoodWorks introduced its participative management (PM) program as a partial solution to turning around the fortunes of the plant and increasing the morale of workers.[3]

By 1992, anxiety and a deep feeling of insecurity were palpable in interviews, at team meetings, and in casual conversations around the plant. WoodWorks' parent corporation—a large, multidivisional firm with international operations—had announced that they eventually intended to get out of the wood-products business.[4] The company considered the timber- and building-products market niche to be unprofitable and viewed wood-producing workers as a regrettably but unavoidably endangered species. Executive management reported that it was going to concentrate its corporate resources on paper products instead and recently had put the plant where I conducted my research on the auction block. This plan, and the broader downward trends in the timber industry, seemed to mock the slogan of the plant's employees: "WoodWorkers for Life!" The concerns of many were crystallized in the words of the business representative of the local union when he told me, "I think we, as far as WoodWorks is concerned, are dead ducks, with or without participative management."

In distinct contrast to Reproco, then, work reform was introduced under conditions of economic and organizational crisis. Specifically, Reproco's employee involvement program and decentralized control system took hold in a period of rapid growth, while WoodWorks' participative management program was introduced after several years of contraction, at a time when the plant faced a real possibility of shutting down. In further contrast to Reproco, work reform at WoodWorks didn't fundamentally alter the centralized organizational character of the site. Rather, the PM program focused nearly exclusively on making *individuals* more flexible, heightening their engagement and holding workers more accountable for production and output.

In this chapter I seek to explain participation and resistance as plant-level management attempted to bring workers into the fold of a new industrial relations paradigm. WoodWorks represents a telling comparison case to Reproco because work conditions at WoodWorks were not in flux, under construction, and emergent as they were in the white-collar business services division. WoodWorks' practices were built on decades of traditional, bureaucratic organizational premises. Hierarchical employment relations between management and workers had been unyielding for decades, framed as they were by union politics and collective bargaining processes. Thus, the woodworkers were struggling to incorporate some of the practices of the new economy into a deeply rooted, hierarchical, and distrustful production system.

The particular outcomes at WoodWorks suggest an alternative framework for thinking about work reform. This framework is sensitive to how new bases for intensification of work and demands on the self are being created and recognizes that traditional forms of institutionalized power are in flux and even challenged, but that simultaneously new opportunities for skill development for workers, and new calculations about the costs and benefits of old versus new ways of working are evolving as well. The woodworkers I studied used new organizational opportunities and personal competencies developed in the participative management program to try to bring their plant into alignment with the shifting markets and accumulation logic of the 1990s.

As was true in the Reproco case, we cannot understand workers' participation in a new industrial relations regime without understanding the complex of meanings that workers attach to changes in production processes and social relations. I do not mean to suggest that blue-collar workers gained substantial or necessarily enduring advantage from work reform—advantage of a magnitude that might offset job loss or plant closure—but that new experiences they encountered as a result of work reform complicated their responses and force us to move away from simple formulations of participation *or* resistance. The case of WoodWorks illustrates the depth of temporariness and insecurity that have become business-as-usual for American workers, but it also demonstrates ways in which workers strive to gain control over and confront this new way of life.

Social Science Research on Participative Management: The "Theoretical Straightjacket"

The industrial relations, sociological, and economics literatures are replete with examples of unionized industrial workplaces such as WoodWorks, in which workers have felt pressured to cooperate with management's agenda to abandon traditional work methods and subsequently have lost political and financial ground. Researchers have viewed workers as reluctant participants in new work arrangements that demand greater involvement, force them to take greater risks, and generally make them more accountable for quality, productivity, and corporate profitability. They have also viewed participative management, employee involvement, and self-management as thinly disguised attempts to make workers absorb the cost at the plant level, when CEOs disinvest, diversify, and reinvest in profitable but nonproductive enterprises.[5] The bottom line, many believe, is that American capital has the freedom and the ability to withdraw from industry, and this prospect hovers over workers, virtually coercing them to move to a new framework for industrial relations.[6]

Indeed, it is in the study of industrial and production workplaces that the cynical perspective about employee involvement emerges full-blown and most unambiguously. Observers such as Bluestone and Bluestone (1992, chaps. 6 & 7), Graham (1995), Grenier (1988), Parker and Slaughter (1988), and Wells (1987) have noted multiple ways in which participative programs have been used to exploit, extract greater effort from, extend control over, and coopt industrial workers. Such programs may demand that workers do more without additional compensation or resources—learn new skills, take on new responsibilities, or monitor and manage their peers—but then fail to confer on workers real benefits or advantages. From the cynical point of view, top managers enlist workers' involvement to stave off profit crises but then undertake layoffs nevertheless (Wells 1987); companies use quality-circle schemes to coopt workers' political efforts and fight unions (Grenier 1988) or weaken unions (Fantasia, Clawson, and Graham 1988); and quality of working life programs in manufacturing firms have at times intensified work, reduced staffing levels without reducing work loads, and compelled workers "to internalize the company goals of efficiency and quality" (Shaiken, Herzenberg, and Kuhn 1986:178).

Milkman's research on auto workers (1997) is a seminal and nuanced contribution to understanding worker involvement in industrial companies purportedly moving toward a new industrial relations paradigm. Her monograph illuminates a widespread pattern in both the use and reception of new, purportedly participative work arrangements. *Farewell to the Factory* documents the unrealized potential in an employee involvement program at GM-Linden, a modernized automobile assembly plant. After buying out part of the workforce as a staffing reduction strategy, management introduced to the remaining workers new techniques for participation and new rhetorical claims that stressed the value of worker input. Yet managers and supervisors failed to abandon traditional, hierarchical ways of controlling and excluding workers, leaving them discouraged and cynical. *Farewell to the Factory* thus supports the cynical view that while management may officially endorse employee involvement programs and other types of work reform, managers don't necessarily provide the support or resources that workers need to successfully implement these reforms. Other researchers confirm the finding that managers and engineers ignore or minimize worker knowledge and input regarding production methods, materials, and quality processes (Graham 1995; Lamphere and Grenier 1994; Vallas and Beck 1996).[7]

At the core of the cynical view of new work arrangements is a zero-sum conceptualization of participative management in which management's gains are equated with workers' losses. Working within what might be termed the "political power" model of work reform, researchers either explicitly or implicitly adopt a narrow assumption about the nature of transformation in industrial unionized workplaces. *Farewell to the Factory* aside, much of this research has been firmly entrenched in an industrial-era perspective on labor relations and has privileged formal, institutionalized collective power, embodied in the labor union and the bargaining table. Management-initiated, collaborative-based worker participation programs are believed to undermine that power by doing away with the need for shop-floor stewards embedded in hierarchical approaches to work, by challenging the authority of unions, and by aligning workers' interests more with management's. Thus, by extension, these programs sap workers' power. In this model there has been little recognition of other forms of collective power, of individual forms of empowerment, or acknowledgment of conditions under which workers don't lose if they unite their efforts with those of managers.[8] Workers' agency—their perspectives on workplace change and the actions they take in light of change—has all too often been ignored. As Hodson (1991) has persuasively argued, much of the critical research on workplace transformation is bound by a "theoretical straightjacket," wherein workers either acquiesce to management's directives (the "false consciousness" perspective) or straightforwardly subvert them. Little has been done to explore more multifaceted dimensions of workers' actions.

While at Reproco uncertainty was muted and counterbalanced by a sense of tangible and short-term payoffs, at WoodWorks uncertainty and tenuousness were immediate, staring workers right in the eye; measurable payoffs for participating in new work schemes seemed distant, if not unattainable. Indeterminacy about the future if the plant was sold was a permanent feature of their everyday landscape. What was striking in this case study was the finding that despite uncertainty and pessimism about the

future, many of the workers nevertheless participated in the new
agenda—some reluctant, some skeptical but creative, some enthusiastic—
in order to maximize their chances to keep their jobs and to hold onto
their plant, the mainstay of the community.

Unique to the WoodWorks situation and workers' responses to it was
the lack of opportunity in the community and region, labor-market conditions that sharply constrained workers' options. Comparing WoodWorks
to the GM-Linden plant that Milkman studied highlights the importance
of this factor. Many of the auto workers Milkman interviewed held contempt for and refused to go along with work reform because they, too,
had a "profound sense of insecurity" over the future, a sense of insecurity
that "made the always formidable task of building a new relationship of
trust between labor and management nearly impossible" (1997:178–79).
Like the woodworkers, the auto workers worried that their occupational
futures with the Linden plant were fated to end. As at WoodWorks, significant numbers of Linden workers had been laid off; more were laid off
after Milkman completed her research. The Linden workers were convinced that a nearby competitor would undermine the security of their
plant, a threat continually thrown in their faces by the electronic signs,
posted throughout the workplace, comparing the production outcomes
for both plants. Yet prevailing labor-market conditions meant that workers at this auto plant had many more alternatives to employment than did
workers at the timber plant. Indeed, many of the workers in Milkman's
sample accepted the buyout package because they were willing but also
able to take a risk—to walk away from union wages and benefits, start their
own businesses, seek training in new fields, or take other entry-level jobs
with the hope of climbing up through the occupational and wage ladder
in other businesses.

When choices are constrained, however—as is the case when the core
business in a company town shuts down or when an entire industry declines in a region—workers' preferences and aspirations, their compro-
mises and resistances, and their willingness to struggle against clear odds
can take on a very different cast.[9] The mix of economic insecurity in the
workplace, coupled with lack of opportunity in the surrounding labor
market, may lead workers not to reject but to embrace what Cole (1979)
has called a community of fate, in which workers come to view their own
futures as deeply enmeshed with those of local management and are willing to align and adjust their efforts accordingly. I argue in this chapter
that the woodworkers tentatively moved away from adversarial workplace

relations to such a community of fate. It was an imperfect community, one that accommodated ambivalence and optimism, resentment and enthusiasm, but it was a community in which workers became purposive actors, self-conscious about their commitments, all the while cognizant that in the long run their efforts to participate in work reform might come to naught.

Neither in Madison nor in the surrounding area could workers easily find comparably paid jobs. Thus, workers had a significant investment in trying to keep the plan open. Many of the woodworkers believed that the survival of the plant—concretely, the probability that a "good" employer would buy the plant and enable it to stay open indefinitely—depended on their ability to demonstrate their adaptability to the new competitive environment. But that is only the larger plot, in which smaller segments tell about the new skills that workers acquired that took them far away from their traditional, production-oriented skill set. In turn, new skills and experiences created novel expectations about what was possible and served to deepen workers' commitments to making sure the plant survived. In their experiences we find a larger story about how stable, once-prosperous industrial workforces with decades of shared employment history struggle to come to grips with the changed conditions of business and production of the late twentieth century.

A Declining Industrial Sector: Setting the Stage

Driving through northwest Montana to reach the WoodWorks plant, I see pervasive evidence of the preeminence of the culture of timber, but also of the decline of the timber industry. Small town after small town displays the visual representations of life in a timber-oriented wilderness region: billboards announcing annual Logger Day celebrations; schools whose mascots, painted in murals and spelled out on marquees, are owls, bears, and badgers, the residents of the forests; restaurant windows along the main roads, often with elaborately painted pictures of male loggers with bulging arm muscles, holding a chain saw in one hand and an ax in the other.

On my journey I compete with fast-moving logging trucks piled high with precious trees, recently felled. In fact, according to local lore, one shouldn't even try to compete. Timber truck drivers are the indisputable, although not necessarily beloved, kings of the road. Residents of the area speak of the many, and occasionally fatal, accidents that have occurred when visitors, ignorant of or cocky about roadway norms, try to pass logging trucks on the main roads, collide with them on the back roads, or aren't watching carefully for trucks entering onto the main roads and highways.[10]

Beneath the surface are traces of a formerly robust industry. While individuals' commitments to their identity as members of a logging community seem strong, it is quite likely that this identity is flamboyantly displayed precisely because its material foundations are eroding. Vivid demonstrations of "being loggers" partly reflect nostalgia, anxiety over the loss of the basis of a shared community, and fear of the future as jobs have disappeared and plants have closed. And indeed, although I see operating plants, I see plants whose doors have been shut and locked permanently. As often as I have to contend with logging trucks on the road, I am told that twenty years earlier, their numbers were much higher.

It is obvious flying into the nearest regional airport that there has been extensive logging of the dense, difficult-to-penetrate forests, but even as I travel the main roads throughout the Idaho panhandle and the spectacular mountainous terrain of northwest Montana, I see gaping, dried-up swaths on the hillsides, clear-cut areas that evoke a sense that the supply of trees in the area is dwindling. And for all the proud and confident representations of loggers I see in public places, behind the scenes children of loggers have been leaving the region in droves, unable to find jobs in an industry that historically provided good employment to their fathers, and sometimes to their mothers, for decades.

In this part of the United States—rural, with a heavy dependence on extractive industries such as forestry and mining—there is no new vibrant economic base to supplant the old. Unlike Philadelphia, where manufacturing largely died but thriving service and financial sectors surged forward, many communities in the Northwest have been hard-pressed to develop new industries. Most profitable are tourism and the retirement industry, but this is not a dependable economic base. Tourism is hotly debated in Madison, for the town has much to attract visitors—glorious regional beauty and opportunities for hiking, boating, camping, and fishing. But as nonsupporters rightly note, jobs in this part of the service sector are a bleak replacement for blue-collar union jobs. Efforts to attract light industry have been more successful in areas close to an urban economy than in more remote regions like Madison. The stakes are high, therefore, for citizens of the region to hold onto long-standing businesses and industries.

In conversation after conversation, plant managers, workers, and community residents sound a familiar litany of explanations for why the timber industry has declined and why logging and timber production have become unprofitable and unwieldy. Mainstream environmentalists like the Sierra Club and other conservationist organizations are blamed for having restricted access to much-needed forests and for tying the hands of the industry in law suits to protect endangered species or old-growth forests. Radical environmentalists like Earthfirsters are blamed for wreaking costly damage on the industry when they sabotage and destroy construction equipment, rip out the markers laid in the ground to create new roadways reaching ever further into the woods, or drive metal stakes into trees to make them useless for timber production. Market prices for timber products have been volatile because of swings in the housing industry, periodically creating near-depression conditions for the region as a whole. Many believe that the supply of timber is quite simply running out, and most people are aware of the blunt fact of automation in this industry and the degree to which it has eliminated jobs.[11]

Reading the proclamations of timber industry leaders, one thing is clear: WoodWorks business executives have concluded that being in the timber, wood-products, and building-products industry is no longer profitable. In the mid-1980s, the CEO of WoodWorks International, headquartered on the East Coast, announced the closures of several plants in the region, explaining this development in a way that crystallized the complex calculations about the state of the timber-products industry. At a news conference reported in Madison's local newspaper, he said:

> We've lost immense amounts of money in this business and couldn't see any end in sight. It's been a major drain despite extensive cost saving efforts over the past several years. For the last five years, the building products industry, particularly in the western United States, has been unprofitable. In spite of intensive efforts to cut costs and improve productivity, external economic forces continue to frustrate any immediate prospects for a reasonable return on the capital invested in WoodWorks' western facilities.

It seems likely that many factors led to this conclusion, but the important fact for the woodworkers of Madison is that WoodWorks International has been closing shop, withdrawing from timber, and reallocating capital into other industries and product markets.

Madison's WoodWorks plant is a work site in transition, caught between old and new paradigms of industrial relations. Its modest towers and smokestacks, pouring out steam against the backdrop of a small hillside, are decades old. One sees from the main road a sprawling industrial complex of small and large buildings and sheds. Further off the road is an enormous logyard with piles of recently harvested logs and several small, murky log ponds. Enormous yellow wagners, rumbling, thirty-three-ton pieces of equipment on wheels, use their pincers to pick up logs and put them on piles or in the pond. They seem to be charging chaotically through the logyard, although I discover shortly that their drivers are engaged in a purposive, collaborative dance with and around one another. A short train track, connected to the Burlington-Northern rail line, runs throughout the complex, transporting across the nation the boxcars loaded with studs, plywood, and wood chips that will be sold to paper pulp plants.

But the administration building, the point of entry for any visitor, symbolizes the plant's efforts to move to a new framework for thinking about workers—how they do their jobs and how best to gain their cooperation in the industrial enterprise. Low-slung and modern, it houses a sizable, recently built physical fitness center, testament to health and exercise fads, and to the current mantra that the company needs to pay more attention to its workers' physical and emotional health. Housed here also are conference rooms where workers—who ten years ago never sat down to talk with their managers away from the bargaining table, who historically were primarily concerned about protecting their interests *qua* workers—undergo a training process with fellow workers and with supervisors and managers. The training is intended to convert them into more involved participants, workers who are expected to step into the shoes of management and view their jobs and their work relations with an eye to managers' dilemmas and constraints.

A modest library comprising some of the latest management and self-help books about the changing economy, new trends in work, and career management occupies one room. John Naisbet's tome to the future, *Megatrends*, is displayed prominently, as is a binder of the regular newsletter—*Timber Flash!*—put together by the PM trainers. The latter feature occasional columns with titles like "Confessions of a PM Skeptic," in which workers write about their positive encounters with PM, mostly in the tone of the testimonial and trumpeting personal conversion. The optimism about the future that is signaled by this cheery setting is at distinct odds with the underlying gloom regarding the plant's future.

Formal Participative Management: Reconstructing Workers

The framework of involvement, a new emphasis on cooperation and communication, poses a dramatic point of departure from traditional bases of interaction in the plant. At Reproco, employee involvement was a novel approach to work for many of the workers, but it was an approach that was organically built into the facilities from their inception. The organization of facilities and the subcontracting of photocopying work came about as a new business strategy, was customized to fit differing business environments, and was repeatedly reconstituted in new settings. Workers were brought in at ground zero, work groups were continually reconfigured, and the clientele was diverse. WoodWorks' new program, in contrast, overlays long-standing, hierarchical labor processes and employment traditions.

WoodWorks' participative management program has both formal and informal components. On the formal side, new organizational spaces have been created for training workers and supervisors and for soliciting their input. All employees initially go through awareness training seminars, two-day sessions held at a local church.[12] In these sessions, they learned about the market status of the company and of the changing nature of the globalized economy (especially factors that are reshaping their work, such as the pressing concern for quality, for customers, and for customization); principles of clear, nondefensive communication; and skills associated with participating in and running meetings. These sessions serve as the orientation for participative management. One can take a seminar in situational leadership, in "financial training" (where they learn how to read budgets and profit and loss statements), and in procedures such as statistical control. The trainers coordinate the publication of *Timber Flash!*, the monthly newsletter exclusively devoted to participative management issues. The newsletter contains articles written by the trainers about PM in general, about experiences with PM in diverse work locations inside the plant, and about outside seminars they attend. It also reprints articles on PM from other sources and occasionally runs columns, written by workers, about successful experiences in training and successful outcomes of their task forces. In formally organized task forces, workers ideally implement the skills, insights, and techniques learned in PM training. Task forces are often cross-functional, bringing together individuals with different areas of expertise, such as planning, marketing, sales, and production processes. WoodWorks' task forces are roughly the equivalent of quality circles: a "study group, which concentrates on solving job-related quality problems, broadly conceived as improving methods of production as part of company-wide efforts. At the same time, it focuses on the self-development of workers... development of leadership abilities of foremen and workers, skill development among workers, identification of natural leaders with supervisory potential, improvement of worker morale and motivations, and the stimulation of teamwork within work groups" (Cole 1979:135).

Informally and culturally, the message of participative management is that the historical divide between workers and managers must contract. Programmatically, PM is concerned with transforming workers into neophyte managers. Much of the substance of the training brings to the surface the tacit rules of managers, translates them into guidelines for workers, and urges them to adopt the point of view of managers, to move away from the "hourly" perspective. Seminars emphasize the dysfunctions of traditional, hierarchical ways of communicating and interacting and highlight the benefits of new approaches to communication that allow for more give-and-take, less defensiveness, greater understanding in trying to resolve problems, and relaxation of rules governing grievances.

A description of the Collaborative Skills training program printed in *Timber Flash!*, indeed, sounds much like the communication principles that Reproco's machine operators learned: It "[s]hows people how to understand better why people act and react as they do. It not only helps with understanding, it helps us deal with people and situations in a positive manner, to help relieve tension and make a clearer picture of what people are saying and doing. [It] shows how each of us have or may have different perceptions, how we communicate, both verbally and nonverbally, how to listen better, and how to give positive, constructive feedback."

These practices and emphases flow from the plant's definition of participative management as a "team approach in decision making, in which a team is given the latitude to determine and influence its job, as the members of the team carry out the requirements of their jobs and meet the goals of the organization." To realize these goals, workers should:

- be responsible for their own actions;
- be accountable to the organization, the team, fellow workers, and themselves;
- encourage input and ideas from individuals in planning and decision making; and
- emphasize self-supervision with minimum direction from above.[13]

The overall effect of PM, therefore, is to encourage workers to move beyond a "positional" or them/us mentality; get them to step into the shoes of managers; and disrupt traditional adversarial patterns of (not) interacting and communicating. In this way, management is attempting to modernize the human relations of the plant. Setting up the formal participative management program, company management strives to overcome traditional divisions between workers and managers, to exhort workers to step outside themselves and activate their human and cultural capital to improve quality, innovation, and efficiency.

Participation and Compliance in the Plywood Plant

To learn about the effects of participative management in an automated, industrial setting, I conducted the bulk of my research in WoodWorks' plywood plant. The plywood plant, having been modernized in the 1980s, seemed likely to present the conditions and practices that I most wanted to understand. Specifically, it appeared to be a fruitful site for studying the way that employee involvement programs, production systems, and workers' belief systems (particularly workers whose beliefs had been forged in the previous industrial era) interacted. Present also at the Madison plant was a stud mill that operated with old-generation (circa 1950) processing systems, a saw mill, a planar, a finger joint plant, and a logyard, sites at which I interviewed additional individuals.[14]

In the plywood plant—a warehouse-sized building in which the production process snakes along for hundreds and hundreds of yards, through dozens of different treatments and pieces of equipment, culminating in towering piles of plywood—state-of-the-art log treatment and processing technology has radically reshaped the conditions of work. Production in the plywood division was labor intensive until the early 1980s; by 1993 nearly every step of the production cycle had been reorganized with cutting-edge, computer-based technology. At the "green end," or beginning of the cycle, undried logs are heated, then peeled down with super-fine lathes that are directed by laser. The lasers precisely focus the lathes and allow them to pare away massive, thin sheets of veneer.

A new-generation stacking machine (a machine that replaced thirty workers who once sorted by look and by feel, according to the operations manager) prepares the veneer for the gargantuan steam dryers, automatically sorting the sheets by width and moisture content. (The amount of time the veneer sheets will spend in the dryer depends on how dry or wet they are.) Three workers later whip sheets of dried veneer off a rack, gluing them to chunks of veneer that are spewed out by a gluing machine, to create plywood of different thicknesses. If necessary, the plywood is sawed and sanded to improve the grade. Finally, a massive press cinches batches of plywood sheets, and they are mechanically sorted into stacks by quality and dimension. All the while, forklift drivers move veneer and plywood from one stage of the production process to another.

The jobs in the plywood plant vary, from the unbearably hot and boring job of the drier who sits and monitors the ultra-large drying machines, the arduous but respected physical job of the spreader who manipulates the sheets of glued veneer, the mind-numbingly tedious job of the "plugger," who sits at a small machine that punches knots out of sheets of plywood and replugs the holes with better-quality wood, to the coveted job at the beginning of the whole stream, where an operator sits at the head of the "green chain" in an air-conditioned room and oversees the logs when they come in on the conveyor belt and begin their journey down the line. All the while, he or she watches for bottlenecks and keeps an eye on monitors to make sure that logs don't get jammed and that all machinery operates smoothly.

Of the approximately two hundred workers in plywood, about one-quarter are women. *Within* the plant, some jobs are highly segregated by gender: spreading and green-chain work is nearly always done by men; women work at the finishing end and staff the dryers. This division of labor is malleable, however, with women crossing over to do men's jobs when needed. But even with this considerable number of women, the plant is palpably a masculinized, blue-collar work environment, embodied in the sweaty, manual labor required for most jobs, the positioning of men in the high-status jobs (the green-chain operator, the spreader),[15] and the proliferation of unequivocally macho task-force names such as the "Wood Lords," the "Survivalists," and the "Stud Runners."[16]

The machinery and conveyor belts that move logs and processed wood conform to Fordist organizational principles. The product moves down

the line from start to finish, and although wood products have to be fed
into and moved through different pieces of machinery (the lathes, the
sorters, the dryers, the stackers, and so forth), and although the pace ebbs
and flows, surges rather than streams continuously, this process nevertheless consists of a series of discrete points through which the veneer
and the plywood sheets must pass to be processed uniformly. The division
of labor among the plywood workers similarly follows the principles of
the assembly line: workers are stationed at each point, and when they're
on the line they remain stationed there. Their tasks are extremely individualized; with the exception of the spreaders, who work in groups of
three to glue and move veneer, all other workers perform their jobs on
their own, doing the same tasks continually throughout the daytime, the
evening, or the graveyard shifts. As I walk along the line, observing each
stage in the manufacture of plywood, interaction between workers is minimal, limited mostly to the introductions my guide makes. The unrelenting flow of the line, coupled with the deafening sound of machinery, re-
stricts opportunities to chat casually with any individual.

How Participative Management
Changed Production Workers' Jobs

While the production line was organized on Fordist principles, an overlay of neo-Fordist principles of interactions and worker involvement
(Vallas 1999:77–84) distinguished the social-relational side of the factory
floor. Plywood workers were strongly urged to participate in task forces,
on which they identified and solved a variety of problems and issues pertinent to the facility and brainstormed about ways of carrying out tasks
with which they were unfamiliar.

One task force had designed a cord that in emergencies could more
safely and conveniently switch off the conveyor belt leading into one of
the stackers; one created a "log deck" that allowed workers to safely cross
over the lathe operation; another designed a safe and accessible route
into the plywood plant for ambulances; and yet another found better ways
of storing veneer.[17] The task-force structure had left the technical side of
work—the highly automated assembly-line production process—intact.
Later, workers and managers in this plant hoped to have workers routinely
rotate through different jobs. But the primary goal of this phase of work
reform was to change workers' mindsets about who was responsible for
production and how production might be improved, to raise workers'

awareness as participants who had an impact on the prosperity of the firm. Plant management and the PM trainers were intent on getting workers to recognize the constraints and barriers that managers faced every day and to think about ways to cope with and overcome them. Task forces were the vehicle that would take workers closer to this goal, and participating in a task force required workers to engage in a new array of interactions with coworkers, with supervisors and managers, and with workers (from other parts of the plant) and customers, "clients" who were "upstream" and "downstream" from them.

Having to develop a broader view of and responsibility for creating and selling their products had, in some instances, expanded the scope of workers' responsibilities away from the line. An emphasis on making production more immediately responsive to the market had led to the formation of work groups that customized small-to-moderate batches for customers. This expansion of tasks and responsibilities had opened up new doors for those involved. One team's project exemplified the thrust to get workers to step into management's shoes, to view business from managers' perspective, and to expand workers' knowledge of the pressures and dynamics of the market. This team had been authorized to oversee the completion of a large customized order from beginning to end, from taking the order to fulfilling it and shipping it out to the customer. In doing so, the workers had executed tasks and entered into business relationships with parties with whom they traditionally had little if any contact. For example, they had calculated the cost estimates of the order and placed bids with the customer to get a contract for the order (dealing with external clients); they had procured the materials at a competitive price, a process they had to work through with purchasing agents (internal clients); they had worked with the maintenance crew to establish a schedule for completing the order (another set of internal clients); and they had even had to contract with an outside firm to carry out one phase of the project (external clients).

Here is an instance in which traditional hierarchical arrangements were altered. First, these workers were now negotiating with customers outside the firm, as well as with inside parties who once coordinated a transaction such as this one. Previously, these workers had been positioned at the bottom of the "transaction loop," relegated to executing the order after the bidding, materials procurement, and scheduling were done by others. Second, these workers were making judgment calls about how to fulfill the task. Although they needed to obtain final approval for their plans from supervisors and managers, they had been authorized to collect and select the data, and plug in the variables for their plan, relying on their assessments of price, quality, and timing.

It would be incorrect to conclude that workers perceived these new demands and experiences as simply onerous and unrewarding, or that they felt unduly coerced into taking on new responsibilities. Matt, one of the members of this team who had found this project challenging but surprisingly enjoyable, remarked that "we had to go through all the steps, all the paperwork and everything, to see to it that the project was carried out and then do a follow-up report, which was another part of the learning—so it was a real educational experience." He went on to say:

That's what the real value of the task forces have been—that people learned how to work the system and we learned that sometimes it's not as easy as we thought it was. Now, when the ball is thrown into our court we realize why. It's not just a matter of saying, "This needs to be done." We had to find somebody to do it. We had to procure the materials. We began to realize that it's not just a matter of having a good idea and then telling management and it was gonna happen . . . It was a lot more involved than just those steps. A lot of us look at it a lot differently now. When management has to make a decision that's not so popular we can understand why these things come about because we've gone through, particularly with our task forces, gone through and started a project from the very beginning.

Another team remedied their lack of experience dealing directly with customers by organizing a daylong visit to two customers in the area to whom they regularly supplied wood products. Touring the premises of a molding plant and a newsprint operation, the men on the team talked with workers and managers of both companies, observing how each used wood stock and chips from WoodWorks, gaining firsthand knowledge about how their own product was evaluated by those consuming them. Team members reported feeling energized by their exposure to other operations and by their new insights about how their products were part of a larger business stream. Al, who had worked at the Madison plant for over twenty years, as had his father, claimed to have gained confidence from working with his task-force comrades to plan and execute the trip and from meeting people out in the field. He ended by saying:

I think partly, too, I'm a Madison native, and my father worked at the mill and it's just a family-type thing [the tradition of working for WoodWorks]. And he was here for many, many years. So I will probably be here for many, many years, too, doing the same thing and not thinking I should go out and do something different. But *now* I think a lot differently. I'm not afraid now to go out and pursue and try different things. So it's been a big deal difference to me.

To a lesser degree than was the case at Reproco, but with no less meaning, given the dramatic shift in emphasis away from blue-collar skills to white-collar, communications skills, WoodWorkers identified ways in which they used various aspects of the communications process away from their daily jobs at the plant. Much like those Reproco workers who used their interpersonal and conflict-resolution skills in their homes, churches, and community organizations, a few woodworkers volunteered that they had used the OMR process—Outcomes, Methods, and Resources, a problem-solving process—to figure out how to complete projects they were executing at home. Gene, a plywood-plant worker who was especially enthusiastic about the training he had received in the PM program, described a situation in which he had been called upon to use his new communicational and presentation skills in the community:

There was some kind of bill (legislation) for truckers that was going to change, and the representative from the area called our union to find out if there were some people in the union who could help them conduct that meeting [taking place about one hundred miles away from Madison]. The union asked for volunteers to go down there and do that for them. We went to the school where they had their community meeting and set up our flip charts in the back of the room because we really didn't know what was going to happen or anything, and everybody turned their chairs around to where the flip charts were, and when the speaker started talking he was in the back of the room. And we organized that meeting and broke it down into smaller groups, and they got through that with very little conflict and a lot more understanding, and that's the kind of thing—WoodWorks, we donated our time and WoodWorks donated the transportation to get there and so, like I say, it's even larger than the community. It's larger than the county.

At a safety task-force meeting of about thirty workers, I observed two men, who had never run meetings or given public presentations before, try out their leadership skills, doing so in a way that was a break from but consistent with traditional norms of communication in the plant. Mike and Allen were two first-time group facilitators. They were visibly nervous and self-deprecating as they walked all the participants through the agenda. The goal of this task force was to come up with a survey on safety issues to be distributed to work groups throughout the plant. Using the obligatory flip chart, they wrote down some of the ideas generated in the brainstorming session, awkwardly flipping page after page of suggestions.

The participants—with only one woman in attendance—continually made good-natured fun of the facilitators. Putting it diplomatically, there was a lot of give and take between facilitators and participants, and much banter between those attending. I struggled to keep myself from laughing as people randomly shouted over each other, yelled at the facilitators to repeat things, and talked among themselves. Much of the conversation, such as it was, consisted of humorous jabs at managers. In one corner of the room, a group of men were teasing Mary, who was every bit as raucous as her male counterparts. At one point, Mike, one of the facilitators, shouted over the din, to everyone and to no one, "Did you all get that?"

At first, I could see this chaos only through the narrow lens of my own involvement in meetings in middle-class institutions. Whether working on the editorial board of a journal, sitting in a department meeting or on a professional committee, or participating in a volunteer organization in the university town where I live, my experiences have always been shaped by a commitment, shared by other participants from similar class backgrounds and political values, to follow an agenda in an orderly fashion, allow people to speak and be heard, and maintain a respectful tone toward other people's comments. Observing these blue-collar workers, I had to resist making sarcastic comments to my contact person, who was sitting next to me, about how disorganized the meeting was. But it soon became apparent that what looked like utter chaos and what I initially interpreted as disrespect constituted, in fact, a functional and cooperative approach to finishing the business of the day. The meeting was a place to vent and to bond, to carry out the goals of PM in a way that allowed the participants to have some ownership of the process, to put their stamp on the new PM agenda. A smoother, more polished facilitation effort, or an insistence on stricter adherence to prespecified guidelines might have been counterproductive, and would not have continued long-standing ways in which these workers interacted with one another.

When the meeting ended, the group applauded Mike and Allen. The two men blushed and gathered up the mess of papers they had managed to strew all around the front of the room. Others came up and congratulated them afterward on having run their first successful meeting. Both Mike and Allen seemed relieved to have it over, bashfully pleased about their accomplishment. They had achieved the goal of the task force: a draft of a survey intended to measure the frequency and usefulness of safety meetings and workers' perceptions of safety features throughout the plant.

I later interviewed one of the men whom I met at the safety task-force meeting. He worked in plywood at the front end of the production line and had found himself having to negotiate with coworkers more than he could remember ever having done in the past. I pushed him, asking whether the new principles of interaction and communication represented a break with the past. His response—emphasizing the need to take the role of the other, to see things from their perspective—reminded me of the way that the Reproco workers talked about their new communicational skills.

> There *was* communication, but I guess part of this [the new guidelines for communication] was giving feedback, you know; and there's a lot of ways to get feedback. There's sign language, you know, which a lot of people get, and there's verbal, you know.
>
> And that's gonna happen all the time and that's fine. But now I'm just trying to understand people. Try to understand, like, with my fellow worker. If there is something bothering them and that for one reason or another they're not themselves—I try to understand. Everybody has an off day. And it used to be, "He's trying to screw me." Well, that's not necessarily it. You've got to understand the people that you work with because there are numerous personalities. I mean, every kind you could possibly imagine you have them out there.

In part, reconstructing workers was a mutual effort in which plant-level management, union leaders, and other workers all tried to transcend the Fordist principles of work organization. Consistent with the fears of the critics of American work reform, this collective regrouping was not political, not defined by workers' status *qua* workers. Indeed, the goal of the PM leaders was the opposite: to abandon the hierarchical, narrow, and limiting relationships of traditional labor/management relations, in which workers were positioned on one side of the divide and managers on the other. A secondary goal was to dissolve divisions between workers and managers by enlisting workers in the managerial project of increasing efficiency, effectiveness, and quality. One of the trainers highlighted these goals when I asked him what effect he thought the new PM program had on the plywood workforce.

> They [the workers] start to see themselves as a unit. In the past they would see themselves as individuals and really not communicate with anybody else on their team. For example, in the plywood plant, on the green end the team may start at the bark area where the logs come in off the pond, and go all the way through to the end of the green end [phase of the line]. Well, the person who pulls the veneer at the end of the green end would never communicate to the person at the other end. It just wasn't done. If there was any communication that needed to be done, they would call the supervisor, the green end supervisor, and the green end supervisor would either handle it himself or he would call his supervisor, and *his* supervisor would go out and talk to the bark operator, and the bark operator would come back and the process would reverse itself, and the message would go through three or four steps before it got to be person-to-person.
>
> The team concept says that the person at the end can go directly to the bark operator and talk to him himself; he doesn't have to go through his supervisors, and that's one of the differences.

In this respect, the new framework has achieved what most pessimists would have predicted: that employee involvement and participative management are little more than schemes for putting a greater portion of the burden for efficiency and productivity on individual workers' shoulders. Furthermore, these teams anchor a system of "concertive" (Barker 1993) or "tyrannical" (Sinclair 1992) control, in which workers monitor themselves and their peers more intensely. But if we are to understand why workers are cooperating in the new agenda, even if sometimes reluctantly, why they extract a different meaning from these activities and don't resist being enlisted in management's goals, it is important to place their perspectives against the backdrop of traditional methods and sensibilities.

For one thing, many of the workers I spoke with have ambivalent or negative feelings about the hard lines drawn between workers and management in the past. As was true with Milkman's auto workers, the tradition of adversarial labor/management relations left much bitterness in the memories of the WoodWorkers; few were attached to what one man called "positional politics," a black-and-white way of looking at shop-floor activities of earlier times. When relations between workers and their managers were more positional, he said, "[t]here wasn't a whole lot of discussion about what's fair and what is appropriate. It was like, well, what does the contract say, and then both sides would argue their side of what the contract says. The company would take a position...and the only alternative in our dispute procedure was to go through that procedure and then take it to the membership for a vote." Workers on the shop floor were nearly completely excluded from deliberations about everyday production processes. Men and women variously spoke of the old mode of working in which they "left their brains at the door" when they came to the job, and, at the end of a shift, left work and tucked it away in the back of their minds. Sue, a fifteen-year veteran of the plywood plant, said "we came in and we did our job and then we went home and that was it. We weren't paid to think, we were there for our backs." She commented that:

> I think PM has affected people a lot. People used to say, "That's not my job, I don't do that." And I think people are tending to do more. There's always gonna be some that do the fine line—"I'll do exactly what I have to and not a thing more." But I think there are a lot—they want to be involved and they want to work on...this is *their* future, you know, and doing things better or different, you know, means our livelihood. So I think some people, for that reason, might move forward.

Like Sue, many workers decided to experiment with the PM program because they were convinced that it would ensure the viability of the plant itself. They didn't challenge the logic of profits, markets, or capital accumulation; rather, they sought ways of ensuring that their plant would adapt to the turbulent, precarious market logic of the 1990s. Their primary focus was on increasing the value of the workforce and creating a set of work relations and skills that would be marketable to prospective buyers. Their reasoning strongly reminded me of the laboring and devout Puritans, blindly but hopefully striving to be one of God's chosen (Weber 1904/1958). On one hand, they hoped that through their good-faith effort to move into a new era of labor/management relations, they would stay profitable and, in so doing, convince corporate-level management to change its mind about selling the plant. On the other hand, they calculated that, if WoodWorks' parent corporation *did* sell it, their efforts would signal to whoever took over that they were willing and able to cooperate and were a viable industrial enterprise. Various workers formulated this equation to me in interviews.

One man, who had worked at WoodWorks for over twenty years, remarked: "If we work together, maybe WoodWorks will keep us. If we work together and be more profitable and keep putting out quality products and what not, maybe the new buyer will be more apt to keep us running rather than to buy us for real estate property or something."

Pamela, employed at WoodWorks for twenty years, rationalized why she and fellow workers decided to disregard the news that the plant was for sale and pour their energies into improving the way they did their jobs:

> You know we've talked about being sold…so when that first happened [the announcement of a possible sale] we kind of all went, "Whoa." You know, "Where does this put us with the (PM) process?" Do we just say, hmmm, "We'll be WoodWorkers anyway?" We felt we needed to continue to do things the best that we possibly can because if somebody comes in to look at us, it's like when you're gonna buy a new car, you want to buy the one that looks good and performs well. You don't want the one where the parts are picking on each other and, you know, it looks like crap. We have to do things the best that we can and continually try to improve. Max [the plant manager] said, "You never know, they *could* pull us off the sale block." He doesn't think that's gonna happen, but you know, it's there.

Another man commented directly on skill upgrading in the industry and the need for WoodWorks employees to stay on par: "We're just trying to be in business, to stay in business, to work smarter, be the best in the business, beat the competitors. The competitors are the Boise Cascades, and some of those are even involved in this kind of process, too. So, you know, it's just a matter of staying one step ahead of them."

The union vice-president spoke of the need for union and management to work together to upgrade the mill workforce, saying, "We've discovered we've got to work together, you know, that otherwise outside elements are gonna destroy us or whatever. If you look at it as, we're working together, it really won't be a problem."

Wanda was particularly expressive and adamant in her belief that it was the collective efforts of the workforce that had prolonged the life of the plant. She'd worked at WoodWorks for nearly twenty years and had witnessed firsthand the profound changes taking place in labor relations. She said:

> If we hadn't had these changes I don't know if we would have survived. We went through some real hard times and lost a lot of money. Just because of the times and the way things were. And I think we're doing a lot of things different and a lot of things better. I think there's a whole lot *more* we could do a lot better, still. I don't know if it's a never-ending thing. But the actual announcement of the sale hit a lot of people, like boom. And, "I don't want to have anything to do with [PM]." But a lot of us said, "Well, let's make the best of what we have and continue on."

Participative management was neither uniformly successful nor unilaterally embraced. To some people in the plywood plant PM felt forced, and its artificiality as a top-down innovation was obvious and resented. Some workers here exemplified what Hodson calls "reluctant participants": that is, they took part in the "official" aspects of PM—the task forces—but they often begrudged the extra time involved and had little confidence that on the whole what they did made much difference. The limits to *requiring* that people change, that they continually seek to innovate and brainstorm in the absence of concrete problems, were painfully clear in the descriptions of plywood task forces whose purposes were nebulous and open-ended, that didn't resolve obvious and immediate problems but sent workers on a hunt to *find* problems. Looking at such task-force mission statements as to "study veneer carts and characteristics," "outcome not yet picked," "study profitable ways of handling $1' \times 4's$," I imagined the resentment sparked by "having" to come up with new ideas to improve efficiency and performance. One man I spoke with, who had worked at WoodWorks for twenty-two years, railed against the "busywork" that the PM program was forcing on him.

This finding is consistent with research specifying the conditions under which employee involvement programs are or can be successful in American workplaces. EIPs that are formally designed from above and foisted onto workers but that don't allow workers to change their work or decide how to do their work, are either viewed more cynically by workers themselves or will patently fail (Bluestone and Bluestone 1992; Kochan, Katz, Mower 1984). Milkman (1997) documented a similar outcome in her study of auto workers. While workers initially endorsed employee involvement, their enthusiasm turned to distrust and skepticism as they realized that management wasn't committed to creating an environment in which their input and deliberations would genuinely make a difference.

Varano's (1999) study of the Weirton Steel employee buyout corroborates this view. One mandate of the buyout was that workers had to participate in a new involvement program, which had the ironic effect of creating new rigidities and reinforcing bureaucratic procedures, rather than eradicating them. Not surprisingly, this outcome left the steelworkers deeply disillusioned, soured on the optimistic rhetoric about the benefits of marching into the new industrial era. At WoodWorks, teams and PM were met with most enthusiasm when workers were allowed to use their insights and decision-making tools to tackle problems in meaningful ways. If a team project required that workers brainstorm on substantive issues and authorized workers to carry forward with their deliberations, team members tended to espouse the goals of PM to a much greater degree.

Reluctance is understandable, given the personal risks that workers take when they put themselves out on a limb, try to get involved, and have to exercise new skills. One individual tried to decipher his own feelings of ambivalence about the new program, pointing out that:

> We have more focus now on the "we" or the "us," rather than "those guys" versus "us guys." We try to build our leadership skills, and it's a little scary for some people. Some people would rather, you know, they've never admitted it before, but they would rather let somebody else do the things and they can just ride it out and do the things that they're told to do. Others are more than eager to get a chance to really do something like leading and to take responsibility and accountability.

Sue's comments after Mike's and Allen's presentation were poignant in this respect, explaining why she thought it took courage for them to volunteer to lead this meeting and become visible group participants: "They don't have the ability to communicate in an effective way because they've never been trained to do it. They have a hard time going back and putting all their sentence structures together and all that kind of stuff, to make it look like something that they could be proud of presenting."

Another reason for reluctance emerged in interviews with some male workers who expressed discomfort with the interactive dimensions of these new organizational innovations—brainstorming in task forces, communicating with coworkers directly about problems on the shop floor rather than indirectly through shop stewards. They were under increased pressure from supervisors and coworkers to explain and express themselves, to engage in direct interactions. Under the new regime of workplace relations, on-the-job communication required yet another level of personal involvement that many had been all too happy to avoid. The trainers recognized this reluctance for greater interpersonal engagement, one noting that, "I think one group of people that are a little hesitant are people who may feel that they're unable to demonstrate their thoughts or feelings to anybody."

Pat's narrative, about how generations of his family had lived and worked in this region, highlighted the degree to which a masculinized ethos of one-upmanship had permeated relations between workers and their managers.[18] The context in which he relayed this to me was our discussion about the new guidelines for communication that he'd learned in his training seminar. He had expressed frustration with his struggle to enact the new rules of interaction because they ran counter to, not only his traditional approach, but to the approach of earlier generations in his family. He told me, as background to his frustration:

> I'm fifth generation to live in this community. My grandfather wasn't working for this particular outfit at the time, but he worked on the river runs when they ran the logs down to Lincoln's Ferry; and when he was, I think, about seventeen years old he got his first job working on the, what do they call it, running the logs down the river.
>
> And the foreman, to prove that he was boss and to prove that he could whip him, he got him out on some logs and knocked him in the water; and every time he [Pat's grandfather] tried to grab a log to get back up, he'd step on his fingers. So, "I'm the boss, you listen to me and do what I say." It was that kind of a situation. And so, the reason maybe he didn't communicate was that maybe you wouldn't want that person to know that you had any weaknesses, so you wouldn't ask any questions and you would be very protective of anything, particularly your weaknesses, so nobody learned anything from one another because they all wanted everybody to believe that they knew it all.
>
> And so, that's kind of been the history. [People] still have a suspicion that, "I don't want to let him know something that I know or something that I don't know because he may take advantage of it. The union was probably formed because of people like that."

This narrative, undoubtedly originating from an actual event but also probably containing elements of a legend about his grandfather that have

grown as the years have passed, touches on a core finding. Many
WoodWorkers identified with a traditional, confrontational framework
within which they related to supervisors and managers. An extremely masculinized framework, it was based on conflict, polarization, and distrust.
Many workers felt ambivalent about making the leap to a new way of thinking about their position in the plant, but as the example of Mike and Allen
(the neophyte facilitators I described earlier) illustrates, many are also
willing to try.

Finally, the terms and discourse of PM had opened up new lines of
counterstrategy for workers. Many workers were willing to experiment
with and participate in task forces, take responsibility for new tasks, and
struggle with new communicative norms. I also uncovered instances
where workers attempted to use participative management to their own
advantage, to strike out in a more global sense to grasp some control over
the fate of the plant. The business manager of the local union recounted
to me how a group of workers had written a letter to corporate-level management, asking to open a dialogue about the possibility of carrying forward with a worker buyout of the plant. A task force had been devoted to
analyzing this prospect. At the time of my study, nothing concrete had
transpired, but the core issue is that workers tried to use the tools of PM
to take a more active role in the plant's future.

Along these lines, several people I interviewed referred to an incident
in which a group of workers had been angry when they weren't able to
get access to profit-and-loss statements for the plant. They wanted to use
these statements to learn more about sections in the plant that weren't
productive, in order to argue for improvements that would improve the
overall prosperity of the plant. Pamela observed:

> There's more and more people getting involved. In fact, a lot of them are to
> the point now that once it started, you know, the thought processes, now they
> think that they're entitled to it, that they're entitled to the information. You
> know, they get the profit-and-loss statements and they get the production runs
> and all this kind of stuff, and now that they've been getting that information,
> when it doesn't come they get mad because they think that they're entitled
> to it now.

Even as workers were carrying out their jobs in different ways, however, they maintained a critical perspective on WoodWorks management.
They didn't absolve corporate-level management of its responsibility for

the good of the firm and the bottom line; they didn't forgive management for making the dire decision to sell the plant. They were cynical and
uneasy, even if their cynicism was submerged, about the forward-looking
emphasis on participative management, given their well-founded
suspicions about corporate management's commitment to them. For example, Brad, the union vice-president who early in our interview said that
he thought all the workers were "dead ducks," later modulated his
opinion:

> Well, I think participative management can work. I think that because of
> what's happened in the last year—even if WoodWorks stays on board or if
> somebody else comes on board, I think there will need to be a reassessment
> of what it's about, as far as, you know, if WoodWorks stays on board there has
> got to be a recommitment from upper management that says that this is going
> to work, and we'll help it work. People were told that they [corporate man-
> agement] were committed before, and a year later they were up for sale. So I
> think there's got to be a recommitment and a reassessment of procedure and
> the process in order for it to work.

This in-depth look at workers in the plywood plant sheds light on the
range of workers' experiences, the meanings they derived from a new approach to industrial relations, and hints at why workers consented to the
new platform of participative management, even when their prospects
appeared dim. Based on interviews with a small number of workers in
other settings—the stud mill, the planar, the saw mill—the plywood workers' reactions seem fairly widespread. Significantly, however, there was one
area in the plant where workers spurned the cautious optimism and the
willingness to suspend distrust and experiment with new ways.
Understanding the circumstances surrounding their refusal highlights
the conditions for others' consent, whether reluctant or zestful.

"Perspiration Management": Natural Collaboration and Resistance to Top-down, Formalized Participative Management

The superintendent of the logyard, Harold, picks me up in the company
pickup truck, in which we follow muddy and rutted roads around mounds
of logs, heading for the far reaches of the WoodWorks property. Making
good on his promise to let me observe and talk to workers with different
perspectives on PM, he had arranged for me to go out to the logyard to

speak with and observe the men who moved newly harvested logs off logging trucks, deposited them in the logyard, and later moved them to one of the production sites. Harold pulls up in front of a beat-up, small, white shack. He suggests that I spend some time with the "men" out here to get a taste of the organization of work and the impact of PM in a very different work setting. When I realize how isolated this is, I start to feel nervous, but when I enter the shack and it sinks in on me that Harold is leaving me here, I begin to have serious doubts that I will be able to pull off this particular component of my research.

The shack is nothing more than a small room with refrigerator, coffeepot, microwave, and large square table around which six men are seated. The room has the smell of hard labor—a mix of sweat, cigarette smoke, and oil. Indeed, the men's hands and faces are shaded with dust and oil; it is an amalgam that also has settled deeply into their denim and flannel work clothes. The walls do nothing to increase my comfort level, covered as they are with pinup calendars and sexist cartoons. The gender, educational, and class divide between myself and these men is wide, and I feel distinctly ill-equipped to gain their trust or make them feel relaxed enough to say anything at all. My clothing—sturdy tailored slacks and shirt, nearly new running shoes—felt reasonably comfortable back in the site administrative office and in the plywood plant; here, this outfit makes me feel like a ridiculous and naive foreigner. Tricks that typically serve me well in drawing out research participants utterly fail me here. My opening questions, meant as informal icebreakers, are met with shrugged shoulders, monosyllabic answers, and smirks indicating that they share a private joke about me and my mission—a contempt that, I am more convinced by the moment, I richly deserve.

Having no choice, since my ride has left, I struggle to talk and resign myself to the belief that this visit will yield nothing. I am the butt of a big joke at WoodWorks, I am certain, and I tell myself that I should just cut my losses, ride out my humiliation, and wait for Harold to return and rescue me. I fantasize that Harold has returned to get a good laugh, at my expense, with his coworkers, as they imagine how this female, urban academic is coping on her own with the "men" of the logyard. Probably because I succumb to this belief, I relax and the tides begin to turn; something of a spontaneous focus group springs forth. I stop trying to get the loggers to talk about their perceptions of participative management through the lens of my "standard operating procedures" manual about work reform, start laughing at their snide cracks about the company, about their manager, and finally come back to PM, which they refer to as "perspiration management."

Nowhere else in WoodWorks has participative management inspired such contempt and rejection. These men articulate a clear, if abbreviated, understanding of the politics and economics of PM. For them, the considerable resources being poured into modernizing the human relations of the plant are a waste of budget and time. Moreover, they represent a major attempt by the management to coopt workers and get them to bear the brunt of top management's greed for profits and efficiency. To the logyard workers, the bottom line is that workers are being asked to buy into the new program but then to live with the possibility of ultimate death, the sale of the plant itself. They are especially scornful of corporate managers that are so out of touch with what goes on in their own industry that, as one man claims, they "can't even tell the difference between a larch and a fir tree." To the logyard men, this is a deficiency of meaningful and unforgivable proportions.

This critical perspective has been shaped by their direct experience as the plant has restructured, reorganized, and shrunk. All the men once worked for WoodWorks in the forests, as loggers and as truck drivers. Logging is a fiercely masculine and independent enterprise, and as loggers, they had near-complete control over their dominion. But WoodWorks long ago externalized the logging function and now contracts it out to small operators, self-employed loggers, or "gyppos." WoodWorks pays for the logs, but they don't buy or maintain the logging trucks; they don't pay wages or benefits to the loggers; and they are not responsible for injuries incurred on the job. The workers chatting with me around the table had, since their logging days, entered the fold of WoodWorks as employees.

The organization of work in the logyard is a world unto itself, one that plant-level managers find extremely difficult to penetrate. The drivers' work is on-site, but they could have been working a thousand miles away, given how little managers have to say about how the logyard workers actually do their jobs. I learn, as I am driven around in a wagner (the thirty-three-ton vehicle I mention in Chapter 1) and then find out how to drive one myself, the level of complexity entailed in this particular job. This complexity makes it extremely difficult for management to expropriate skills or dictate anything to these men. To my surprise, it is not getting the wagner to move or shifting its gears that is challenging and unique. Rather it is the skill required to avoid a careless movement of machinery; the ability to accurately gauge the distance between the wagner's pincers and the ponds into which logs are being dropped, to avoid driving this huge hunk of machinery into a pond; the knowledge of all the places, crooks, and corners at which one needs to be alert; the forethought required to anticipate and interpret the movements of other wagners and to continually choreograph movements around them. One thing is clear: inexperience and carelessness could wreak great and expensive damage. (When I ask my "instructor" whether anyone has ever died in an overturned or drowned wagner he looks at me, grinning, and says, "Oh yeah, dozens." I believed him then, but in retrospect I suppose my anxiety was all too transparent and too difficult to resist making fun of.)

The drivers possess extensive knowledge of these monstrous vehicles; they are skilled in manipulating gigantic pincers to lift multiple logs off trucks and transporting them to piles and ponds; the job is surprisingly interactive in that they have mutually worked out schemes for bypassing one another as they briskly drive about in a tightly constrained area, shouting to one another over their CBs using a cryptic code system, warning other drivers of their locations or of dislodged log piles and logs in unexpected places. These insights and skills, coupled with the nonstop, arduous nature of the labor, combine to make them a tightly knit group, a grudgingly respected workforce that for the most part management leaves alone.

These men are equivalent to the miners of Gouldner's (1954) study, the workers whose skill, risk, and interdependence led them to bond, to collaborate, to figure out the best ways to do their jobs. It seems fitting that because the logyard workers *are* autonomous, self-managing, continually brainstorming workers, they have successfully deflected management's vision of a top-down, formulaic agenda to turn workers into more involved participants. Here, workers don't even bother to pay lip service to PM; it is only a target of their sarcasm. They refuse to participate in task forces (for example, cross-functional task forces that might bring them together with workers from other production sites to discuss more efficient handling of logs from one location to another). The PM trainers, responsible for spreading the gospel of PM, long ago discontinued their treks out to the yard to try to get the logyard workers to buy into this modernized approach to the social relations of work, a conspicuous indicator of PM's failure that had become legendary throughout all ranks and all production settings. Beyond the reach of management to dictate how they should conduct their work, workers spontaneously and of necessity take initiative, self-organize, and live according to the spirit of self-management, realizing it even as they carry it out in rejection of management's letter of the law. In other words, they self-consciously resist management's definition of involvement and participation.

In sum, the logyard workers rejected the new plan, and management could not make them participate. Unlike workers in plywood, the logyard workers were not vulnerable to coworkers' or managers' pressure to "get involved" on the shop floor. The logyard workers' jobs already entailed a high degree of initiative and autonomy; they used their brains continually and so could only view PM's call to get more involved as lip service, as empty rhetoric. Unlike workers in plywood, logyard workers were not easily replaceable or transferable, and management is not willing to pitch a battle with these workers to force them to participate in the PM program. On top of all this, logyard workers found it impossible to believe that if they would only go along with the program locally, in their work site, something positive globally, with regard to the fate of the whole operation, would work out. They'd already been caught up in the retrenchment processes of the corporation, having lost their jobs as company loggers. Their cynicism and disbelief were right on the surface. When I asked them what they might do if the plant closed, they spoke vaguely of becoming gyppos (independent logging contractors) or retiring.

The logyard is not merely "decoupled" from the main plant; it is severed from its apparatus of control and social organization. The minimal attachment of the logyard to the plant explains, it seems to me, why the logyard workers' resistance stands unchallenged. Not only do they lack on-site supervision (the yard is highly decentralized and self-managing, much like the facilities at Reproco), but the logyard workers are invulnerable to the group processes and peer pressures that lead the plywood factory workers to accept and internalize the terms of the new participative management program. The logyard workers don't interact with workers throughout the plant who now have a greater and shared commitment to retooling the workforce so that a "good" employer will save them. They don't interact with external clients, because their work is geared only to those who are located in the internal machinery of the mill. These dynamics and experiences mean that logyard workers are out of the loop of the internalized and group control so common in restructured and reformed workplaces.

Farewell to or Retooling the Factory?

I argue that many of the woodworkers in the plywood plant made a good-faith attempt to learn about participative management and to exercise the techniques and skills gained in their training sessions. While their cooperation was founded on a range of feelings and opinions about the program—from reluctant to enthusiastic—they were nevertheless willing to experiment, to implement some of its practices, and to suspend doubts about the long-term efficacy of their efforts. In so doing, they weren't simply acquiescing to management's vision but were striving to turn it to their own gain. Neither were they myopically buying into a false optimism about what rewards they might reap in this venture.

However qualified their opinions of participative management, their actions embodied an effort to alleviate and control an extraordinarily high degree of uncertainty. Setting goals and achieving them in task forces, enlarging the scope of their work, incorporating management's perspective, making new demands for information about running the business were all ways in which plywood workers attempted to gain some degree of advantage over potentially crippling circumstances, to redirect and shape the outcomes: for the plant, for their jobs, and for the very life of their community.

These efforts at work reform offer an insight into the struggle to cross the great divide quite different from those at Reproco. Reproco workers faced experiential uncertainty within a framework of structural security: economic growth, reasonable expectations of job security, and a modest but meaningful package of benefits and training opportunities. The employee involvement program was a tool that enhanced their sense of efficacy and advancement—a logical, near-organic approach that allowed them to adapt to stress, conflict, and unpredictability in their jobs.

The woodworkers, in contrast, faced tremendous structural and employment insecurity in a declining industry. Participative management was not built into the conditions and features of their jobs but was rather a social construct mapped onto existing production arrangements. The map was borrowed from the outside world of professional consultants, trainers, and writers who had developed new models of involvement that were supposed to hold universally across diverse work settings. Compelled by fears of losing their jobs and way of life, many workers "bought into" this particular version of work reform.

Because of this process, a shift was occurring. In the earlier period of adversarial, "positional" labor relations, workers found formal, collective voice in their union but were extremely individualized in their relations with one another on the shop floor. Disconnected by virtue of their positions on the production line, and by a bureaucratic and hierarchical grievance procedure that inhibited them from spontaneously identifying and solving problems with immediate coworkers, the woodworkers lacked voice and empowerment to change their daily experiences. The "success" of this participative management program was a long way from ushering in "true democratization" as envisioned by the most forward-thinking labor leaders (see Bluestone and Bluestone 1992, chap. 7 and Kochan, Katz, Mower 1984 for a fuller treatment of the potential of the employee involvement trend). Indeed, the new framework of industrial relations contained the very real possibility of gradual, long-term weakening of union power. Yet it presented substantive opportunities instead for working collectively with others in everyday work and business activities.

Herein we see the double-edged sword of the new work arrangements. Embracing participative management can mean that workers' attachments to unions will change and weaken, but that their commitments to a broader community, including managers, supervisors, and coworkers, will expand. Participative management calls for workers to take on more responsibility and to be held more accountable for success and failure, for quality and efficiency, yet it also creates the organizational opportunities for learning skills and insights that workers view as a means to engage with the work world—both in the plant and outside it—in novel and often rewarding ways. For these reasons, the woodworkers did not reject new, flexible work arrangements out of hand; rather they tentatively explored them, appropriating aspects that were consistent with traditional norms of communicating and working within the plant, hoping that these efforts would bring them security and an enduring basis of community. In other words, they appropriated participative management in their efforts to control structural uncertainty.

Conclusion

In the summer of 1999, the WoodWorks plant was still open, but it had undergone major reconfiguration. As it had hoped, WoodWorks International had sold the plant. The buyer, Birch Creek, is a small private timber company. Birch Creek split the holdings up, purchasing the Madison plant while another timber business bought the timber lands that WoodWorks had owned. Birch Creek has a ten-year contract with the U.S. Forest Service for timber, but two facts keep the former woodworkers up in the air: it isn't clear that the timber will last for the full ten years, and it isn't clear what the company will do after ten years if the timber does last. Thus, the fate of the plant as a whole still hangs in the balance. The remaining woodworkers received a new lease on their employment lives, as they had hoped, but their position in 1999 was arguably as tenuous as it had been in the early 1990s.

The only remaining operation of any significance was the plywood factory. It employed approximately two hundred people, an increase of 25 percent since 1992. When I toured there in 1999, operations on the shop floor looked much the same. The environment was still deafening, the machinery overwhelming, the workers engrossed in their jobs as the site manager walked me through the facility.

The modernized administration building, the most visible tribute to the new industrial regime, was no longer part of the facility; it was now separated from the original facility by a cyclone fence. Birch Creek gave it to the city of Madison. Its office space is now inhabited by the workers of city hall, its fitness center used as a rehab center for patients from the local hospital. One now enters the plant through the modest old building that, at the time of my first research stint, was simply the place where the truck drivers checked in as they took their logs out to the logyard. The planar, a massive curved structure that had been in operation earlier, had been sold off to a private party by Birch Creek. It had passed through the hands of several owners and by the time I revisited, it had for all intents and purposes been abandoned. The roof had caved in and the walls had fallen through, allowing me to see clear through the structure, now little more than the eerie remnants of an industrial age. Birch Creek sold off the machinery and tools in the saw mill and the stud mill to other businesses. Workers had completely dismantled the stud mill, shipping the machines off to their new homes; as they were dismantling the saw mill, sparks were created as workers dissembled the machinery, fueling a huge fire that totally destroyed the building and its contents. Where the stud mill once stood was an empty space; the saw mill was now a charred heap. The finger joint plant employed about thirty people, and the logyard employed six. The logyard was now a skeletal operation, with a fraction of the log piles, and the ponds were gone because of environmental regulations.

There was no longer a formal participative management program in place but I was told, in casual conversation, that many of the workers continued to informally follow the precepts of the program. The workers still had a union, and there had been no strife to compare with that in the late 1980s. Presumably, workers had been chastened by the experiences of tenuousness and insecurity that they have endured for the last decade.

What can we conclude from the example of the woodworkers and their experiment with participative management? Can the survival of the plywood operation be *explained* by their willingness to give it a shot, by improvements in their effectiveness and productivity gained as a result of PM? It would be difficult to definitively make this argument. The plywood plant was a productive enterprise, and company management had invested millions of dollars to modernize its equipment in the 1980s. To a potential buyer, this would probably make the plywood division appear to be a profitable investment. This explanation makes sense when comparing the fate of the plywood plant to the fate of the stud mill, to take one example, which by all accounts had a hard-working and dedicated workforce but was severely constrained by its outdated processing system. Overhauling the stud mill to modernize it, or building the new stud mill that had been envisioned by the task force, would have presented formidable costs to the new buyers.

It is plausible to suggest that workers' involvement in the participative management program may have sweetened the pot, that Birch Creek could have seen the workforce and its orientation to a new era of industrial relations as potentially profitable, value-adding, much as it viewed plywood technology and infrastructure. Although it would be hard to draw direct causal linkages between worker involvement and the continued life of the plant, it is easy to imagine that, had the workforce overtly resisted current management or expressed hostility or passivity to future managers, any potential buyer might have decided that this modernized portion of WoodWorks was not going to be a reliable investment. Certainly, in this case, workers did win a temporarily desirable outcome. But, given the capriciousness of management and markets, and the instability caused by capital withdrawal from this industry, in some ways the woodworkers were simply plain lucky that their plant wasn't shut down and its machinery sold off, to be shipped piece by piece out to surviving wood-product plants.

In the next chapter I examine another population of workers in the American economy who are striving to make it to the promising and enabling side of the economic/production divide and to secure stability, attachment, and challenge in work. Temporary workers in the United States occupy an insecure position in our occupational structure, and the growth in their numbers raises significant questions for social scientists theorizing participation and resistance, power and control, and organizational effectiveness. Their tenuousness, in the employment relationship and in their jobs, would lead us to predict that they would have minimal attachment to firms, considerable resentment toward employers and coworkers, and little commitment to the quality of their work. Using the case of CompTech, a firm that manufactures computers and other cutting-edge technology, I ask the question: how is it that, despite the circumstances of temporary employment, workers can maintain a stance on the world that leads them to strive for the improbable outcome of a permanent job in the continually changing postindustrial workplace?

4

"I'd Work Forever as a Temporary Worker at CompTech": Temporary Work, Attachment, and Aspirations

CompTech, a leading high-technology company that designs and manufactures a wide range of computer-based products, has received much acclaim for its products, employment practices, and work culture. Like Reproco it is based squarely on the other side of the industrial divide from WoodWorks: CompTech is a thriving, profitable business located in the most dynamic sector of the U.S., if not the world, economy. A progressive or enabling approach to worker involvement, collaboration and team work, constant learning, and career development is deeply ingrained in the organizational employment practices at CompTech. Although the company, like many others, has experienced a squeeze on its products and profits, top management has endeavored to preserve the company's progressive work traditions.

For a sociologist who studies work and corporations from a critical perspective, it is difficult to get beyond an initial cynicism about the progressive employment relations framework at CompTech. CompTech's philosophy of engaging its employees in work and in decision-making processes, of offering them a broad range of benefits and amenities, and of positioning workers as neophyte managers (realized in such policies as having groups of workers participate in interviewing and hiring new employees and in evaluating one another's job performance) can, on the surface, be viewed narrowly as a paternalistic or hegemonic system of control, a way of regulating workers and getting them to throw their best efforts behind the goals of management. Yet such an appraisal, while containing a kernel of truth—that CompTech's policies do in fact fuel a high degree of worker consent, effort, and loyalty to the company agenda—

fundamentally misses the depth and the nature of identity, meaning, and security that employees derive from this type of employment. A cynical or dismissive appraisal also discounts the degree to which working in a company characterized by progressive management policies has become a privilege in the tumultuous, churning labor market environment at the turn of the century.

This perception of privilege explains much of what I learned in my study of the workers in the underbelly of CompTech's system: its temporary workers. As has been true in the high-tech industry in general (Carnoy, Castells, and Benner 1997), CompTech has experimented with the restrictive side of flexibility and work reform by hiring greater numbers of temporary employees. In the early 1990s top management directed managers to start using temporary workers, a staffing strategy that hopefully would allow the company to survive in an increasingly volatile economy. Stopping short of laying off permanent workers, top managers imposed a hiring freeze; when business prospects improved, the workforce was expanded with the addition of temporary workers. CompTech's employment of temporary employees contains in microcosm the national trend in the use of temporary labor. Temps were brought in both as a flexibility strategy—the company gained new capacities for immediately accommodating the ebbs and flows of demand cycles—and a cost-saving strategy—the company could avoid having unnecessary workers on the payroll during periods of slack demand.[1] In 1996–97, when I conducted my research, approximately one-quarter of the several-thousand-member workforce at this particular site was employed on a temporary basis. Thus, while leaving intact the progressive employment model, another model of employment—of temporariness, of seeming marginality and detachment—was built alongside it, a sharp and sometimes painful juxtaposition for permanent and temporary workers alike.

The merging of two employment systems at CompTech—a progressive system founded on substantive flexibility, generosity, and security for permanent workers, and a restrictive system founded on insecurity and impermanence—raises novel questions for work and employment in the United States. Specifically, like the case of the Reproco photocopy workers, it compels us to ask what flexibility means or offers to disadvantaged workers, as well as to ask why disadvantaged workers might work for and align their commitments with companies that seem to use them in far-less-than-ideal ways.[2]

Comparing workers at Reproco and CompTech enables us to zoom in on the problem of disadvantage and consent. Reproco's workers, like those at CompTech, had had limited and disadvantaging labor market experiences prior to entering this core company. As indicated in the discussion of Reproco, many of the photocopiers were people of color who had had low-status jobs in the secondary labor market, and the majority had been unable to pursue their education past high school. The photocopiers worked on the premises of professional business organizations, learning white-collar, middle-class interactional skills that conceivably were transferable to other work settings that offered training and mobility opportunities, albeit limited ones. Their jobs were stable. In this context their cooperation and optimism were comprehensible.

Temp assemblers and clerical workers, in contrast, were officially excluded from the advantages and opportunities available to photocopiers. Officially, they were not to attend training seminars or spend their time hunting for a permanent job in the company; they were not allowed to step on even the lowest rung of an internal job ladder. That they nevertheless cooperated requires explanation, as does their view of the larger economic system and its narrowing, perplexing opportunity structure.

At Reproco uncertainty and change were inherent in the flexible, decentralized organizational conditions of the jobs but were ameliorated by temporarily secure employment and exposure to new organizational settings. At WoodWorks a sense of uncertainty and temporariness was ubiquitous but substantively unrealized. But for the entry-level temporary employee at CompTech impermanency and uncertainty are stark and inescapable facts in the structurally most disadvantaging combination. Temps anywhere experience the highest degree of structural uncertainty. They shoulder the greatest and most palpable risks: the risk of not receiving a paycheck or health benefits and of not being able to support and protect a family, buy a house or a car. Given the dramatic transformation in the paradigm of temporary employment in the 1990s and the increase in the use of temporary workers, it is crucial to explore their situation and to look at contemporary employment from their standpoint. Specifically, why might the long-term temporary worker in the postindustrial economy at the turn of the century—who arguably experiences the most deleterious conditions of temporariness, risk, and uncertainty—develop aspirations and commitments typical of attached workers? Why and how would they accommodate but simultaneously resist marginalization and subordination?

Visiting CompTech: A Stratified Occupational World

The CompTech site that I studied is located in Northern California, and it resembles many of its sister high-tech campuses throughout this part of the state, with numerous nondescript facilities housing administration, design, and production centers.[3] As I enter through the security gate I notice that the guards at this post wear purple identification badges but the significance of this does not strike me until after I've begun my research, when I learn that one of the distinguishing features of the temporary employment system is that temps are assigned differently colored badges from the permanent workers. I discover this is a widespread practice when I visit other local high-technology companies, whether to conduct other interviews, receive a tour, or negotiate for access to conduct research.[4]

Once I'm attuned to the color hierarchy, I realize that the entire site is color coded, awash with temporary and contracted workers everywhere I go: from food service workers through security workers posted at the entry of each individual building, assemblers, and clerical workers, mailroom and other business service workers, and janitors, up to the well-paid software engineers and programmers.[5] Within the ranks of impermanent workers there are salient distinctions. Many of those with purple badges work for companies to whom CompTech has outsourced specialized functions: security to Pinkerton, food preparation to Marriott, travel services to American Express. These outsourced workers are counterparts of the Reproco photocopiers, who are employed by Reproco but work on the premises of other companies. I have come to study a different category of contingent workers: workers who are hired by less specialized temp agencies which send individuals out to perform a wide range of work tasks in numerous business settings.

After receiving my own temporary badge at the front desk of my first research site (but a different temporary badge, the visitor's pass), I'm admitted to the heart of business. Neither temporary workers nor visitors are allowed to take their badges home with them, so the front desk hums with activity as permanent workers slide their worker identification passes through a scanner, and temps and visitors like myself negotiate with the desk personnel as we obtain our passes and sign in. The color-coded system means that space, movement, and activity are perpetually monitorable: it is very easy to single out a person whose badge color doesn't entitle them to be in the area or corridor in which they are located.

My initial sensitivity to the hierarchy implied in the badge signifier re-
cedes as I begin to grasp how comfortable and generous are the accom-
modations of the site. The signs of CompTech's paternalism are everywhere. The company takes care of its permanent employees, providing
automatic teller machines for employees' convenience, cafeterias that
serve genuinely healthy and tasty food, a work-out room, volleyball and
basketball courts, and even a travel agent's office. In several of the offices
and departments I visit, I see brightly colored balloons and banners hovering over workers' cubicles, greeting workers with "Happy Birthday!" and
"You did it!" Passing by a supervisor's cubicle, it is not uncommon to see
plaques and certificates applauding the most recent employee of the
month or recognizing employees for various creative contributions and
accomplishments.

At CompTech, permanent employees, from the lowest rungs of the
occupational ladder through the highest, enjoy generous benefits packages, amenities, training and mobility opportunities, and secure employment. Production arrangements afford even the lowest-level assembly
workers some degree of autonomy, and multiple opportunities exist for
employees to make decisions and give their input to managers. Managers
historically have managed by incentive, using symbolic and material rewards to positively reinforce workers' performance. This participative system creates a highly positive culture for CT's permanent employees. In
itself, it is an exemplar of a decentered, self-managed control system that
has been extremely productive for managers. Permanent employees are
rewarded for self-monitoring, taking risks and assuming responsibilities:
their mobility in the company indeed depends on it. Authority is dis-
persed throughout the organization, in teams and in brainstorming and
problem-solving workgroups, with workers enthusiastically assuming responsibility for the prosperity of the company.

Temporaries' experiences are embedded within this paternalistic
context.[6] They are paid slightly above minimum wage and formally work
for their temporary-help agencies. As noted, temps wear differently colored badges. They also have an eighteen-month cap on the length of
their employment (although they can be and often are hired back after
a mandated three-month leave), and they are excluded from various
work-related meetings and social events for permanent workers. In light
of recent legal cases around the nation in which temporary employees
have challenged their economic and employment marginalization,
CompTech management takes quite seriously the imperative to enforce

the boundaries between permanent and temporary workers.[7] Yet despite their exclusion from the formal, symbolically meaningful occasions for participation (such as business or brainstorming meetings), they are in practice and experience integrated into the decentralized and participative system.

Many temporary workers have opportunities to acquire a range of skills and decision-making responsibilities, the lines of authority and hierarchy in everyday work life are blurred, both between temporary workers and their permanent coworkers, and within the ranks of temporary workers themselves; and temporary workers' understanding of their employment status is destabilized. By virtue of these arrangements workers' perceptions of opportunity rise to the top of the mixture of uncertainty and risk. Formally marginalized by restrictive corporate policies, temps' experiences are substantively saturated with enabling flexible practices. Within this constellation of factors it becomes easy to understand how temporary workers develop an abiding commitment to and investment in employment at a "good" company like CompTech.

Temps on the Line: Two Production Models

Before being permitted to visit the production lines at CompTech I have to "ground" myself so that my body's electrical discharge won't neutralize the computer components. Boyd, a temporary worker and my escort on the first day of my visit to the lines, skillfully helps me fit an electrical static discharge strap over the heel of my shoe and ground another strap onto my body with a bit of water. He leads me to a metal plate on which I stand while holding my fingers to a small metal bar; when the green light indicates I am successfully grounded we both cheer, and I proudly announce "I'm grounded!" to Boyd's bemused coworkers.

Boyd is a thirty-eight-year-old white man who has worked as a temporary employee for seventeen months. His ardent hope is to be hired on as a permanent worker and my gut feeling is that he would be a strong candidate for permanent employment. He is enthusiastic, articulate, and obviously responsible, evidenced in the fact that he has been trusted to work as the team leader for a work group that is composed of temporary workers. These qualities make him a superb field informant, an individual who is able to alert me to fine distinctions in the work that his team mates are doing and to provide telling insights about the hierarchy of status and security at CompTech. He leads me to his work area, explaining that his work group has ten temps, nine men and one woman.

As we enter the area where Boyd's team assembles computers he points out an older man at the head of the line. What Boyd tells me about this man instantly jars my assumptions about the marginalized and detached circumstances of temporary workers. As already noted, CompTech imposes an eighteen-month limit on the employment of temporary workers in order to clearly establish boundaries: between the temporary and permanent workforce, and around the identity and employment status of the temporary. Mason, the man Boyd has singled out to me, has about one month to go before his temporary contract expires. The problem, according to Boyd, is that Mason is six months away from being eligible to receive social security. To make it possible for Mason to avoid economic hardship in the intervening period, Boyd has been negotiating with *his* manager to find a way to keep Mason on as a temporary. Taken aback by what Boyd tells me, I later query his manager about this claim and learn that, in fact, Boyd has accurately represented the situation. My initial black-and-white expectations that temporaries would lack voice, and that their efforts and participation are confined to a simple expenditure of physical labor, start unraveling.

Boyd's production area is best characterized as a serial production process. It is technologically Fordist, although much less rigid than the work system at WoodWorks. Although the skill level required here is not high or complex, the organization of the line does provide opportunities for brainstorming, collaborating, and improvising. The product lines can be changed easily, depending on the particular model this unit is charged with assembling. Assembly begins at one end of the line and, as components are added, each unit is moved to successive stations. Mason, the first "builder" on the line, faces a PC that is perched in front of him. He reaches for a empty computer case from a storage cart, places it before him on the ball-bearing conveyor belt, and scans the bar code on it with a scanner attached to the PC. The bar code generates specifications and code numbers, displayed on the PC, dictating what he is to install in the case. The task of whoever is positioned at station number one—at this point in time, Mason—is to insert memory modules. Mason turns around and retrieves the number and types of modules specified from the shelves behind him. Each module has a bar code that he also scans in order to register the serial number. Information about all the added components will be centrally recorded and stored in this way, important information if flaws and defects are later detected. After drilling the boards into the case, Mason pushes it on the conveyor belt to station number two, where another family of components will be added.

Various phases of production include the insertion of components such as power supplies and hard disks; a baking process in which units are rolled into a huge ovenlike piece of equipment and exposed to varying degrees of temperature, dryness, and humidity; and a diagnostics session wherein each unit is plugged into a testing bank that searches for defects or incorrect installation of parts. One individual installs software. The final stage is "buttoning up," when a worker places a hard plastic cover on the computer, screws on a company identification tag, presses on appropriate labels, and wipes off obvious smudges and stains. From there, the units go to packaging and shipping. One man sits in the corner installing upgrades, both software and hardware, for customers who already own this particular model.

In contrast to the comparatively traditional Fordist line at WoodWorks, the line at CompTech has more variability. Although temps by and large don't rotate positions here, they do determine the pace of the line; the type of computer they assemble periodically changes; they double up to help one another when one station gets backed up; and they spend a moderate amount of time evaluating problems and glitches in production.

"Gigabob," so named by his fellow temps because of his impressive size, is a young (twenty-one years) white man who today is installing hard drives into and screwing the backplates on the units. Prior to working in this unit at CompTech Gigabob had had another temporary position with a different company which he claims was the worst, most exploitive job he had ever had. There, he worked in a large warehouse breaking down discarded materials that were going to be recycled. The temperature of his workplace, he claims, was poorly regulated, the ventilation inadequate, the work exhausting and unbearably dirty. As Boyd gets in Bob's face and lobs questions at him as though he is Oprah Winfrey—"Bob, what DID you think of working at Recyclone?"—Gigabob swears that his current job at CompTech is a complete and unequivocal improvement. In addition to enjoying assembly work in this unit, Bob, it turns out, is a crackerjack, self-trained computer programmer, and occasionally he uses his knowledge of CompTech's production processes to help fellow workers write code and fix bugs, both in his immediate unit and for units in near proximity. He fervently wishes to become a permanent member of this work organization, to start as an assembler but then to move up the job ladder, and to gain new opportunities for further development of his programming skills.

Boyd's work area presents new twists to common assumptions about the degradation of temporary workers. These temps work semi-autonomously, make decisions, and are part of a work system whose progressive culture for permanent employees strongly permeates their own work experiences. Time spent in Erin's work area reveals different principles of assembly, but similar expressions of enjoyment of the job and desire to move beyond temporary status.

Erin is a thirty-two-year-old white woman who had temped at CompTech for over ten months until recently, when she was converted to permanent status. In contrast to the serial production process of Boyd's unit, Erin's is more aptly characterized as a parallel or integrated production process and is much more skilled and craftlike than serial production. Another of my assumptions—that temporary workers are primarily used to staff unskilled jobs in which alienation and turnover pose minimal cost to companies—is dashed when I learn that in Erin's comparatively skilled work group of about twelve, about one-half are temps and the other half permanents. One-third of these workers are women.

This is a larger work area than Boyd's. It consists of five stand-alone work stations where each unit is assembled, start to finish, by one individual. Each station has a small hydraulic lift next to it, which is used to elevate a chassis onto the station's work platform. All assemblers have their own trays of screws, drills, various tools, blowers to eliminate dust particles, parts, and a PC with a scanner. Inventory shelves run alongside the stations. All workers, temps and permanents alike, go through elaborate record-keeping procedures to check out memory boards, so that the company can keep track of exactly who takes the boards and how they're being used. The units they are assembling are far more complex than the computers in Boyd's area. Each unit is customized to meet the specifications, displayed on PC screens, of individual clients. The complexity shows in the images and instructions that workers follow on the PC. They scroll back and forth between screens, study maps of areas where they install components, and read instructions that are of much greater detail and length than any I ever witness in Boyd's assembly area. In a process that takes hours, sometimes an entire day, Erin installs disk drives, CD-ROM drives, CPUs, tape drives, power supplies, peripherals, LAN cards, and memory and mother boards.

Erin's boss doesn't want to do their troubleshooting for them. His dictum is that the assemblers should solve any problems among themselves. He wants to know *why* production gets held up, but he doesn't want them to expect him to solve the glitches. This means that these workers, in addition to assembling units, have to calculate time tables and schedules for completing orders, handle parts shortages, remedy product or process defects, replenish inventories, and assign workers to particular jobs. It is they who call the appropriate engineers or materials handlers when the need arises. Like Boyd's unit, here the units are baked and run through temperature and moisture stress tests. After a unit is assembled, it is tested and run through diagnostics: common problems, Erin explains, include the discovery of bent pins inside the machine, faulty solder joints, and contamination of connectors.

On occasion, she mentions, she and fellow workers meet with vendors when there is a recurring defect in the vendor's product, something she did when she was a temporary worker as well. Making very clear the complexity of employment dynamics in an era of outsourcing and the use of contract workers, Erin describes one such meeting where she learned that the vendor had himself outsourced for the parts, thus extending the network of production well beyond the formal boundaries of CompTech. Matt, the temporary assembler who works at the station next to Erin's, has trained other employees, including Erin, to work in this unit. Matt is so enamored of his job that he claims, without my having specified that I was interested in this particular angle, that he enjoys "a *real* form of empowerment." Currently, Erin is working on a college degree, with financial assistance from CompTech. Like Boyd, Gigabob, and others, Matt patiently works away, devoting time and effort to his job. It strikes me that he goes well beyond what the company might reasonably expect from a temporary worker, hoping his turn will come to be converted to a permanent employee of the company.

Obscured Inequality

Decentered Authority and Organizational Integration. As these descriptions indicate, temporary workers at CompTech are situated in a range of jobs, differing by skill, responsibility, autonomy, and degree of integration into the ranks of permanent workers. This was a significant and surprising finding. Researchers typically expect temps to be degraded, deskilled, segregated from permanent workers, and least likely to be granted autonomous work conditions with decision-making capabilities. Boyd's and Erin's production settings typify the variation and complexity in the tasks temps perform and in their relationships with coworkers and managers on the shop floor at CompTech.

A thirty-six-year-old Hispanic woman described a typical day on the job, and her description illustrates the degree of temporaries' integration into the participative system, the amount of on-the-spot decision making, and the level of their knowledge of the line and inventory planning. In this team process, she and her fellow temporaries had to handle a production line organized on just-in-time principles:

> We all help each other out. Um, like, we rotate. The units come down to us but through different people, a group of people. And they set 'em there, and then we figure out how many parts go to that order, and then we go ahead and package it and send it down. So there's, like, four; there's about four different productions that are, like, actually going down the same line. And sometimes we get, like, it gets overcrowded, and it depends on how fast the line's moving, the people on the line are moving. Sometimes there's a parts shortage on the line, and so they have to, like, remove the order from the line and...and so they have to return it back to us later. And so, like, we all have to, like, get together and find out who's got what before we send things down and who's not gonna be there, how fast the line's gonna be flowing. You know, there's a lot of things that we have to discuss.

As this woman suggests, temps confer with one another, and with work groups preceding and following their line. They make calculations about the pacing of order fulfillment and coordinate the production of multiple orders. Another temp who worked on an assembly line commented on the unpredictability of the work flow and the committed effort required to handle flux, observing that, "They [temps] do produce good quality work. We have some that fall below the average. But most of the whole crew does a fantastic job, uh, producing quality and quantity, too. We get big orders coming in. And when it comes time to ramp up, it's like, 'OK, folks, this is what we gotta do today.' And they buckle down and *everyone works as a team to get that out*" (my emphasis—V. S.).

Marina described an event that defied common expectations social scientists might have of workers believed to be marginalized. Her positive description of how temps mobilized to clear up a backlog of orders is consistent with her comment to me that she would "work forever as a temporary worker at CompTech": "My boss is in charge of a lot of people, and, like right now, he is way behind in [producing] units, and he let us know, 'I'm three hundred units behind,' and he was worried. And we said, 'Let's go.' You know, we clapped our hands, 'Let's get as many as we can out.' And we're doin' fifty a day, which is a *record* for us" (my emphasis—V. S.).

Many of the temporaries spoke of situations in which their boss had given them an opportunity to learn, to handle challenging situations, and had generally entrusted them with information and responsibility for planning and coordination. Consistent with Kanter's (1977/1993) structural opportunity hypothesis, workers felt they'd been given an opportunity to prove themselves and had intensified their efforts to do so. A young, white, male temporary worker in his late twenties, for example, had come to CompTech after a string of casual jobs and an unsuccessful job search. His employment experiences working as a day laborer for a landscape firm and his high school diploma limited him to a possible future of secondary-labor-market jobs. After starting as a line worker at CompTech, his boss had moved him into a high-security work setting and given him the responsibility of maintaining an accounting system for keeping track of expensive memory chips and doling them out appropriately. He spoke of his gradual personal growth and his sense that he was rising to the demands of his new position:

> I was moved into that cage, and this is what I was told, um, my supervisor had a lot of confidence in my ability, so he felt I was the best person for the job, and he moved me in there. It was very good that he did—it just made me kind of feel good about myself, I guess, and so then that made me work, not harder, but it just made me think about, think about it more, what I was doing, and I guess, I guess you could say it increased the quality of my work a bit more.
>
> I've been given more responsibility along the way, I've felt more confident in my abilities, and I felt my supervisor's confidence in my abilities, so I've just taken it upon myself not to make it [temporary status] such an issue. It all depends on a person's position. I have a higher position than when I came in here, and, um, I see friends of mine, coworkers that work around in lower positions, and I think if you're not given the responsibilities from your supervisor who's a regular employee, then you don't, that feeling of *separation* lingers [my emphasis—V. S.]. But the thing that changed my attitude [toward the positive] about [being a temp] was that they moved me into the cage. That's what changed my attitude. They gave me more responsibility and more control over my work area.

Another temp, a white male in his mid-thirties, had been a routine assembler and then moved to the position of group coordinator. He described a similar trajectory: "Well, I think more of an issue for me than the money or the title, anything like that, was basically the respect that I got from the management team, that they felt that I had the skills to lead the team and that I was capable of doing the job. And I was very proud of that. You know, that was what made the job, that they had faith in me to do that and that I could do that to the best of my ability."

A white woman temporary who worked in a warehouse coordinating and clearing the way for company products to go through customs, mentioned her gratitude that her manager had developed her into a valued employee, and that such positive treatment had led her to work hard and effectively at her job despite her formally tenuous status.

> Being in the positions that I've been in and stuff, I've seen how other employees, temporary employees, have been treated. And sometimes it's unfair. But then again, I think it all has to do with the individual too. So, certain incidents where I have been treated very well, it's just that they really take good care of me as a temporary employee. *They helped me be successful* [my emphasis—V. S.]. They helped me get into positions that are worth being in. And they just treated me like a permanent.

Marvin, a white man who had worked as a temp for eight months, stressed the elements of the job that deepened his own desire to stay at CompTech: "The company holds a lot of stock in empowering its workers and basically presenting the task and allowing the worker to complete the task in whatever way they see fit, as long as it's done in a timely and quality-acceptable manner. So, it's a very enjoyable environment."

In these ways the company's participative system tapped temporary workers' desire to shine and to rise to new, demanding work situations, further deepening their commitment, intensifying their work efforts, and aligning them with their immediate supervisors. Marla, holding a temporary position for eleven months, was adamant when she told me that: "Here, they give you anything you really need to achieve the job. So it's just, you really feel like the company is committed to making you the best kinda person you could be."

Thus, the day-to-day experiences of many temporary workers were comparable to those of permanent workers in their work sites. Temporaries had accumulated much organization-specific knowledge in the course of their employment. Everyone I interviewed had been cross-trained for a variety of positions. While many positions required simple skill levels, temporaries had had the opportunity to develop a cross-organizational perspective, gaining knowledge of many different functions in their production area. Temporary workers had trained new workers, labored in a variety of work settings, worked side-by-side with permanent workers, and were occasionally divided from other temps when they were positioned, by managers, to monitor and supervise their temporary coworkers. These findings illustrate the complexity of power relations among temporaries and their diverse organizational statuses, all of which eroded the basis for a singular group experience. Temporary workers were organizationally integrated into a participative work system in ways that gave them unanticipated authority and skills, rather than being segregated and marginalized in overt ways. In some cases they even had the upper hand over permanent workers who depended on the temps for their experience and knowledge.

I discovered other unanticipated features of temporaries' work. Piecing together observations of people doing their jobs and interview data with managers and temporary workers, a picture emerged of the "valued temp" whom managers and supervisors tried to keep over the long run (see Smith forthcoming/B for fuller analysis of managerial strategies in this setting). The average length of time that people had worked as a temp was twenty-seven months, indicating that supervisors and managers trusted them and relied on them as a source of institutional memory. Managers cited numerous instances of having recalled their temps (bringing a temporary worker back into the company after the required three-month leave), and temporaries spoke of having been recalled. Some managers maintained relationships with valued temporaries when they weren't employed at CompTech, and some found ways to extend a single work stint beyond eighteen months. As a result, many temporaries developed strong ties with their managers and strong commitments to the company. They developed informal bases of authority based on accumulated experience and knowledge.

The downside of working in this environment, however, was that these conditions served to obscure the basic facts of inequality—that temps were earning lower wages than permanent workers for the same or similar jobs, that they weren't allowed to move up the job hierarchy, that they literally could not be certain that they would have their job from one day to the next. The obfuscation and even silencing of these facts are a basic ingredient in managers' success in gaining commitment, trust, and participation. Obscured inequality was deepened by two other factors: temporaries' understanding of whom they worked for and their previous and potential labor-market opportunities.

The Employment Contract. Temporaries' understanding of who had power—who was responsible for their formally marginalized employment status and who shared their marginalized status—was obscured not only by production arrangements but also by confusion over who their employer was. This murkiness was the result of routine changes in temporary agencies used by CompTech and by temporaries' location in the complex web of outsourcing arrangements. In fact, their view of employment represents the subjective, experiential side of a postindustrial economy characterized by change, downsizing, and outsourcing (Harrison 1994). Sixty-two percent (fifteen of twenty-four) of the temporaries and former temporaries whom I interviewed identified *boundary changes* in their employment: one or more changes in their employment status during their affiliation with CompTech.

The range of confusing employment arrangements were multiple. Some temps started as members of an internal temporary labor pool (a now-discontinued system in which CompTech directly hired temps)—they wore the same colored badge as the permanent workers, received no benefits, and had no job security, but they were able to participate in company events and shop-floor award ceremonies). These workers had then become employees of a temporary hiring agency (meaning that they wore differently colored badges, received no benefits, and were excluded from company events and meetings). Others started as employees of one temporary hiring agency and were transferred to the payroll of another when CompTech ended its relationship with the original agency. Some temps worked on CompTech's premises, ostensibly for CompTech and with CompTech coworkers but in fact were employed by one of its vendors/outsourcers, who was also using temporaries and had hired the individual from an outside agency. When an individual worked at CompTech but was formally deployed by other firms, it became difficult to disentangle who actually had power and authority over them.[8]

A few interviewees were utterly unable to specify who their employer was. One interviewee initially couldn't answer the question, "Who are you employed by?" He and I mulled over the question, tracing through the organizational arrangements of his job. When I queried, "So you think it's CompTech?" he said "Yeah, I *guess* so" (emphasis his). In fact, as I found out later talking to his manager, his employer was one of the temporary agencies. And even in cases where it was easy to identify precisely who one worked for, a final layer of complexity originated in symbolic attachment: workers mentioned how they achieved status by association with CompTech and therefore would tell people that they were employed by CompTech regardless of who formally employed them (both managers and workers reported this phenomenon). Status by association was captured in the comments of one white woman who, years earlier, had worked as a clerk typist, file clerk, and warehouse worker but had been out of the labor force raising children for fourteen years. She told me that her temp job was "the best she'd ever had" and that she would work at CompTech "forever" on temporary status. She described what employment at CompTech symbolized for her:

> [After having been out of the labor market for a number of years] I went to [a temporary agency] 'cause I was havin' a hard time findin' permanent employment that, well, I could have gotten a job at quite a few places, but it wouldn't have been what I enjoyed. I'm the kind of person has to enjoy what I'm doing or I just can't do it. So I went to [the agency] because I figured they could give me a wide variety of jobs, and they gave me the realization that: "If you don't like this job, you don't have to take it. You can turn it down. We'll still keep you posted on other jobs." So I liked that. And they called me one day and said "Would you be willing to work at CompTech?" And I said, "Oh, that would be great," because it's so, well, I mean it's reputable. I mean everyone knows CompTech. And I said "I would be honored," 'cause I, I'm the kind of person that if somebody asked me in a cocktail lounge or somewhere, "Where do you work?" and they don't know what it is or never heard of it, it's kinda, oh, you know, you have to explain. But you say "CompTech" and they know right away.

She derived personal dignity and status because of temporary employment at CompTech. Other interviewees repeated this sentiment.

A white male temp in his early forties claimed,

> I would much rather tell people that I worked for CompTech rather than saying that "Oh, I'm a temporary worker. I work for *TempsRus* or *WeStaffYou* or whatever." You know, I would much rather of said, you know, "I work for CompTech." And it's just the way it sounds. I mean people know that

CompTech is a good company, and it does look awful good on a resume to have worked for CompTech. So I can see, I think it's more of a *self-made discrepancy*. People would rather put CompTech down as a job reference than a temporary company [my emphasis—V.S.].[9]

Thus, employment identities created within this system of employment were not stable, continuous, or unambiguous; rather they were disjointed and often institutionally obscured. Temporaries' work and class identity in part have unfolded within these material arrangements of production and hiring contracts. Coupled with the ways in which power was "creatively" redistributed throughout a flattened hierarchy and found in unexpected places like the hands and minds of temporary workers, temporary workers' sense of group solidarity was fractured and their interests were more likely to coincide with the interests of their managers than with those of their temporary colleagues.

Extra-organizational Determinants of Consent: Labor-market Experiences and Personal Aspirations. Some might predict individual recalcitrance or collective opposition to company management, if temporaries were to share their feelings about managers' high level of expectations for good work performance and contrast that with their anxieties or resentments about being excluded from CompTech's permanent workforce. My evidence, however, supports the view that most temporaries were "good" and "valued" workers on whom supervisors and managers came to rely extensively, and that temps kept any resentment to themselves. Should we conclude that these individuals had been coopted by the positive company culture, uncritically abiding by the inequality, the rules and procedures, or that they were coerced into working hard and well but did so sullenly and grudgingly? Much as the commitments of photocopy workers and woodworkers were conditioned by the local labor market and opportunity structure, temporary workers' aspirations, commitments, and goals were strongly shaped by these external factors as well. They are also coated with an optimistic and persistent faith.

As many of the foregoing quotes indicate, temporary workers' "enthusiastic participation" (Hodson 1996) in the work systems at CompTech is explained by their own occupational trajectories—where they have been, where they hope to go, and what they perceive as possible. The vast majority of these temps ultimately sought permanent employment with CompTech. For many of these workers, even a temporary job with this good company was more secure and gratifying than their previous tenuous labor-market positions.[10] These prior labor-force experiences and current aspirations combined to lead temporaries to work like permanent employees and to engage in profound self-discipline. At the intersection of workers' own occupational goals and managers' mandate to use temporary workers in a participative system was forged a work system in which temporaries worked intensely but for their own personal gain. Like Reproco photocopiers and WoodWorks timber workers, temps at CompTech were striving to control pervasive uncertainty—in their case, structural uncertainty.

Thirty-two of the entry-level workers I interviewed (twenty-four formally, ten informally) desired permanent employment at CompTech. Four temporaries volunteered that they had turned down offers of "permanent" jobs at other companies, choosing instead to stay at their temporary jobs even though there was no guarantee of permanent employment at CompTech. Any optimism about, faith in, criticism of, and resentment toward the company centrally revolved around workers' aspirations for staying on at CompTech and concern that these aspirations would go unrealized. I asked workers about their plans and aspirations in different ways. I asked directly whether they were interested in staying on at CompTech—a question which typically evoked an adamant "Yes!" or "Doesn't everybody?!" although sometimes simply quiet affirmation— and I asked indirectly by querying them about their long-term personal plans and goals. When I asked managers and workers for their best "guesstimates" about what proportion of the temporary workforce desired a permanent job, I was given figures ranging from 70 to 100 percent, and none of my interview or observational data contradicted their estimation.

In a practical sense, these workers believed that temporary employment was a route to permanent employment at CompTech. Their faith and hope that they would be one of the chosen few to land a "good" job is strikingly similar to the woodworkers' faith about salvaging their plant through their hard and unquestioning labor and persistence. The belief was grounded in their concrete observation that others before them had been converted to permanent status, an outcome confirmed in other studies of temporary workers (Cohen and Haberfeld 1993; Henson 1996; O'Reilly 1994) despite the fact the conversion rate appeared to be only somewhere between 10 and 15 percent.[11] Of the individuals for whom I have reliable data about pathways to entry into the company (twenty-one), the majority (seventeen) purposely sought CompTech employment, not temporary employment alone, and believed that the only way to enter CompTech was to go in through a temporary agency.

One white woman—who had had a series of jobs in retail sales prior to joining CompTech—summarized this point of view (of which I heard many versions) in somewhat dramatic, but nevertheless pointed terms, saying that "There's a big incentive to just get your foot in the door. As the saying goes, when you're a contract worker, all you're looking for is *any* job, absolutely any job, whether you are scrubbing the floors or picking up papers, whatever. As long as you can get that badge (the perm badge) you've got it made." Indeed, "getting my foot in the door" by taking the temp route was virtually a master narrative for temporary workers, even though they were told, in their "official" orientation to the company, that there was no guarantee of such an outcome. I heard multiple versions of one temp's calculated gamble in staying in a temporary position: "It's a way to get experience in the job; like, you're already doing the job, so when an opening comes in it should, you know, logically you'd be, you'd have an edge to get into that opening."

Another confirmed his belief that: "It's not necessarily something that is held out in front of you like a carrot on a stick but it's more of a, you know, 'I'm here. I have the opportunity to impress these people and if, hopefully, if I do a good enough job, if I impress them well enough, then you know, they may see fit to bring me on if they have the opening.'"

Erin called this risk calculation: "like rolling a dice. You don't know, you don't know what's going to happen. So I took a shot at it and I figured, 'Well, while I'm working here I'll learn whatever I can about the company and find out where I can fit in as a CompTech regular employee.' And once I got my foot in the door as a temp, then I wanted to expand where I wanted to go."

Yet another temp, a white man in his early thirties, deployed the same metaphor, saying: "I was hoping for a shot at a real job here. It's like rolling dice. You don't know, as a contract worker, you don't know what's gonna happen, so I took a shot at it."

Looking at the educational background and labor-market histories of people in temporary jobs helps make greater sense not only of their involvement in CompTech's participative system but also of their willingness to line up and wait for long periods of time in a "queue" (Reskin and Roos 1990) for permanent employment. The vast majority (83 percent) of past and current temps in the sample of individuals whom I formally interviewed did not have a college degree. (Four individuals had an associate of arts degree from California community colleges, and two were working on their A.A. No one had a higher degree.) The vast majority (79 percent) had had a series of unstable, entry-level jobs prior to working at CompTech: men and women alike had worked in low-paid jobs in the service industry, retail sales and health-care industry, or had had other temporary assembly jobs in less progressive companies (described as "sweatshops" by some).

The frustration of finding decent employment in a turbulent economy, when one possessed only nonspecialized skills, was pointed out by a Hispanic man who had been at CompTech as a temp for twelve months:

> I think for my whole life I've kinda looked for a company that would let me do my job the way I saw fit. I had been laid off the year prior to coming here and then gotten some more training, a little more focused training on repair of computers. Then I just went out job hunting. Basically, I sent a resume to every address and fax number I could find and I, the first call I got back was from a temp agency, and they're very quick to respond, and they asked me if I'd like to take a position. Um, of course, they said, it's not permanent. It was a maximum of an eighteen-month contract. I asked 'em who the company was and when they said, "CompTech" I said "Oh yeah, I would definitely like to give that company a try." And of course, from that point I felt, you know, I could get in there and hopefully impress somebody and get a position.

Their employment histories also reflected the larger gender- and class-stratified occupational system: all of the women had worked in "feminized" occupations, and five had worked primarily as full-time parents, reentering the labor market when their children were older; nine of the men had been located in secondary-labor-market jobs characterized by instability and low pay; three men had left unionized, male-dominated positions and were struggling to resituate themselves in "good" jobs in the labor market; one other man had worked as a market researcher. Given these employment histories, CompTech employment, with the possibility of a permanent job, represented a genuine advance for the workers I interviewed.

One story recounted to me by a young Hispanic woman was a poignant illustration of the baseline from which many workers began, as well as a reminder of a genuine divide in the postindustrial occupational structure, between poorly paid and degraded service workers and the

better-positioned knowledge and manufacturing workers they serve. This
woman, in her late twenties, was a single mother with two children, working on her third stint as a temporary assembler at CompTech. She had
previously worked in day care, fast food, and elder care. She recalled the
chain of events leading her to seek temporary work at CompTech:

> I found out about [temp work] through a friend of mine, a friend of mine
> that was working... (at CompTech). I was working for Carl's Jr. at the time.
> She says, "Why don't you come and apply for a job out there to see if they'll
> hire you?" And I'm like, yeah, OK. So I was at the window, at the drive-through
> window at Carl's Jr. And I was like lookin' at all these cars going by, you know,
> [I was thinking], like, what must it be like to work in one of those factories,
> you know, big computer factories? And I used to be at work early in the morn-
> ing and see all those cars go by, and they were nice-looking cars. I'm like,
> "Goodness, maybe I'll, maybe I could have one of those jobs one of these
> days," you know.
>
> And then I got to meet a lot of people, 'cause... [my supe] would place me
> up in the front too. I would take the orders in front, in the lobby, and I'm,
> like, I would talk to all these people coming in with their badges [permanent
> workers, since temporary workers were not allowed to take their badges with
> them after work—V. S.]: "Is it nice working out there?" And they'd say, "Yeah,
> you know. You should go apply." And I did. One day I said, "OK, I'll take a
> chance," and I went and applied at the agency.

Another woman, a white woman who had been a full-time parent for
many years, identified the kinds of skills and knowledge she was acquiring in her stint as a temporary worker. She felt that these new skill sets
were transferable and positioned her more advantageously to find other
jobs; this perceived benefit reinforced her commitment to the company:
"I've really liked working here because I'm just glad to've had the opportunity to learn what I've learned as a contract worker, because, um,
it's something I feel that I could've went out and paid for to learn how to
assemble a computer, how to fix a computer, how to do all those things,
seems almost I shoulda paid them to learn it, but they paid me to do it.
And I feel very fortunate, *very* fortunate."

Others viewed permanent employment status at CompTech as a
means to slow down their declining occupational opportunities, a straw
to grasp at in their attempt to regain the benefits and security that they
had once possessed. The global story of the decline of status and privi-

lege associated with being a white male with little education in the postindustrial United States (Faludi 1999; Fine et al. 1997; Stacey 1990) emerged
in microcosm in interviews with several white men in their late thirties
and forties, temping but striving for permanent jobs. The pain and bewilderment resulting from the disappearance of certainty were stark. A
forty-year-old, white, male temporary assembler, for example, had previously worked in construction, in a union job. He spoke at length of the
disparity between his current and his past status, of the downward mobility he and his family had experienced after he had to quit the union
job because of health complications. In response to my question about
whether he bought a benefits package from his temp agency (he didn't)
or whether his wife had a benefits plan (she didn't), he commented:

> Well, it's expensive [to buy benefits] and it's, well, that really drops your wages
> down to nothin' now compared to what I used to make, you know. There's a
> lot of people on the line that they're makin' good money to their selves and
> they're buyin' the benefits through the, the temporary agencies. And I hear
> it's fairly good. But it's nothing compared to what I had. And the benefits they
> have here [at CompTech] are just wonderful. And at our age this is somethin'
> that you want. You *want* this. It's not really secure but you want this type of
> benefits. You want this type of job. I don't wanna get into construction again
> and haveta work myself way back up.

His bewilderment about his temporary status captured his frustration
with the loss of the male model of the career (Acker 1990; Hochschild
1989), one based on full-time, year-round, secure employment. He said
"[t]hat's pretty much why I went into this temporary service. I had the idea
that if you work out, you turn into a permanent right away. If you don't,
they send you on your way and you go to another place. That's my idea of
temporary service; I had no idea that you could be a temporary the rest
of your life." His remedy to this situation, seemingly as insecure as being
a temp, was: "I'll start my own business and have people work for me."

In evaluating temporary employment, it is important to look at a
number of factors, including the location of particular temporary
jobs and the labor-market experiences of those in temporary jobs.
Employment at CompTech, even as a temp, lifted the ceiling on many of
their work experiences. For most, CompTech employment was better than
the companies and jobs in which they had been located, where employment was comparatively degraded and unstable, and workers lacked op-

portunities for training, involvement, and trust. If *temporary* employment at CompTech was superior to the earlier employment experiences of most of my interviewees, permanent employment was like striking gold, a secure step onto the bottom rung of a secure, well-buffered, and promising mobility ladder.

At the Epicenter: Self-discipline in Temporary Jobs. Temps viewed temporary employment as a screening process, a location within which temporaries could prove that they would be reliable employees. It was a difficult position for temporaries because, although many did work for long periods of time, they shared the belief that temps were rarely "given a second chance." Thus, if they behaved badly, did sloppy work, worked slowly, or sparred with a coworker, supervisors and managers would request their "nonreturn." These factors—the pressure for mistake-free performance coupled with the belief that such performance increased their chances of obtaining a permanent job—acted as a powerful tool of control over temporary workers and served to cement their acceptance of marginalized labor market status. Their desire for a "real" job led them to engage in strict self-discipline that well served a production system based on individual initiative, decision making, and responsibility.

Temporaries' own view of how their self-discipline and effort affected their quest for permanent work emerged in interviews. Boyd, for example, was striking in the degree of effort and involvement he demonstrated in his job. I observed him in his capacity as team leader for a group of temps: he planned every shift, assigned jobs to each worker, oversaw their work during their shift, and was responsible for this unit's output. The depth of his knowledge of the division in which he worked was impressive, and his relationships with CompTech permanent workers around him were relaxed and good-natured. He observed,

> You know, you certainly don't want to be labeled as a troublemaker or a squeaky wheel. You just wanna go with the flow, don't wanna rock the boat, so you just zip your mouth and keep on goin', you know. As for myself, I really like CompTech, and I like the products. And because I've worked for them, I have a bit of pride in the products that I produce and ship out of my area. So I take more pride in the work and stuff that I produce. And, ah, I really wish that either the agency and/or CompTech in general, um, I don't know about CompTech, I should say my, my managers would see that.

Another temporary worker, whom I introduced before as a single mother who had previously worked at Carl's Jr., talked about this issue with greater desperation in her voice. She was in her third year of employment and, with two young children, felt deeply frustrated at not having been hired into a permanent position. She recalled: "I was telling a friend of mine, I was, like, I wish that, that one of these days that I could have a permanent job here. You know, if anything, they've bypassed us. Yeah, they did. And we've really done a lot for the company, and we've shown a great amount of responsibility that we can be here and be dependable. And I would, I would love for them to just take into consideration that—that we have tried hard and, and we deserve a permanent position."

A white male temporary worker in his early thirties who had taken the CompTech temp job because "I was having a hard time lookin' for a decent job," identified how he had gone far beyond the immediate tasks at hand to stretch and learn more about the organization. In response to my question about how to increase the chances that he would be hired permanently, he answered: "Just continuous high-quality work, I guess. Um, the processes where I'm in [his production area—V. S.], I'm makin' a point to learning and becoming familiar with in case it becomes a need to know, then nobody else knows, I'll stand out, 'cause I know this, you know. They notice things like that."

Converts similarly reflected on the degree of self-regulation to which they submitted in efforts to penetrate the ranks of the permanently employed. Describing himself as having been "on both sides of the fence for about the same amount of time" (six months as a temp, six as a permanent), a technician recalled his temporary experience:

> You know, we would do daily tasks and down the road we knew that, ah, employment-wise, the size of our line was gonna grow, which it has, to about twenty people now. We also knew there would be permanent positions open, and so there was a lot of jockeying for the ah, you know, who could do the, the best job, you know, who could perform the best. There was a lot of ah, there was *a lot* of competition between, between the temps to kinda develop, not necessarily a pecking order, but develop a who's-impressed-the-most-people-type order, and who is thought of more highly. And that was our goal. And then I, I believe that really, based on that competition, that's how the decisions were made to hire.

Another male convert who had worked in the "food services industry" for fifteen years prior to joining CompTech remembered his strategies for gaining permanent status: "It was like, I'm here, I have the opportunity to impress these people, and if, hopefully, if I do a
good-enough job, if I impress them well enough, then you know, they
may see fit to bring me on if they have the opening. And certainly that
does happen."

For other temps, the belief that it is management's prerogative to use
temporary labor to resolve business downturns underwrites their self-
discipline. These individuals didn't question the logic of capital accumulation or the fact that large companies need organizational flexibility
to meet the demands of changing markets. For example, Amos, a temporary assembler in his late twenties, posited that:

> Temps are great because they're a great resource that you can add on if you
> need 'em and take them right away. And although it may seem heartless to
> the person, that is, the temp, it's great for business because it [the workforce]
> can grow with the business or shrink with the business really quickly.

He held to this view despite acknowledging the drawback, to the temps'
morale, when he or she knows, "Even though my manager likes me, they
[*sic*] can get rid of me tomorrow without any response, they can just let
me go for no apparent reason whatsoever, even if I've given my all."

Another temp predicted that if she "ran a big business, I think I would
do it probably the same way. They can pretty much just say, 'Don't show
up for work tomorrow.' They are not obligated to tell you why. It's an easy
out for the big corporations. Now for *us*, no, it's not so great. I've seen
people all of a sudden just not be there the next day and they didn't have
a clue" (she laughs out loud).

Finally, an individual who had worked as a temp for thirteen months
theorized management's perspective quite cogently. His observations go
to the heart of situations where corporations attempt to protect their core
workforce with a buffer of temporary workers, the shock absorbers of economic volatility: "CompTech doesn't wanna go the way of IBM or Digital
or any of those places where they, you know, where suddenly 14,000
people are lopped off the payroll. They're more responsible to their workforce than that. So, I mean, if you're going, if it's inevitable you're going
to have some *pain*—where do you have it? With the people that you've
had for twenty years? Do you want it to go there? Or is it to the people

that you willingly and knowingly hired on a limited job? Now do you whack them or the other people?!"

Finally, however, to this textured picture must be added the ways in which some temporaries refused to accept a definition of themselves as marginalized participants. Specifically, many earnestly worked to build their profiles as committed workers and searched for inroads to the system to try to land permanent jobs, in ways that had been officially prohibited by corporate management's policies. Thus, temporary workers' strategies to land permanent employment were not confined to regulating themselves only to stay silent and enact behaviors that would make them stand out. Rather, they actively undertook informal measures to affect their outcomes.

The list of informal procedures included going through web pages from different company units and divisions to gain information about permanent job openings (something forbidden in the exclusionary framework); taking preemptive measures by routinely circulating resumes to managers who might be hiring in the future; seeking mentoring from supervisors and managers; deliberately making themselves available to learn new skills and knowledge bases so as to make themselves indispensable on the shop and office floor; and appropriating the CompTech work identity for their own (telling outsiders they were employees of CompTech rather than of a temporary agency) rather than letting the label of "temporary worker" be hung on them by the company or by the oscillation of the labor market. And if management were to put its foot down about these practices, it ran the risk of delegitimizing an entire production system that in theory relied on participation and trust and in practice was dependent on the compliance and involvement of a critical mass of temporary employees.

The temps I interviewed also articulated a discourse about the "bad" temporary worker (much like the temps that Henson [1996:165] studied). In this discourse they constructed images of bad temporaries who were "deviant" and "immature." Interviewees saw themselves as more like permanent workers and distinguished themselves from temps who fit prevailing negative stereotypes about temporary workers today. The negative stereotype in essence blames individuals for their temporary employment status, arguing that transience and marginalization of employment is explained by individual-level variables such as a weak work ethic, laziness, lack of commitment, deviance, and even criminal behavior.

Rosaria, a thirty-two-year-old Hispanic woman, talked with me about her self-consciousness with regard to working hard to impress her manager. She worried that the behavior of some of the "useless" temps, as she called them, boded poorly for temps in general. In her estimation, "There's a lot of people that just can't keep a job. That's why they go to temporary services. And you realize it when you work with 'em. They don't wanna come to work, or when they come to work, they don't wanna work. They're just punchin' their hours in the time clock." Another temp, Marcy, categorized all young temps as bad temps: "I see a lot of young eighteen-, nineteen-, twenty-year-olds that this is their first job and they don't care. And then you've got the older workers, you know, that are thirty and more that this [job] means the world to them. You know, they have goals and this means the world, and you'll get caught up around teenagers that are, don't care, and you're associated with 'em. You say, you know, these people don't really care about their jobs."

Ironic in Marcy's statement is that in the five production settings in which I had the opportunity to observe several hundred people, very few of the assemblers and none of the clerical workers appeared to be very young at all. My sense is that Marcy has had experience working with some younger temporary workers, either at CompTech and in other settings (she had had several temporary jobs before joining CompTech), and young, irresponsible temps were a vector for her larger anxiety about not getting hired as a permanent worker.

Temporary workers at CompTech, striving to land permanent jobs, actively worked to distance themselves from this stereotype. Many of the temps I interviewed expressed their anxiety about being associated with bad temporary workers, and sometimes they blamed "bad" temporary workers for everyone's difficulty in landing a good job. In this way, temporary workers seeking long-term jobs refused to internalize the label of the untrustworthy and transient temp; instead they constructed a point of view in which they had much more in common with permanent workers than with certain temporary counterparts.

Conclusion

Reproco workers cast a positive light on jobs that weren't highly paid or socially valued but were nevertheless part of an occupational hierarchy in a paternalistic, core firm. The woodworkers struggled to keep a positive view of their futures. Their definitions of permanency and their understanding of the traditional social contract were continually morphing, and they dedicated much effort to keeping their plant open because they believed that such a goal was within the realm of the possible. CompTech's temporary workers maintained hopeful aspirations about becoming a member of a paternalistic firm as well; for them, even a firm like WoodWorks, with dwindling expectations for employer obligations to employees, would appear to offer good jobs that they'd never had. Through their activities they labored to gain control over uncertain employment conditions.

CompTech temporary workers' situations reside in-between those of Reproco and WoodWorks. Temporaries' responses were conditioned by factors found in the two cases discussed so far, but these factors were recombined and thus bore different causal weight in workers' calculations of uncertainty, opportunity, and risk. As was true for the service workers at Reproco, CompTech's temporaries were integrated into a more or less organic employee-involvement and flexible work system. Their jobs, even when low-skilled, presented challenges and opportunities. Thus, like the Reproco workers, CompTech's temporary employees benefited from experiential uncertainty and unpredictability in a setting where work conditions and employment relations were progressive for the companies' "permanent" workers. At the same time, temps faced the structural/employment uncertainty of the woodworkers. In the case of the temporary workers, the potential of losing their jobs was pervasive and inherent in the nature of the temporary contract. The temps, I argue, participated in CompTech's work system because they hoped, against obvious statistical odds, that their situation at CompTech was only temporarily temporary, that the job was merely a rung on the ladder to permanent employment with a good employer.

In remaining dedicated to becoming a member of CompTech despite the low probability of entering the permanent ranks, temps in certain respects stood a chance of earning a much larger payoff than either of the other groups. Ironically, their consent and cooperation may make the most sense of all. If they became permanent members of CompTech, they would gain access to a more open mobility ladder, many training and educational opportunities, a culture of respect and inclusion, and comparative job security. For these reasons I would argue that temps were not quiescent, subjecting themselves to an employment relationship that would never work to their advantage; rather they viewed their jobs as a proving ground, an opportunity for demonstrating the behavior, the attitudes, and the ambition that might lead managers to take on their case and become an advocate for them in their quest to obtain a good job.[12]

Their resistance to structural disadvantage played out in refusing to internalize stigmatized definitions of themselves as marginalized workers, and they actively endeavored to turn their aspirations into concrete outcomes by donning the profile of an attached, valuable worker. If temporariness and uncertainty were ubiquitous but unrealized among plywood plant workers, permanency and security are ubiquitous but unrealized to CompTech assembly and clerical temporaries.

Clearly, the conditions under which one works as a temporary worker in the late twentieth-century United States matter enormously. Day laborers, hired off a street corner for a day of hard work on construction sites or in fields; temporary clerical workers who work three or four days in a small business office (Rogers 2000); or low-wage temps who work at extremely peripheral jobs in firms dominated by despotic management practices (McAllister 1998; Parker 1994)—all these situations would draw the temporary employee into a very different web of experiences, social relations, and policies than those faced by the CompTech temp. Clearly, the findings from this study of temps in a progressive, paternalistic work setting are generalizable primarily to similar settings.

Nevertheless, the importance of the CompTech case cannot be underestimated. Large core companies in the United States have been using temps to an increasing degree. As small a proportion of the workforce as temporary employment commands, the rates of its increase have been substantial, and there has been a paradigmatic shift in the way that employers envision using temporary workers. Indeed, changing expectations for impermanence and unpredictability, which have seeped deeply into U.S. employment relations and culture, are embodied in the experiences of the long-term temporary worker, whether long-term in one company or moving from temp job to temp job over time. While it would be difficult to make the case that CompTech's situation is representative of what all temporary workers face, it is plausible to argue that a new template is emerging and gaining strength, one in which using temporary workers to perform recurrent (nontemporary) tasks is seen as more viable and in which the costs of such arrangements may increasingly be perceived as less onerous than once believed.

I have considered three cases in which the combination of uncertainty, risk, and opportunity have played out and permeated work life for U.S.

workers. I now turn to unexplored terrain: unemployed individuals who previously held stable jobs, who now struggle to reestablish themselves within the postindustrial employment relationship. Conducting in-depth interviews with them and observing their experiences in a job search organization highlights a troubling dilemma for those trying to cross the great divide into the new world of employment.

5 Structural Unemployment and the Reconstruction of the Self in the Turbulent Economy

Hi, my name is Harvey Dixon. I specialize in human resources management and have extensive experience working in the telecommunications industry. I've been responsible for up to 750 people. I'm credentialed in teamwork and want to work in a professional environment that values working with others. I especially seek challenges, change, and opportunities for making innovations. So if you know anyone seeking a person with my skills, tell them to call Harvey Dixon.

A professional introduction, scripted and delivered by Harvey Dixon (a pseudonym) at the general membership meeting of Experience Unlimited, a job club for unemployed professionals and managers.

Being a Manager, Being a Professional, Being Unemployed

Employed photocopiers, woodworkers, and even long-term but temporary assemblers have jobs and are located within employment institutions where they experience varying degrees of uncertainty and risk, but also opportunity. What does the uncertainty/risk/opportunity equation look like to people standing outside employment institutions, fervently wishing to become attached and stable members of one? How do these unemployed managers and professionals, once untouched by layoffs, displacement, and corporate restructuring, interpret the new rules of the employment relationship or feel about having to reevaluate and put a new gloss on their employment identities? How do labor-market intermediaries, such as job training agencies and job and career search organizations, insert themselves into these processes? What kinds of signals do they give the unemployed about corporate restructuring and impermanency? In short, what messages are being transmitted to people who have fallen into an abyss, who are stuck in the great divide itself and striving to reach the more promising terrain of the new economy?

Lack of a job in the latter years of the 1990s has had humiliating implications for unemployed professionals and managers. Many of the individuals whom I interviewed and observed at a job search organization, who were experiencing in blunt form the dynamism of the labor market, understood that they were up against challenging institutional changes: the decline of the permanent job model, erosion of internal labor markets, and the pervasiveness of employment insecurity.[1] They were deeply discouraged by their sense—often grounded in protracted, painful experience—that emergent structures were impenetrable to them, that the rules of getting and keeping a good job were increasingly indecipherable.

Unemployed professionals and managers labored to learn new job-search, interviewing, and negotiating tactics that they believed would position them advantageously in the turbulent economy. Desiring respectable employment that would offer a modicum of security and opportunities for mobility, dignity, and a reasonable wage, they craved the chance to demonstrate to employers that they could learn new skills and would be committed employees. They articulated well the master narrative of the new, destabilized economy: a story with subplots including routine corporate downsizing, employers' preference for adaptable workers with general rather than firm-specific skills, employers' desire to depress wages by downsizing older, long-term workforces, and the growth of contingent employment. It is a story that reassured them that their personal problems were structural in nature.

Yet, in counterbalance to this version of economic change, they read of astonishingly low unemployment rates. They read newspaper articles citing the leading employers in the area, who lament the shortage of available skilled labor. The skills employers say they can't find are the skills that unemployed managers and professionals are willing to learn, and they believe they have the organizational and cultural capital to do so from their previous employment experiences. They also read of the so-called work revolution, the dazzling range of income and work opportunities, seemingly just out of their reach in the information- and communications-based dot.com economy. These labor-market facts don't add up, but they do create a deep sense of personal insecurity and failure. Interpreting and being at the epicenter of these contradictory trends constitute the daily experiences of the experienced but unemployed professional or manager.

Studying lived experience in intermediary labor-market organizations yields much sociological data about these questions and issues.[2] Chapters 2–4 center on employment organizations and the ways in which different organizations structure participation and surprising levels of aspiration. In this chapter I focus on how an organization for the un- and underemployed—a professional and managerial job search club organized under the auspices of the California Employment Development Department (EDD)—framed the dynamics of job searching and labor markets to its clientele, and how members of the organization responded to this framework. It is within such organizations that people learn about and map out the dynamics of labor-market processes and job acquisition procedures, identify particular career paths or occupational fields, strategize to identify, build, and improve their job skills, and come to grips with unemployed comrades, with rejections from employers and with discouraging holding patterns such as long periods of temporary employment.

The framework that is the subject of this chapter was inscribed in the organization's entry criteria, written rules, training practices, and collective discourses. This hegemonic framework presented a consistent view of economic transformation and how unemployed managers and professionals could overcome its most deleterious effects. Taking an in-depth look at what such organizations actually tell and do for the unemployed sheds light on the contemporary discourse of flexibility, turbulence, and temporariness. It also opens up opportunities for examining how unemployed participants interpret and respond to the types of labor-market changes I have analyzed thus far, how they seek to transform the self (Hochschild 1983; Leidner 1993) to adapt to those changes, and how they struggle to gain control over situations that are highly uncertain and feel painfully out of control.[3]

Sociologists, organizational researchers, and industrial relations theorists lack in-depth data about how individuals attempt to affect employment outcomes and about activities they undertake in spheres and organizations that fall outside formal employment and labor-market organizations. Much research has focused on structural factors shaping entrance to or rejection from jobs and labor markets, such as biased recruitment processes, in which organizational gatekeepers routinely engage in statistical discrimination and in so doing make access to jobs or labor markets difficult for some, or organizational determinants of inequality and mobility. Yet we lack systematic investigation and understanding of the circumstances under which individuals attempt to manipulate structures: the work they undertake to gain access to labor markets and firms and to manipulate mobility opportunities prior to acquiring formal employment. The structural emphasis on job acquisition, "in bypassing the process by which workers evaluate their market prospects and actively construct their careers... renders the mobility decision analytically unproblematic" (Halaby 1988:9). The structural approach is cognizant of the different choices individuals may make about jobs, but the issue of choice and agency has by and large "been relegated to the background" in the study of job search activities and mobility strategies (ibid.).[4]

Understanding agency and choice is pressing in the current industrial, economic, and labor-market transformation. Of central concern in this chapter is the way in which strategies for finding work are shaped and constructed by perceptions of the broader economic, institutional, and cultural context in the United States. As I suggest throughout previous chapters, transformations in work and employment relations increasingly signal to adult workers that they must confront the shifting practices and structures of postindustrial labor markets in novel and unorthodox ways. Here, I examine how these perceptions and strategies unfold in a job search club.

I highlight a paradoxical effect of participation in this organization. One goal of the members of this organization was to reproduce their class position in the reconfigured economy. Yet the rhetoric of the club and the individualized tactics the unemployed used to reposition themselves in jobs and labor markets had the ultimate effect of depressing their aspirations and setting them up for downward mobility. I argue in this chapter that while managers and professionals understood and endorsed the point of view that structural factors accounted for the origins of their unemployment, in their view it was their individual flaws and presentation of self that accounted for their inability to land new jobs. Thus, their personalities and their impression-management skills became the final frontier for finding jobs and gaining control over structural *and* experiential uncertainty.

Labor-market Organizations and Their Role
in Constructing the Terms of the Great Divide

Labor-market organizations such as state-sponsored training or job search agencies play a vital role in smoothing the uneven interface between shifting labor markets and people looking for work.[5] Agencies for the unemployed present a selective view of how labor markets work, propel particular groups of people toward particular types of opportunities, and act as a link between formal institutions and an aggregate of individuals who desire employment. The type of organization I studied— going by the names of both Experience Unlimited (EU) and the Sacramento Professional Network (SPN)—is part of a population of organizations that has been researched and analyzed by others in a search to understand how displaced managers and professionals navigate through the labor market. Newman (1988) pioneered a groundswell of interest in these organizations in her discussion of downwardly mobile managers and professionals who utilized the services of the exclusive 40 Plus Club, a private career search club that provided services to a select clientele of the unemployed.

Torres (1996) studied a branch of the same EDD organization as I did, but in Santa Barbara. The Santa Barbara club, like the Sacramento club, was accessible to a broader socio-economic swath of the unemployed public than was the 40 Plus Club. Torres quite innovatively investigated why unemployed professionals and managers didn't use weak ties to find jobs to the degree predicted by Granovetter (1974/1995). Strohschein (1998) studied a similar club in Ontario, Canada, exploring the "little" things people did to cope with unemployment and increase their sense of efficacy in their job search endeavors, many of which mirrored the individual-level solutions that people were pressed to undertake in the Sacramento club. Finally, Crouse (1998) examined a private outplacement agency, Transitions, looking at the way downsized managers struggled over the loss of the old and the rules of the new social contract.

While all four studies explicitly situated themselves in the context of corporate restructuring, they did not explore how the organizations they examined deployed discourses and practices that promulgated the new rules for maneuvering in specific labor markets, nor did they discuss the ironies of such clubs emphasizing individual solutions to structural problems. Indergaard (1999) has advanced this area of inquiry considerably, presenting an insightful, fine-grained analysis of a retraining and job placement agency for displaced blue-collar workers. Using field research data, he showed how the agency's treatment of workers was specifically geared to the particular features of local labor markets in the deindustrialized Detroit area. My analysis of a job search club shows how "resocialization" procedures in this job search club were biased toward getting members to adapt to the exigencies of changing labor market institutions and practices, and to adjust to the likelihood of downward mobility. Participants were pressed to remake and recraft their employment profiles, encouraged to "settle" for less desirable entry-level, nonprofessional, or temporary jobs, and urged to act as if they were responsible for their own occupational fates.

The analysis offered here strives to advance the discussion of these labor-market organizations and the experiences of managers and professionals in them beyond the widely shared insight that professionals and managers typically grasp the structural causes of their unemployment but inexplicably adopt individual strategies to find new jobs. This formulation unnecessarily mystifies why managers and professionals resort to their own devices to remedy problems that they have not created. Here, I make the case that managers and professionals viewed only *one* side of the equation—the *cause* of their unemployment—as structurally determined, but viewed the *other* side of the equation—their search for and inability to find a new job—in purely individualistic terms. Despite cognitive recognition of change in economic institutions, these individuals internalized responsibility and blamed themselves for lacking what it took to reposition themselves in the labor market. Their remedies for change are consistent with an individualist American ideology of meritocracy that reassures us that the starting point in our mobility trajectories is not as important as what we do to move us up and through them.

Experience Unlimited: A State-sponsored Job Search Club for Professionals, Managers, and Technical Workers

In 1959 the California EDD established Experience Unlimited because the department felt that it could not adequately serve the needs of the managerial and professional unemployed. Correctly, EDD pointed out that employers typically didn't list announcements with them about professional and managerial job openings, and that the managerial and professional job market tended to operate more through networks and connections than through formal job listings of open positions. EDD also believed that unemployed professionals and managers needed to be actively involved in their searches to a degree that was not possible in the traditional bureaucratic and hierarchical organization of EDD. Utilization of Experience Unlimited declined dramatically in the 1970s but began to pick up in the late 1980s and exploded in the 1990s.[6] When I conducted my research, EU paid the salary of one full-time staff person (Karen) and provided resources such as computers, telephones, furniture, and office space.

Following on the principle that different conditions and resources were required to facilitate unemployed managers' and professionals' quest for jobs, the EDD designed an autonomous professional space for their use. The physical layout of the Employment Development Department architecturally stratified the job seekers using its services from the unemployed of other classes. When other unemployed people went to file for unemployment benefits or obtain information about available jobs, they entered through the main door of the EDD into a large impersonal waiting area. These "regular" unemployed—the large numbers of people looking for entry-level service, production, or construction jobs, mostly people of color, people who dressed casually and informally, some sprawled out and fast asleep, others who didn't have the "luxury" of napping because of small, impatient children—were separated from and ranked below the agency workers by a thick wall of Plexiglass. Standing in front of the tiny opening in the Plexiglass, individuals were fed narrow bits of information from the frontline workers. Until then, they sat in rows of hard plastic chairs, waiting for their names to be called, for the "privilege" of being grilled and processed by the EDD employees.

The members of EU, however, were cushioned from the stigma and the experience of unemployment in various ways. The unemployed managers and professionals had a separate entrance that led into a large and comfortable suite. It was fully equipped for members to conduct job searches with comparative privacy and autonomy. Their hours and days at EU were self-organized, often filled with friendly and supportive interactions with their unemployed colleagues. They were free to explore reams of information at their leisure. Here, there were no spatial or administrative hierarchies inscribed in the everyday arrangements of the organization: no bulletproof Plexiglass repelled and reminded them that they were to be managed with apprehension, if not contempt; no bureaucratic cadre suggested that the professionals and managers were in an organizationally subordinate or socially stigmatized position. Although Karen, the paid staff member, was responsible for the general functioning of the center, EU was otherwise completely coordinated and governed by volunteer participants themselves.

The stigmatizing label of "unemployed" was obscured by the name always cited by any volunteer answering the main telephone: "Sacramento Professional Network." Members often gave this telephone number to potential employers so that when an employer needed to contact a member about an interview or a job offer, they left their message at what sounded like a professional answering service. On its surface EU had the feel of a friendly professional club.

In separating the unemployed professionals and managers from and privileging them in comparison to the unemployed from the ranks of those who are working-class or lack skills and education, EDD also spun a class-specific rhetoric about the unique needs of the former groups. In the EDD's *Fact Sheet* describing the rationale for EU, the department connected the goals of the organization directly to the currents of the 1990s economy, noting that "many professional, managerial, and technical workers…have unexpectedly found themselves out of work" and that the organization's services are "a response to the needs of communities faced with an increase in corporate mergers, relocations and downsizing, or an increased number of people forced to change jobs due to technological shifts."

A Profile of the Membership. The membership of Experience Unlimited was predominately male. Karen, the staff member, estimated that the ratio of women to men was approximately thirty-five to sixty-five, and that the racial and ethnic ratio was approximately 20 percent nonwhite to 80 percent white. The membership was also mature. A quick gaze across the room at any time suggested a group with enormous collective experience, with many people, both men and women, looking to be in their late thirties, forties, or fifties. The sixteen members who were in my introductory workshop averaged in age forty-five years, while the seventeen individuals in my interview sample averaged forty-four years of age.[7] For individuals who had had what could be called long-term, permanent jobs prior to coming to EU, the average length of time they spent in their job was fourteen years. This group constituted about one-third of the total in my workshop and interview sample; the remaining two-thirds had had shorter tenure at a greater number of jobs.

The occupational status of nearly all EU members was professional and managerial, broadly defined. Previously, most of them had held lower-to-middle staff and line management positions or belonged to less specialized professions and semi-professions. I met no doctors or lawyers, although I did interview a woman who had a law degree but had never practiced law and was seeking a new career line. In fact, only four individuals held higher degrees: the woman with a law degree, a man with master's degrees in engineering and in business; a woman with a Ph.D. in chemistry; and a woman with a master's in public health. What is important here is that these individuals were in a position where personal/professional networks were failing them, where demand for their labor was weak, either because of their limited skills, age, and seniority or because they were handicapped by previous employment experiences, a matter I discuss later in this chapter.

Many of the people I studied had had direct experience with temporary employment, in several ways. Eleven of the seventeen people in my interview sample had worked as a temporary or contract worker. Nearly every one of the eleven had been employed by an agency, not directly by the company. Of those who had worked on a temporary basis, five were what I would call "serial temps": they regularly held temporary jobs, ranging from a period of months to several years, and had used EU when they could afford to devote their energy toward hunting for more regular employment.

Three others had worked on the *staff* of temporary firms. Their labor had, in small but nevertheless significant ways, contributed to the destabilization of the employment structure. For example, one woman helped her employer—who owned a legal-services temporary help agency—to market, sell, and set up franchises of that agency, thus building the temporary-help service industry. Another individual, employed by a temporary agency and working for a large regional utility company, had conducted "Activity Value Analysis," wherein he analyzed detailed company data to conduct a cost assessment of various companywide functions. The company needed this information to determine what functions were most suitable for outsourcing to vendors. Thus, he, as a temporary worker, was collecting and analyzing the data that would allow this company to downsize *its* permanent workforce.

Seven of the individuals in my interview sample had acquired additional degrees, credentials, and certificates in their quest to expand their options and make themselves more marketable. For example, two individuals had gone through the career search program at a national company called Haldane, paying approximately three thousand dollars of their own money to do so. Three other people I interviewed had considered using Haldane, had attended Haldane's preliminary workshop to determine whether they wanted to go through the whole program, and had decided against it. They were discouraged by Haldane's steep price and the program's vague promises of actually landing a job. One man had obtained an MBA, and one woman working in the field of insurance and investment service had acquired four licenses and had paid four thousand dollars to complete yet another career evaluation and search program. Others had obtained certificates (in quality management programs and professional conference and meeting planning, for example), while yet others had taken various courses to hone their computer skills, such as word processing, web page design, desktop publishing, and database management.

Finally, nine of the people I interviewed, and an indeterminate number of people in my workshop, were compelled to use EU after they had been caught in the cross fire of corporate restructuring. That is, the direct causes of unemployment were widespread layoffs in a single company (in some cases, people had experienced multiple layoffs) or layoffs caused by their company's merger with another company or by technological/organizational restructuring and displacement.

While a slim majority of people I discuss here lost their jobs through corporate restructuring or downsizing, some of the remaining group had been fired for what appeared to have been poor performance or personality conflicts. I make no effort to compare the two groups or to suggest that one group was structurally victimized while the others were "losers," the latter a negative stereotype held even by some of the unemployed themselves. (One woman's comments typify an ambivalence I heard in many interviews. "I know this is very bad of me to say but I felt, I looked around, and you heard of everybody's personal needs, and it was like, Why can't these people get jobs? I mean, if they are this skilled and qualified, why can't they get jobs, and why can't I get a job? On the one hand, I understand it because I was having trouble too, but on the other hand, I didn't get it.")

In this chapter, I hope to avoid perpetuating the categories of "deserving" and "undeserving" unemployed that have plagued discussions of poverty in the United States. Nor do I wish to simply report the personal injury and frustration that interviewees and workshop participants described to me. To be sure, such injury and frustration prevailed; discussions of it dominated one-on-one interviews. I focus instead on the fact that, for whatever reason, people using the organization's services shared the circumstances of unemployment. They had to maneuver within similar labor-market constraints. They were the recipients of a common set of messages and practices endorsed by a state-sponsored job search organization, and they selectively interpreted, appropriated, and rejected those messages. Indeed, EU participants reinforced these messages in the way they planned their workshop curriculum and made use of many of the tactics that were promised to help them "terminate" their unemployment. While many criticized the tactics as being superficial, transparent, or desperate, nearly all experimented with them and even persistently continued to exercise them despite the odds that they faced in the job market. This chapter addresses the way these messages were framed to EU participants and how participants reacted to and filtered them.[8]

Professionalizing Unemployment or, Daily Life at Experience Unlimited, aka the Sacramento Professional Network

On the sweltering summer morning on which I am supposed to make a pitch to recruit interviewees for my project, I drive to Sacramento, park my car in the vast, steamy parking lot of the California Employment Development Department, and go through an unmarked door to present "proof" to the volunteer at the front desk that I am authorized to attend the EU general meeting. Not just anyone can enter the EU facility. As if to continually remind themselves of their professional norms and identity, members have erected administrative and symbolic shields around their premises, barriers of entry to any casual or inappropriate visitor to the center. In so doing, they recreate professionalism: they define the boundaries of their professional field and apply well-defined criteria to determine admission to their ranks.

First, anyone not authorized is not admitted. EU members jealously guard their resources and their turf. While I am filling out information for my visitor's pass, I hear Ramon, the sentry, deny one man entry and explain to him what he has to do to gain entrance. Obtaining authorization either means having the permission of the single EDD staff member or filling out extensive paperwork enumerating work history, personal data, and career goals. Even when a potential member completes the required paperwork, he or she is only allowed to initiate participation at an appointed date specified by the sentry. Each prospective member must take their place on a lengthy waiting list.

Other measures create the aura of professionalism and reinforce the professional shield. If a member is inappropriately dressed—that is, not dressed professionally as defined in the manual of rules—he or she is not allowed to enter. The exception is if the dress-code violator agrees to don an article of clothing from the surplus professional clothing supply, a coat-rack hung with men's ties and sports jackets and women's linen jackets. Bare legs on women are frowned upon, as are slacks. The dress with ny-lons is uniquely considered the evidence of women's professionalism, as the tie is for men.

The center hums as members perform the work they believe is nec-essary to find a job. Searching for a job, I come to see, is a job itself. As I learn in the following weeks of workshops, job searching is taught as a near-scientific process (represented as a pyramid of ten ascending steps one must follow to get a job), with specified tasks, a prescribed and sys-tematic methodology, schedules for meetings, and collective expectations for performance. To conduct this work, EU has a significant amount of open, communal space for large meetings and cozier cubicles and work areas for small group meetings, individual tasks, and one-on-one conver-sations between members. When I arrive at 8:45 A.M., some members are setting up folding chairs for the mandatory weekly general meeting. Although some people jovially share stories about their weekends with fellow members, most seem to be carrying out tasks that are part of the daily and weekly work in the organization. Several sets of people confer about their plans for workshops to be held that week.

Some individuals thumb through job announcement binders and clip-boards, while some work on their personal organizers. Others station themselves at one of many computers available for on-line job search ac-tivities, make calls at the bank of phones to schedule appointments or in-quire about openings, or read informational and inspirational news sto-ries on the bulletin board. Articles with headlines such as "Understanding the Hidden Job Market," "Job Search Stress," "Changing Careers," "Fatal Mistakes in Interviews," "Should You Lie to Land a Job?" "Creating a Better Life after Topping Out Early," and "Mantras to Make Yourself Feel Positive" confirm the realities of the treacherous job market but suggest that the reader can minimize or overcome such treachery. By engaging in these activities, EU members sustain a sense of autonomy, industriousness, and professionalism, but the activities also serve as vivid testimony to the hard realities of why people are members in the first place.

Regular attendance at EU provides members with a salient connection to a stable institution. They find the resources they need to do their work—the job search. They learn skills that for some are new: how to facilitate meetings, write newsletters and reports, improve their public speaking skills, network, and learn the theory behind cross-training and multitasking. They engage in regular events and rituals; they are part of an organization with a history; and they are embedded in a set of ongoing social relationships. The faces of those with whom they interact may change (and in fact, everyone hopes they will change, since it is inspiring evidence that people do find jobs), but there is a general stability to EU's population. Hence, joining EU confers membership in an ongoing social and professional unit, while the work the unemployed do there affords them a sense of control and efficacy under circumstances in which they have little control. Coming to EU everyday, as the leadership of the organization advocates, anchors people who have no active relationship to any other stable, collective entity or project. As one woman said to me, EU "kept me going through a time when I was kind of like searching for some kind of identity" after working for AT&T for nine years. Unemployed people who have invested much time and effort to carve out their professional niches face enormous challenges to their sense of identity.

Becoming an active member of EU also serves to break down people's sense of isolation, to minimize their feeling that they are alone in their plight, and to fuel collective critique of the structural determinants of their circumstances. Ironically, EU normalizes rather than pathologizes the causes of professional unemployment in the 1990s. One woman had been downsized out of two human-resources management positions in Los Angeles and had moved to Sacramento to work as a recruiter for Packard Bell, only to lose that job during its fifth round of layoffs. She said:

> SPN has helped because it really helps get rid of some of the negative associations [with unemployment] that many people have. It was ironic because I had had negative stereotypes about people like me who couldn't find a job. Then I became one of "Them" with a capital "T." I came to recognize that one of "Them" is not at all what I filled the blanks in with. And it was humbling to realize that I wasn't alone. And that there were really sharp, professional people who, due to downsizing and the condition of the globe and economics and

issues beyond individual control, in my mind, the political situations and so forth, and people who are in really high, respectful, prestigious, well-paying positions—they were all there.

In fact, what had broken down for this woman were stereotypes about unemployed professionals and *not* about unemployed people across the board. The structure and daily operations of EU that I have described reaffirmed her sense of class position; thus, her various layoffs hadn't propelled her to feel greater affinity with *all* victims of turbulence and restructuring. Empathy with what their fellow middle-class unemployed had endured created feelings of support and solidarity, feelings that allowed people not to succumb to viewing their situations in purely individualistic terms. Don claimed:

> I know what it's like to have been forced out of a job. I know there are two sides to these stories. In an average organization, if I may wax cynical here for a moment, scum seems to rise to the top of the pond. So I talked to a number of people at SPN who I know are competent, very generally worthwhile people, very normal, very rational. And then to hear about the circumstances under which they left their previous job, you really have to question the reasons and the motive behind the people who made decisions to let this particular individual go or fire them or do whatever. I, through my own experience, have a very cynical approach to when management, quote, management, decides to get rid of somebody.
>
> We function here as a support group. You get the camaraderie, the professional companionship, so to speak. The people, regardless of being from different fields and stuff like that, you have the fact that you are out-of-work-professionals in common, and most people are willing to contribute that moral support. Just because they're all, you know, we're all in the same boat.

Sara, a white woman in her early forties, echoed Don's cynicism, quiet anger, and bewilderment. Sara had worked for fifteen years as a teen health program coordinator and childbirth educator for a major regional hospital. Holding on to her position through two mergers, she was finally laid off as the final merged unit downsized. Shortly thereafter she was re-hired into what the hospital calls a "term-limited position," their terminology for a temporary position. We talked about what it felt like to work term-limited for an institution she had previously worked with for fifteen years, and she shared the following reflections:

I don't really feel appreciated in the organization. I did get severance. It was
all done by the book. But being a very loyal person I wanted to have more loyalty on the other side and that's just disappeared from business now. They
hired me back on a renewable basis. This just hurts to realize that the employers are not going to give to employees. Because I'm willing to, you know
I'd give 120 percent. Lots of times it takes me longer than my eight hours to
finish my work. [As a permanent semiprofessional employee she received a
salary; as limited-term she receives an hourly wage and is only paid for an
eight-hour shift.] It's very hard for me to say, "No, I need to quit, this can wait
until tomorrow" because I want to just finish it up. You know, it's like I need
to finish it now, so it'll take an extra hour. I know it won't be appreciated in
the long run, so I shouldn't do it, but it's hard not to.

   And I have the sense of being betrayed, feeling like we've all been abandoned, and there's all this emotional feeling that it's hard to be unemployed,
makes us feel not worthy, although it's not our fault, still . . . it's a humiliating
experience.

Surrounding oneself with others who share an understanding of the
public nature of one's personal problems creates a buffer between the
unemployed individual and employed friends and family, and in so doing
it helps alleviate some of the stigma of unemployment. Anthony, a white
man in his early forties, had worked most of his career as a nuclear engineer for Bechtel. In the early 1990s he decided to take advantage of
Bechtel's program for subsidizing the education of its professional employees and went through the MBA program at the University of
California, Davis. Bechtel laid him off shortly after he finished his MBA.
Since that time he had been un- or underemployed, mostly working at
temp jobs. His most recent had been at Packard Bell, doing database management. All the while, he had been searching for a full-time, stable professional job, trying to fend off friends' and family members' perception
that he wasn't doing everything he could to find another position. He described his discomfort with his current status:

   I think there is a certain stigmatism attached to it—not working. Like, for example, one of my friends, he was unemployed for about eight months. Not
   underemployed but unemployed for about eight months. He got laid off from
   Bechtel too. And he was on unemployment, and I remember he told me his
   brother-in-law said, you know, "You get fourteen hundred dollars a month for
   doing nothing," and it's like, we don't do nothing. We spend, we have a full-

time job (job hunting) but we just don't get paid for it. So I think some people who haven't been in this position think that either we're lazy, we're not looking hard enough. Or, we're too choosy, something like that. Since there's that stigmatism attached to being without work, it makes it harder to say, "Oh, I'm not working," if someone asks.

As another man put it, friends were unwilling to talk too much about his unemployment: it was as if a death had occurred. "You know, it kind of struck me that while people are very willing to give you personal support, it's as though a relative passed on. They want to be really supportive but they're very careful not to mention the relative's name or the direct circumstances of the demise, you know?"

When people join EU, they agree to a contract specifying the terms of their involvement. As mentioned earlier, everyone is required to attend the general meeting. All participants must undergo three days of "training," a series of workshops that introduce new members to the major issues surrounding the job search. Topics covered include the changing economy, how to compose effective scripts for introducing oneself to potential employers, the art of interviewing (where one can learn, among other things, "how to respond to tough questions and find out what your body says about you"), resume production, and so forth. One workshop imparts a sense of regional place, alerting participants to the peculiarities of employment and underemployment in the Sacramento area. You can learn "which occupations in the greater Sacramento area you can approach with confidence" (a uniquely subjective assessment of prevailing opportunities), as well as answering the question "How do your skills and talents translate to industries and businesses?" in the area. Special topic workshops are also available. "Riding the Rapids" introduces everyone to the travails of the job search process and to the unpredictabilities of careers in the 1990s. "Network or Don't Work" emphasizes that you can't make it if you don't effectively network and exploit connections. "Compensation Negotiation" teaches participants how to control salary negotiations by reading and manipulating body language, holding one's cards close, and engaging in impression management that conveys confidence and an "I can walk away from this interview" attitude.

The "Applied Brain Research Seminar" offers a biological perspective on one's aptitude for searching for a job. Applied Brain Research is one of the more popular workshops, consistently filling up very quickly; if you don't score well on the 120-question survey that measures aptitude for successfully finding a job, you're given remedial tactics to make up for and gain some control over your genetically based job search deficiencies. The linkages between mental aptitude, employment, and the global economy are explicated in the Applied Brain Research literature passed out to prospective seminar participants.

> Western Society and American businesses are under intense pressure to adapt to a rapidly changing world. The basis of industrial society is shifting from material to information, and the information-based organizations will use labor and technology that can best utilize information as capital. Mental skills, thinking styles, and knowledge will be the new currency that will form a new basis of wealth for individuals, corporations, and our country.... A person's thinking style manifests itself in every human endeavor whether it's working, communicating, creating, managing, problem-solving, or learning. Corporate cultures take on the characteristics of dominant thinking styles that will enhance or inhibit thinking style expression of employees. Jobs and professions have certain thinking style requirements that attract "like-minded" people.... Having access to the totality of human information processing capability represents the ultimate competitive edge for individuals and corporations.... Those who can access and apply the diversity of thinking styles either personally or within the corporate environment are considered to be "integrated thinkers."... Some have this ability naturally and most can be trained in this emerging discipline.

Everyone has to sign up to work on one of seven working committees (such as the computer, communications, or education committees or the committee that produces the weekly newsletter, the "Job Search Times"), and every member is required to volunteer four hours of "work" each week. Members elect their peers to positions as president, vice-president, and members of an executive council.

I have arrived for the weekly general meeting, at which new members introduce themselves and all members share information about job announcements, job placements of former members, and upcoming skills workshops in which members might want to participate. Items on the agenda impart many lessons about what is happening to people searching for employment, as well as how members of the organization view the nature of the 1990s economy.[9] Karen begins by announcing messages sent to her by former members who have let her know why they're no longer coming to EU. The reasons cited make clear that few people are landing desirable professional jobs, but Karen couches the news in a way that softens its impact.

The majority of people who sent in an update have obtained "bread-and-butter" jobs, not their dream jobs. A bread-and-butter job is the organization's standard lexicon for an entry-level job or a job that otherwise represents downward mobility to the job holder. Bread-and-butter jobs, de facto, are temporary jobs in Karen's eyes. Karen reports the bread-and-butter news optimistically, emphasizing the importance of even having a job, as well as her belief that everyone, at one point or another, has to compromise their dreams. She stresses that their job outcomes are either temporary or are bridges to more desirable employment and she is stern about the fact that no one should interpret such a job in negative terms.

Not far behind individuals with bread-and-butter jobs are those who have accepted de jure temporary jobs, a type of employment that Karen frames in similarly optimistic terms. Before she announces where each individual has landed, Karen recommends that *everyone* should sign up with a temporary agency, because, she says, the temp-to-regular job route has become a routine method for landing a stable job. Some of the benefits of working on a temporary basis, she adds, include gaining new opportunities for networking, learning new skills and gaining experiences in new industries, and gathering information crucial to developing a job search plan.

Her words represent an institutionalized opinion about the virtues of temporary work that, as I show in Chapter 4, are real for many workers. The CompTech case study, indeed, demonstrates that we cannot assume temporary jobs are absolutely deleterious based only on surface-level knowledge about them. Yet I can well understand why EU members don't take comfort in the examples that Karen regales us with from former members. She mentions a temporary clerical position with a law firm; a one-month job doing administrative work for the Sacramento County fair organizers; a temporary data entry job; a temp job as a "beauty consultant" at the perfume counter at K-mart; and a subcontracted position "consulting" for an organization called the American Productivity and Quality Center.

The audience nods as she lists the benefits of temporary employment but, as I learn later in one-on-one interviews and in small workshops, they are painfully aware that her perspective makes a virtue out of a necessity. Every single one of my interviewees, and many of my workshop comrades, has been stationed at some point along the temporary employment circuit, having either worked on a temporary basis or having worked for short periods of time as staff members in temporary placement firms. A small number worked as well-paid contract workers, as programmers and systems analysts; the vast majority worked as administrative assistants and clerical workers, and a few worked as assemblers and inventory controllers at local high-tech firms. Despite substantial evidence about the pervasiveness of temporary employment, and although the organization overflows with reminders that the stability of the past has disappeared, EU members' long-range goal is to land full-time, permanent employment.

Members view the temporary job as no more and no less than a temporary strategy, evidenced in Sam's comment that the temp jobs he'd had were "gigs, not jobs."[10] Yet temporary work was a trap for some who were stuck in a cycle of temporary employment. Having been forced to accept a temporary job to make ends meet, they then found it difficult to muster the effort and the time to find a full-time, permanent job. Elana, for example, when first unemployed, had taken a series of clerical and technical temporary jobs, viewing this as a holding pattern until she could land her "dream job." This had ensnared her. She told me: "I haven't the time now to take to look for a permanent job. I made, I think, what my pastor called a short-term favorable decision with long-term negative consequences."

Three individuals had returned to their previous employers, while one appeared to have obtained a well-paying management position. At any given time at EU, there are various individuals who have left to accept temporary positions but have returned to the club to continue their job search. "Retreads," as members wryly call themselves, tell me in interviews that they do accrue some of the benefits that Karen mentions, but that, bottom line, they wish to leave the cycle of temporariness and land a "permanent" job. How normative this range of potential job outcomes is is revealed in the "New Job Information Sheet," an exit survey that newly employed EU members fill out. One can check off "Permanent, 40 hours/week," "Temporary, 40 hours/week," "Permanent, part-time," "Temporary, part-time," "Permanent but not dream job," or "Job is part-time, I wish to continue in program."

Karen also reads off information about new job openings, some of which she's just received in the mail, others from members. Her language reveals her belief that EU members may have to settle for less, but it also reveals her appreciation for members' professional aspirations and concerns. Members at the meeting furiously take notes, writing down names and phone numbers as she informs them of a truck-driving position "with professional-level salary"; bacteriologist; quality assurance supervisor; administrative assistant; cabinetmaker and cabinet finisher, both at "professional wages"; inventory scheduler. As I observe people taking down the details, I find the limits inherent in these job announcements to be both evident and painful. They're either highly specialized (a commercial truck driver, a bacteriologist, a cabinetmaker); or they're low-level and quite likely low-paid (administrative assistant or inventory scheduler). Karen ends this portion of the meeting by asking members whether they'd like to announce jobs that they know about but won't take, hardly an upbeat conclusion to an agenda item that in itself was sobering.

Eighty to one hundred people typically attend each meeting, making for very crowded and intense sessions. The general meetings are considered crucial to ongoing socialization, networking, and building of community. Each week a new cohort, averaging in size about fifteen, joins the organization. It is easy to understand how the total membership of EU is replenished, maintaining an ongoing membership of about two hundred.[11] Members cycle in and cycle out; some members leave to take permanent jobs; some leave for a new job but return to EU when the job doesn't live up to their expectations; others leave EU for temporary positions but return when their contracts expire. From an organizational standpoint EU is in many ways extraordinary, with continual turnover in its membership but a structure, based entirely on volunteer efforts, that is steadily maintained despite membership fluidity. Extraordinary, too, is the fact that the organization puts out particular messages and strategies that are entirely perpetuated by the unemployed themselves. The members do the research, uphold the rules, teach the newly unemployed, and carry the banner that every individual should do whatever they can to eliminate the reason that has brought them to a job search club in the first place.

Mantras for the Job Seeker:
How to Reinvent the Self for Desirable Employment Outcomes

EU participants receive a recurrent and integrated set of lessons about how best to combat unemployment.[12] The lessons are encoded in the content of general meetings, in the introductory training sessions, in specialized workshops, in the bylaws of the organization, in the literature and documents used to educate members, and in one-on-one pep talks delivered by the staff coordinator. All these sources consistently emphasize that employment and labor markets have changed. Members are told that they shouldn't expect to find "permanent" jobs. Due to the shaking and rumbling of labor markets, they should brace themselves for possible downward mobility: the optimistic discourse about the "bread-and-butter job" and the admission that temp jobs may be the only available jobs for the time being both normalize this possibility. Stability and tenure—either of past job experience or of future job expectations—is to be deemphasized and even hidden; adaptability is crucial and, although unemployment may have structural causes, it can only be resolved by individual solutions.

A core mission of EU is to shake up and dissolve members' aspirations for predictability and continuity. At the same time, organizational discourse and logic are premised on getting the unemployed to construe uncertainty and risk as an opportunity to grow personally and professionally. There are several tactics through which members can develop new personae to present to potential employers.

Recrafting One's Employment Profile: The Resume and the Thirty-Second Me. Socialization into the goals and the norms of Experience Unlimited, preparing oneself for entering the rocky terrain of the job market, entails a process of self-reconstruction on several levels. This process aims to reconfigure a self that, for many participants, has held steady over many years of employment. Creating a new professional profile takes place primarily in two venues: writing resumes and scripting professional introductions. EU participants call the latter the "Thirty-Second Me." Using a three-page set of guidelines for a Thirty-Second Me, participants compose concise statements to impress themselves on anyone who might employ them. Each Thirty-Second Me starts with "Hi, my name is…" and ends with "if you know anyone looking for a person with my skills, tell them to contact…" as exemplified in Harvey Dixon's Thirty-Second Me presented at the beginning of the chapter. Both venues supply messages about the self, and participants craft each one seriously, always feeling that their futures are limited if their craftsmanship is shoddy. The information that finds its way into the resume and the Thirty-Second Me constitutes the creative work that individuals engage in as they strive to position themselves for the demands and the peculiarities of emerging employment practices.

Certain principles of resume production are well-known to anyone trying to get a job in the postindustrial economy. Some of the advice EU participants receive about putting together a successful resume mirrors the advice that career counselors and placement officers give students in colleges and universities. An effective resume shouldn't be too long (EU workshop leaders stress that a resume should never exceed two pages; one page is ideal); material should be presented simply and accessibly; and the document should look professional and be printed on high-quality paper. It should highlight key experiences, skills, and competencies and should state job and professional goals. On the first day of our weeklong training, my cohort debated the advantages and disadvantages of differing type sizes, fonts (proportional vs. nonproportional, serious vs. humorous, clear vs. bizarre), the faxability or scannability of different qualities and weights of resume paper, and other elements of resume production that we believed would give us greater control and efficacy in finding a job.

Unemployed professionals and managers at EU, however, face additional, unique dilemmas in trying to land a job. Karen and the workshop leaders stress to us that not only must we find a job, we also face the painful exercise of having to hide, even erase employment histories that will be viewed as undesirable and dysfunctional, that render us uncompetitive for positions in the turn-of-the-century economy. For all intents and purposes we are encouraged to hide our human capital, that bundle of job and training experiences and educational backgrounds that make up our unique occupational autobiographies. The leaders continually point out that employers don't want to hire people who have developed a sense of entitlement forged in previous long-term employment in paternalistic firms, people who might wish to settle into one position for the long haul, or people who have worked in stodgy industrial or military sectors where they have not been forced to be innovative or to change.

This advice guides the reconstruction of the self in the resume. My cohort members, many of whom have not written a resume in years, attempt to repackage themselves to convince classmates and future employers that their skills are transferable across different industrial/sectoral contexts. They strive to demonstrate that they are multitaskers, people who thrive on conducting several lines of activities at once. They endeavor to avoid the impression that they are looking to stay with one company for a protracted period of time. In the resume, the reinvented version of themselves, revealing nothing fixed about who they are or what they do, is ironclad.

There is no such thing, for example, as "a" resume. Our leader advocates writing multiple resumes, versions and revisions of who we are that are adaptable to the diverse organizational and employment settings that we can encounter in looking for a job. Indeed, she boasts that she has produced "hundreds" of resumes, each one carefully crafted to adjust to various positions. No one dares voice the obvious illogic in her point: the fact that *she* is here, still at EU, implicitly sends the message that the high-volume approach to resume production isn't especially effective. The leaders do not suggest that we present ourselves dishonestly but that we package ourselves in less traditional, more creative terms that are consistent with expectations in the new economy. For those who have difficulty pinning down what their skills are, they can read the "skill clusters" list for appropriate and marketable terms.

Exactly how can my unemployed colleagues reconstruct themselves with these lessons in mind? First, "students" recompose themselves temporally by removing evidence of extended job tenure or gaps in employment, both of which are viewed as handicaps. For example, they obliterate dates, from resumes and personal introductions, that indicate lengthy tenure at previous jobs. They also downplay references to companies at which they worked that might sound the alarm to human resources personnel that they were accustomed to traditional, stable work environments. For example, Bruce had worked at IBM for twenty-two years and Ron had worked for the telecommunications giant, GTE, for twenty-one years. Both are strongly cautioned to remove those signifying facts from their resumes. The alternate phrasing that workshop participants come up with, under the prodding of the workshop leaders, is that each has "extensive experience" in the "high-tech" and "communications" industries. Several men and one woman in the introductory workshop I attend have lengthy experiences in the military. After heated discussion they agree that they should deemphasize the fact that they were in the armed forces for twelve or fifteen or twenty years, and they put in the foreground the skills they acquired, such as "experience with international cultures," leadership, delegation, inventory procurement, multilanguage fluency, and so forth (deemphasis on the military itself is achieved by writing it in small type *after* listing their skills).

As another element of such an evasive approach, workshop participants are given a sheet with "red light" answers and "green light" answers that they can offer in response to an employer asking, "Why did you leave your previous job?" An answer that shouldn't be given—a "red light" term—would be "left town" or "fired for tardiness or late to work," while "green light" answers—legitimate explanations—include "forced reorganization or merger," or "contract successfully completed."

Logically following the principle of erasing indicators of lengthy job tenure from one's record, participants are cautioned that they undermine themselves if, in a brief resume section stating professional goals, they say anything revealing a desire for a permanent, long-term job. Instead, they should stress their desire for change, for new and challenging work environments, and for gaining experience in a specific company or industry, rather than for a particular job. Further straining the self-reconstruction process, unemployed participants are supposed to obscure any information that reveals gaps in their employment histories. For this reason, many individuals in the organization mention skills gained through participation in EU, and some cite positions that they have held at EU while unemployed, listing "President" or "Vice President" of "Sacramento Professional Network" as evidence of professional activity.

Others with advanced educational degrees and credentials are advised to leave these off their resumes in situations where they might be handicapped if seen as overqualified or overly experienced. Across the board, men and women are urged to compress lifetimes of work experience into two or three essential skill or competency categories. Great premium is placed on leadership skills, innovations, general rather than firm-specific skills, and all experiences and competencies that would be applied to a variety of situations. We help individual after individual come up with the language that allows them to emphasize general employability rather than specific employment. Although we don't name the process as such, the effect is that we all participate in devaluing and degrading members' past work contributions and histories. Each person has to disassemble his or her own history and repackage it to increase marketability in an economy with transformed institutions and norms. In other words, uncertainty and insecurity force them to rewrite the *representation* of the self, to jettison pieces that may handicap them in the job market, to erase some skills, experiences, and competencies while coming up with new categories to capture their strengths and contributions.

Participants are encouraged to downplay or erase numbers when it comes to years of employment, but at the same time they are encouraged to deploy numbers that underscore their readiness, creativity, and initiative. In reconstructing themselves as multitalented individuals who are ready and willing to take on any challenge future employers might present to them, to display themselves as people who are bold and forward-thinking enough to introduce innovations and change, EU students also add what I call "mythical statistics" to their package of "assets." In a process I call "strategic quantification" students throw around mythical statistics—memorable sound bites—easily and frequently, both in the resume and in their Thirty-Second Mes. The statistics are socially constructed and fantastic, yet consistent enough with common parlance about business practices that they don't initially raise an eyebrow. These statistics, as I ponder them, seem to me to defy reconstruction or validation by any outside party. Indeed, some of the measures seem to defy quantification, period. Ironically, as one interviewee noted, by quantifying their achievements, EU participants are commodifying themselves.

At one general meeting three women deliver their Thirty-Second Mes, announcing, respectively, that they had "improved customer satisfaction rates by 700 percent," "improved customer satisfaction rates by 250 percent," and "supervised five thousand people." In all three cases the statistics are cited without reference to a specific job, employer, or industry. A fourth woman calls attention to the fact that she had "improved sales in her previous job by 3,000 percent," while one man had "handled a five-million-dollar purchase order." A man who had been in management for a fast-food chain claims to have been responsible for "twenty-five thousand dollars savings per fast-food unit."

Others offer not statistics but less obvious, difficult-to-pin-down achievements such as "decreasing the number of lawsuits brought against my company," "saving my company thousands of dollars in insurance costs," and "minimizing waste levels in my company unit."[13] Such statements of accomplishment are not fabrications, but the result of complex and creative calculations deemed desirable and appropriate in EU philosophy. Organizational literature about preparing general yet impressive summaries of skills and experiences encourage this approach, offering up boilerplate examples such as "Supervised branch staff of sixteen on work performance, goal setting, and success measurement, reducing turnover by 20 percent and improving productivity by 8 percent," or "Maintained overview of projects identifying and correcting problems at early stage of development, ensuring on-schedule completion."

This overly general approach to the reconstruction of the individual can be problematic and painful to the individuals involved. In his Thirty-Second Me, an African American man describes himself as an architect who specializes in "management and city building," and works with "multimillion-dollar projects." In the evaluation session that follows his presentation, we struggle to figure out what he actually had done or could do, because the language in his self-description is so broad. The goal is to help him figure out a way to make his accomplishments more concrete so he can present himself more effectively. We fear that he is doing himself a disservice by claiming expertise that is so broadly formulated as to be indecipherable. Increasingly distressed by the pressure, he rephrases, saying he is a "city builder, a team player." He finally refuses to talk, asking fellow participants to back off, saying that "this just isn't the time" to try to pin all this down. The stress level in the group is pretty high at that moment.

Piecing together a Thirty-Second Me isn't always this excruciating, but the more typical efforts to script one do reflect a struggle to find the magical wording that will enable an individual to say the right thing at precisely the right moment. "Perfect" is a Thirty-Second Me that includes buzz words of the new economy and that also conveys some general information about one's skills. This, however, is a difficult balance to maintain. Marianne's struggle to reframe herself compellingly, for example, came out when I asked her what kind of job she was looking for, how specific, how general, and what kind of work she desired. Her answer—which touches on some "hot" areas of expertise such as total quality management, training, and education—is extremely vague, to the point where it is difficult to discern a specific field she has worked in or position that she desires. It illustrates the difficulty of packaging oneself as the multivalent, all-purpose person who can step into any situation but preferably into one that is consistent with her own aspirations.

> I'm concentrating more on teaching and training positions. This is where my Thirty-Second Me comes in. What I'm trying to do is identify a training position, preferably in a large corporation, where I can utilize my communication skills and my teaching abilities, my educational experiences, my management background. And what I want to do is train in management-oriented issues. Because of my experience in total quality management [she had received a certificate in total quality management at her local community college—

V. S.], I have a real interest there in using quality tools to try to make the workplace better. And so that's really an interest of mine.

In an interview Anthony, the former nuclear engineer, touched on why it was so difficult to buy into the mechanisms for rewriting one's occupational self in the ways that facilitators were prescribing. For him, retooling, transitioning, and transforming himself into a more broadly marketable person had been difficult. He believed that the essential facts of who he was as a professional were indisputable, not general stories that could be easily manipulated, with plots that he could just change and embellish depending on the audience. As he noted,

> Probably in about one-third of my interviews, I get a question like, "Why does a nuclear engineer want to work for Packard Bell? Or Hewlett Packard?" That's their first question, because when they look at my resume there's one line that says MBA. Then there's three-quarters of my resume that says "Nuclear Engineer." That's the way they see me . . . that's the hurdle I have to get over in the beginning, to prove that I'm not just a nuclear engineer. I have an MBA. So that's the first hurdle I have to clear.[14]

Anthony's point highlights how important it is to have institutional connections prior to retooling and recrafting oneself. An individual can have the most reasonable, even rational goal—to obtain an MBA, in Anthony's case, or, in the case of another man, a credential in professional meeting and conference planning—but if one does not have connections to the people and the organizations where one gets hands-on experience, a degree or credential doesn't automatically open the doors to getting a job. Neither individual had, at the time of our interview, found a job in his desired field.

Madeline Cox, whom I quoted at the outset of this book, detested the advice to reduce her work life to one dimension, to sound bites and snippets. For her, who she was as a professional consisted of much more than statistics about productivity achievements or cost savings, and vastly more than what she contributed to the world when she was "on the job." Her objections are interesting because she doesn't challenge the organizational rhetoric of a "Me" or the concept of repackaging oneself for future employers, but nevertheless talked about pushing the boundaries to present a more well-rounded, multi-dimensional "Me." She argued,

We need to broaden a Thirty-Second to a Sixty-Second Me. And not only do you need a *work* Thirty-Second Me, you need a *personal life* Thirty-Second Me. You know, we're many facets, and if you can learn how to pull out and talk about yours, about the appropriate qualifications for whatever it is you're doing, it's gonna make your Thirty-Second Me that much better to any employer.

You know, it's ok to try to tailor yourself quickly on your feet and to get comfortable at that takes practice. But we need to be able to incorporate even the personal side of things, where you bring in your church and your community groups and, you know, some of your social activities, and volunteer work....I would like to see it that we get people to think about all these things.

Her criticism of the process of occupational transformation went even further. She was advised to package herself as someone with general skills and interests, yet her bachelor's degree was in environmental science; she had spent her career working in this field in the private sector, and she desperately wanted to stay in the field. Put simply, she loved her work. She didn't want to reinvent herself: she wanted a job in hazardous waste management and rarely found job announcements for such positions. Facilitators in her workshops had advised her to think and plan more broadly, but it was difficult for her to make the leap, in her mind and in her repackaged self. "Part of what I'm havin' trouble with is, 'Well, if I do have to leave the environmental field, what do I call what I want? How do I package me?' Everybody just says, 'Geez, your skills are so great.' Well, if they're so great, how come I don't have a job?" Mike Daly, in contrast, *did* resist the notion of packaging and marketing the self, saying it was his belief that "it is contrary to human nature for many of us to sell ourselves."

Be Instrumental and Attentive at All Times: Working on Self-presentation. The unemployed at EU try to maximize their options by working on formal and scriptable venues such as the resume and the Thirty-Second Me. Increasing the pressure to seize any and all opportunities, organizational literature and workshop facilitators also exhort the unemployed to be prepared for all informal, unscriptable, spontaneous encounters as well. There are many points in everyday life and in the job search process during which an unemployed manager or professional has a chance to present him or herself in the best possible light to someone who might offer him or her a job. Part of EU's mission is to educate participants about such events and occurrences and to raise their sensitivity about all situations where they might unknowingly be auditioning for a job. Members are expected to map out a systematic search strategy for themselves, but they are encouraged at the same time to rationalize casual and leisure time: to poise themselves to jump on unanticipated opportunities, to be constantly vigilant, to view any social situation or relationship as possibly consequential for their career outcomes, and to never drop their regimen of looking for work. The core elements of this philosophy mirror the emphasis on flexibility, adaptability, and unpredictability that workers *with* jobs face to an increasing degree. But in Panopticonic fashion, EU participants anticipate that the gaze of future employers can fall on them at any time, demanding constant self-discipline.

For the unemployed, time when they might ordinarily be able to relax from the pressures of job hunting becomes time where every second contains the possibility for scrutiny, observation, and evaluation. In our job workshop, in a module on "cold-call networking," we are encouraged by the workshop literature to:

> Seek every opportunity to meet people. Don't wait until you actually walk into the meeting room to begin networking. If you arrive at the meeting place by car and notice a group of women in the parking lot, take the opportunity to strike up a conversation. "Are you going to the women's network meeting? Did you run into that traffic on the freeway?" *Whether you are in the elevator, the ladies room, or waiting at the bar, start talking.* [Emphasis in the original—V. S.]

Thus, personal time, regarded as casual and unrationalized, should be saturated with continual sensitivity to unpredictable labor-market patterns and dynamics. This advice also points to the belief in a "hidden market," the notion that most professional jobs aren't obtained as a result of reading and pursuing advertisements in the newspaper or in announcements sent to EU but through connections, networks, or random occurrences. In this hidden job terrain, EU facilitators claim, it is possible for the unemployed to create their own jobs, to present themselves as people capable of identifying a need and a niche in a company, and to persuade the employer that they are indispensable. Despite the many structural causes of professional and managerial unemployment and displacement, all these "tips" about how the hidden job market works put the responsibility for success and failure soundly on the shoulders of each unemployed individual. Being poised and ready calls for individual strategic attentiveness at all times.

Two examples illustrate how central this point is to the everyday rhetoric of EU. First, a recurrent narrative, espoused in both the general meetings and in the workshops of the introductory training week, highlights the need to be prepared by way of negative examples demonstrating the consequences of *not* always being prepared. Significant because it provides a vivid contrast to the mental stance EU members are encouraged to cultivate, the narrative of the "lazy unemployed" is evoked on many occasions, each time containing nearly exactly the same "plot elements."

Karen frequently congratulates attendees for "getting out of the house," not falling back into the "pity pit" and isolating themselves in the privacy of home. According to her, attendees need to do all they can at all times to take action, follow leads, engage in impression management, and be opportunistic in unforeseen encounters. Who knows when one might be asked to come for a job interview in thirty minutes, or just spontaneously accept an invitation to step into someone's office for an informal interview? If a person is not ready at all times to leap into action or isn't dressed professionally or hasn't adopted the professional mind-set, they simply aren't going to be able to roll with the rapid and unpredictable punches that life in the world of employment could deal them.

Karen and others hold up the scenario of the "lazy unemployed" to reinforce this view. Details of this stereotypical individual vary slightly from telling to telling, but certain core elements are consistent. A lazy unemployed person is someone who isn't on the alert, isn't constantly in the job search mode. We would find this person slouched on a couch at home, drinking Pepsi or beer, watching television with the volume blasting, whether it's soap operas or football games. He or she is always dressed in worn, tattered T-shirts or oversized sweatshirts. The women lack makeup and well-tended hairstyles, and the men sport hair on their faces, evidence not of beards but of failure to shave. Everyone has put on extra pounds as a result of their slovenliness. No matter the gender of the unemployed, undisciplined children run screaming in the background, signaling to anyone who calls that they've contacted a highly unprofessional environment.[15] To top it off, the guilty individual can never find his or her appointment book to schedule possible appointments. This individual, according to organizational lore, stands little chance of being viewed positively by employers and would not be able to compete with others who can drop things in an instant and who can, given the opportunity, change their plans without batting an eye.

A milder example sees the unemployed individual as being more professional but still lacking the attentiveness to ubiquitous opportunities. Marvin, a leader, recites the purportedly true story of Ray. Ray drove to an appointment for a job interview. Arriving early, he parked his dirty, messy car right in front of the building where the interview was to take place. As he approached a man leaning against the front of the building, Ray asked him if he had a light for his cigarette. The man replied negatively; Ray asked one or two other people entering the building if they had a light, finally finding one, smoking his cigarette, and entering for his appointment. He discovered that the interviewer was the first man he had asked for a light, the same man who had witnessed the condition of Ray's car, and seen Ray indiscriminately halting people in his search for a good smoke. The leader asks the workshop participants: When did Ray's interview start? Because we've been following the facilitators' logic about the ubiquity of opportunity the point is obvious to all of us: it started when Ray drove into the parking lot. The message to participants is: never relax, never assume you are unobserved, and never take for granted—moreover, take control of—any social interaction.

Don't let your bitterness and frustration defeat you:
emotion work of the unemployed.

Body language! When shaking hands, offer a firm handshake. Erect posture shows confidence. Sit down only after offered a chair. Lean forward in your chair and relax. Do not fidget.

Enthusiasm! Bring a positive attitude into the interview without being too familiar. Avoid being negative. Find something you like about the interviewer. Sell yourself. Remember, the difference between bragging and self-confidence is enthusiasm.

While conducting the work of finding a job, EU members have to hold themselves together mentally and emotionally. Facilitators call on participants to self-consciously perform emotion work on themselves in order to leave unemployment, with its angst and its financial insecurity behind.[16] Yet the unemployed find it difficult to uphold these principles when they are awash in uncertainty and anxiety about employment futures. When Karen speaks of "the pity pit," she names what many members fear: that their negative attitudes can hold them back from improving their situations. People in workshops and in in-depth interviews express their fear that their own negative frame of mind has the power to hex their job search or block their ability to present themselves as a desirable potential employee. Participants fear sabotaging themselves and continually talk about suppressing their fear and anger, trying to remain emotionally detached from the labor-market turbulence surrounding them.

Esther, an African American woman who lost her job as a supervisor in the banking industry, remarked, over and over in our interview, how much she feared blocking herself because of her anxiety. Esther was emotionally scarred from the institutional and technological transformations that had buffeted her. Over the course of twenty years Esther has been steadily pushed out of her work, supervising backroom production operations for various banks, as a result of corporate centralization and automation. Unemployed at the time of her interview, she had sold her house and had had to rely on some money from her son: "I'm looking around and now I'm scared. I can't figure out what's going on. For the salary I'm used to, people have degrees. I'm a dinosaur now. My type of position doesn't exist anymore. Business is changing; it keeps shrinking and places keep getting bigger. And so, for instance, there used to be perhaps a hundred places in the state that did what I did, like, twenty years ago...now, there's maybe ten."

She claimed that she did active work on her attitude to maintain a positive mental outlook on her situation. It was as if she believed that she had to quash her anger or it would follow her through her interviews, contaminating her presentation of self.

> I've had to work so hard at not being bitter and hateful. There's so many people at work who are. I wanted to make sure I had my act together because nobody will hire somebody who's bitter or hateful or anything. So I decided, well, I'm going to see a therapist to make sure I keep balanced on this.
>
> I mean, how can I get a job if I go to an interview and I'm bitter about my last company and I'm scared of my future? I mean, how could I get a job based on who I am? Because no matter what your qualifications are, hiring managers still go by personality, gut feelings about who you are. Whether you are going to be a match or not.

Anthony, who had a fairly realistic understanding of the difficulty of repositioning himself with his MBA in the business world after working many years as a nuclear engineer, actively worked to change his inner sense of who and what he was. He would visualize himself in the role of a business manager rather than in the role of nuclear engineer. His visualization work hadn't yet yielded any gains, and he feared that he hadn't sufficiently aligned his image of his old self—nuclear engineer—with his new skills and capacities. His own analysis was: "I don't want anyone to think that I'm just a nuclear engineer. That's probably what's holding me back."

One woman stressed that she experienced "two kinds of hard" in her current circumstances, explaining that she tackled them at two levels. One was what she called the "technical" part, knowing where and how to look for a job, learning how to maximize personal connections, and how to put on the best professional face. The other, though, was the "personal hard," the emotional labor of simply maintaining oneself, day in and day out, feeling humiliated at one level but participating in an organization where, in the public presentation of self, expressions of humiliation and anger were not tolerated. She felt challenged, in particular, by the work that she had to do on her confidence when interacting with her EU peers.

> The thing that is personally hard for me is I actually know that though I have some inventiveness about me and I've done well within my field or within my skill level or accomplishment level, at SPN I meet people who are more qualified than me. And sometimes I find myself almost marketing myself almost as if I'm as capable or experienced as them. And underneath I feel kind of a little embarrassed or ashamed. The hard part comes when I give my Thirty-Second Me in the class and I see other people and they're basically sizing me up. It's a little humbling, it hurts a little.

Emotion work has limits, however. At many points, participants are unable to maintain the positive attitude "necessary" for playing by the rules of the organization. The tension in their situations pops up for the facilitators, the unemployed who promulgate the culture and the activities of EU. While facilitators and leaders teach new members and lead workshops, they must often grapple with their own distress and ambivalence. Mike designed and regularly offers a successful, well-attended workshop on improving self-esteem while searching for a job: "This was a problem for me. I developed the curriculum for this particular class, and I'm really an inappropriate person to do that because my esteem right now is as low as it could possibly get because of the experiences that I've had. They want me to teach it again and I came up with an excuse why I couldn't do it. I just can't do it anymore." Nevertheless, other members were eager to step in and take over the workshop.

Conclusion

Stay vigilant and alert, relinquish the trappings of the traditional employment model, transform oneself into the flexible professional employee of the turbulent economy, and maintain a modicum of control under unpredictable circumstances. These messages constituted the optimistic perspective imparted by the EU curriculum and rhetoric to empower its unemployed participants. Yet it was impossible to shield the unemployed from the intractable contradictions of their situations or from their fundamental disempowerment.[17] A "scientifically based" job search rarely allows anyone to maintain the kind of control they are desperate to gain. Members were advised to keep their cars clean and well-maintained, because a person with the power to hire them might observe their vehicles and pass judgment accordingly. But their cars were funky because they lacked the money to repair and clean them or to buy a more updated model. Members were to wear tasteful, pressed, professional clothes and avoid wearing clothes that were frayed or out-of-fashion. Yet often they lacked the money to purchase, dry-clean, and otherwise maintain clothes, rarely a problem when they held a job. They were to produce high-quality resumes and should send them out by the hundreds, but producing such resumes (particularly producing multiple versions) and mailing them out in such high volume was often unaffordable.

If given an opportunity for a job interview, an EU member was encouraged to approach it as a fifty-fifty partnership. Don't let the interviewer take the upper hand; exploit the interview as a time where you, the interviewee, can obtain information about the company; act as though you, the interviewee, are going to the interview to let the potential hirer *persuade you* that their company is a place you would like to work. The interviewee should control his or her body language, avoid slumping or giving off any signals of desperation. But many EU participants were worn down and found it difficult to hold back from employers their genuine desire for the job. They also would accept a reasonable job offer in a heartbeat and feared playing the negotiating game because they didn't want the interviewer to call their bluff.

Such elements of a positive mental framework resonated only weakly with the people I observed in workshops and with whom I spoke at length in interviews. The rules of the new economy have changed, and they felt they had little choice but to go along with advice and strategies that presented at least some alternative for improving their circumstances. At the

same time, as previous quotes have illustrated, EU members did not engage in occupational reconstruction uncritically. Throughout this chapter we heard of different participants doing what they could to successfully reposition themselves, all the while resenting employers for changing
the rules, regretting the loss of a more stable occupational base, and fear-
ing an unpredictable future. Madeline Cox's sentiment paralleled that
expressed by others in my case study.

> What are some of the moods here [at EU]? We are the forty-something bunch.
> For the most part we've been climbin' the corporate ladder like the model
> said we were supposed to do. And we've been booted out. But mostly I don't
> think the people here are as willing to do the corporate thing as they were be-
> fore. Now, I don't know if it's out of bitterness and disillusionment. You know,
> "I've played the corporate game. I did everything right. I wore the clothes. I
> did the hours. I did the time. And then you fired me?" And they're saying "I
> ain't gonna let that happen again."

In endorsing a unified vision of what's wrong with the economy and
how people can individually transcend problems that are rooted in structural and institutional transformation, Experience Unlimited played a
quiet role in reconfiguring the class and the occupational structure. It
was instrumental in writing and teaching the rules of the new economy.
It oversaw a process wherein professionals and managers, used to greater
security and financial prosperity, downwardly adjusted their expectations
and minimized their aspirations. Ironically, EU contributed to the de-
professionalization of these professionals and managers. By encouraging
individuals to reinvent themselves as multivalent, employable generalists,
EU told them that previous professional experiences and expectations
did not and could not hold in the new, turbulent economy.

In the experiences of the unemployed we witness perhaps the most
deleterious combination of insecurity, temporariness, blocked opportunity, and personal risk. Although circumstances could change, many of
the unemployed discussed in this chapter seemed faraway from conditions of structural certainty. Most had no paid job. Those that had or have
had temporary jobs primarily have had short-term temporary positions
in small operations, marginal business niches, and seasonal projects. The
EU unemployed lacked even the positive experiential challenges and opportunities that were actually and potentially available to the CompTech
temporary workers.

It was hard for the unemployed to interpret constraint as opportunity when they lacked footing within an employment organization where they might have been able to take advantage of resources or expand and activate their cultural and human capital, as the Reproco and WoodWorks employees did. Even though WoodWorks' entire existence was in jeopardy, there was at least some reasonable hope on the part of the workers that they could positively affect the plant's future. They had decades of attachment to and history with the company, deeply rooted in the physicality of place and industry and in their own industrial identity. That continuity was utterly unavailable to the SPN unemployed.

Perhaps because the discourse of the organization puts the blame squarely on economic institutions and on a new economic order, though, it was easier for the unemployed to resign themselves to the fact that the only way they would scale the heights of the great divide was to generate an individual solution. Even though they were angry and resentful about corporate behavior in the 1990s, they accepted it as inevitable. Fundamentally, they believed that the reason they hadn't recovered had to do with their own inadequacies, their own inability to retool, to reconstruct themselves as employable, and to march ahead into the labor markets of the twenty-first century. To acquire control, even modest control, over structural uncertainty, reinvention of the self appeared to be the only viable option for the Experience Unlimited unemployed.

It is worth repeating Mike Daly's thoughts on the sensitive mix of structural factors causing unemployment, coupled with the simultaneous internalization of responsibility for pulling oneself out of unemployment. His reflections, quoted at the beginning of this book, are more comprehensive in light of the dialectic of structure and agency characterizing unemployment:

> I have to really search my soul, do whatever I can to make sure that unemployment doesn't happen again. We all hear like it's hard to find a job, but I think if a person looks at what the, um, pundits—or whatever the market researchers are called—I think you'll get conflicting information. I was reading in the paper...about how companies now are looking for employees. They can't find the people they want, and it's so bad that they won't even build plants 'cause they can't find any workers they want. So, this is really weird. And unemployment is supposed to be at an all-time low right now. But then you turn around and you read all these articles about how it's impossible to find work. *The upshot is if you manage your career well it probably won't be a prob-*

*lem if you get downsized. But if you get downsized out, haven't managed your career,
it's probably gonna be a real problem.*

Ironically, this whole process can also be a time for personal reflec-
tion that leads to new ways of thinking about what one really wants from
work. I conclude with the comments of a white woman named Caroline,
who was trained and had experience working in the field as a geologist.
After traveling around the United States to follow different jobs in the
private sector, Caroline had settled in Sacramento with her husband but
had been unable to find a job in her field. Few jobs were posted, and her
interviews had not netted her any offers of a regular job. She had, instead,
held several temporary clerical jobs. When I asked her about her dream
job, I was struck by the fact that she didn't mention a particular industry
or occupation. Although during "public" sessions at EU members usually
refrained from citing specific positions, firms, or industries they hope to
work in, in private interviewees usually "confessed" to highly specific
situations they were seeking. In contrast, Caroline lists the qualities of
work and employment that appeal to her so much in comparison to the
temp jobs she's been able to find:

> Well, it would probably be like a twenty- to thirty-hour work week with the
> state. I really like the idea of not having to worry about marketing myself and
> chasing down work all the time. I like the idea of being involved with projects
> where you're involved with them from when you start until it's over. Once
> there, when you're there, you're the one involved with the final decision. Has
> enough work been done? Is the outcome good enough? So you're part of a
> team. You're part of making those decisions.

Being valued for your skills, not your success in packaging yourself;
being involved in work holistically, seeing projects through from beginning to end; working with others collaboratively—such are the characteristics of jobs, both finding one and keeping one, that many people at
the turn of the century would view as ideal.

6

Crossing the Great Divide: Negotiating Uncertainty, Risk, and Opportunity

"The Liberated, Exploited, Pampered, Frazzled, Uneasy New American Worker." This summary of changes in work and employment, the title of a special issue of *The New York Times Magazine* (March 5, 2000), well captures the contradictory elements of working in the new economy. In its ads, features, and advice columns, the magazine communicates that traditional ways of working are obsolete or on their way to being so. It applauds the ascendance of the *free agent*, an individual who doesn't seek jobs but instead is on the lookout for projects, tasks, new knowledge and information bases, and connectedness through the World Wide Web. For the brave new free agents, the economy is their oyster, and they are leading our march to the prosperous side of the great divide.

Free agents don't need or want a single, physical location in which to work. Neither do they need or want promises of security, benefits, or mobility. They simply need a powerful computer, state-of-the-art programming languages and database-management programs, and a password to access the complex, limitless world of the Internet and e-commerce. They have project, not job, contracts and they run their own business operations. They are all too happy to see their start-up companies swallowed by bigger firms. When that happens, they merely recombine their material, information, and human resources, regrouping to fill the next profitable gap in the market. In an e-based economy even Microsoft employees are viewed as obsolete "Resters and Vesters" who complacently put in their time at the corporation in order to maximize their worth when they cash in their stock options. Free agents not only become multimillionaires in the world of high-technology and information-based start-ups but they are the masters of their occupational fates, not "microserfs."[1]

This model of work and "profitable uncertainty" has taken hold in the public imagination. Anyone reading business magazines, newspapers, and popular career advice books might easily get the impression that the traditional occupational world has been entirely reconstructed. In the emerging dot.com world success seems to rest solely on personal initiative, creativity, and the capacity to live with continual ambiguity as the free agent creates and dissolves business units as the market dictates.

Yet, despite the encroaching hegemony of this caricature, most American workers are eons away from the abstract, cutting-edge world of dot.com innovators and agents. The majority of workers, like the photocopiers, the timber workers, and the assemblers, create the infrastructure that makes it possible for free agents to prosper. They continue to serve people in a multiplicity of service jobs; to construct roads, homes, office buildings and factories; to assemble the computers, modems, scanners, fax machines, and servers in those factories; to input and process data in those offices; to care for ill and vulnerable people; and to supervise and manage these legions of employees. They typically carry out these tasks in the employ of an owner or owners and in physical work settings—large and small companies, offices, factories, and other work sites that require bodily presence.

Unlike the mythical free agent, most workers lack the skills, and hence the bargaining power, to make the economy their oyster, to manipulate jobs and labor markets to their advantage. Most workers continue to be located in subordinate positions in hierarchies based on unequal power and to have their activities, efforts, and outcomes measured, evaluated, and disciplined. They are also struggling to reach a part of the postindustrial terrain that is far from the territory of the mythical free agent. I have examined work settings in this unsettled terrain, looking closely at how they are affected by the organizational and rhetorical elements in the new paradigm of work and employment.

Comparing the Case Studies: What Do We Learn?

Three workplaces and one employment organization—four settings that shed light on uncertainty, risk, and opportunity in flexible workplaces. Each setting contains a facet of the new flexible era: ongoing structural change, ideologies about worker participation, and open-endedness in employment futures. Each demonstrates the variability and flux of the opportunity and mobility structure in the United States. They spotlight what is to come on the still indeterminate other side of the turn-of-the-century great divide. It is now time to merge the findings from these case studies into one overview of what is changing for U.S. workers and in U.S. workplaces.

As I note at the outset of this book, when I initiated my research I expected to find engaging and decent jobs, dignity, and opportunity on one end of the employment spectrum and uncertainty, risk, degradation, and frustration on the other. The literature that guided me to this project led me to believe that our job structure was polarized and that it would be possible to develop a clear typology, with convenient boxes indicating characteristics and outcomes of positive and enabling jobs and boxes containing characteristics and outcomes of disadvantaging and restrictive jobs. I assumed that I would construct these differentiated boxes according to conventional social science categories—white-collar service; traditional blue-collar; new, high-tech blue-collar; white-collar professional and managerial—and that I would discover significant variations that would easily lend themselves to clear-cut comparisons across the spectrum.

Traveling through employment institutions in the 1990s necessitated that I develop a very different schema for understanding work and employment in the United States, a schema that is more a fluid continuum than a set of rigid boxes. For, while it is true that I found settings that were closer to one end of a dichotomous spectrum than the other, it is also true that a common thread ran throughout them and that participants shared many key experiences. In fact, what seems sociologically meaningful were the kindred experiences and perceptions of workers in diverse conditions of employment. The employed people in this study, as well as those seeking employment, shared similar perceptions about risk, structural advantage and disadvantage, and their embeddedness in a larger stratification system. They expressed common yearnings for techniques they could use to springboard away from traditional ways of working, to cross and firmly position themselves in the opportunity structure of the new era. It is to these common experiences and their implications that I now turn.

Reproco exemplified both the promising and the limiting sides of flexible arrangements in a new economic era. The manner in which the company structured a system whereby its photocopy workers were contracted out to other work sites, and wherein authority and control were fairly decentralized throughout those sites, came close to an ideal-type, optimistic model of flexibility. Yet the jobs were low-wage, low-status, and low-skilled. Despite this duality and contradictoriness in the employment arrangements, Reproco seemed to offer its workers the most: low risk, minimal employment and institutional uncertainty, as well as opportunities with realizable, albeit modest payoffs to its workers.

The photocopiers, at the time of my study, had employment security in a division with no hint of pending layoffs, in a company with generally progressive employment policies. They were able to take advantage of a variety of training workshops, and they were exposed to and learned about professional organizations by virtue of moving about from facility to facility. Their jobs were not highly skilled, but they were interpersonally challenging. This last fact exacted the highest costs from the photocopy workers, but even here the cost was moderate. When they tried to control clients, when they attempted to assert themselves in the face of clients who viewed photocopiers as low-status workers, it was often at the expense of their dignity and self-esteem. But this result was not structural; unstated personal injuries did not translate into job loss or demotions.

Personal injury could be compounded by positional variability, by the fact that photocopiers had to move about from site to site, had to adjust continually, and had to learn how to work with very different sets of clients. Yet there were tangible benefits to workers who learned how to cope with various professional workers and settings; in particular, workers felt that through this exposure they were gathering information about the way businesses work that they might use in other core-company jobs or in their own businesses. The photocopiers' commitments to go along with these processes and engage in these interactions was deepened by their prior labor-market positions and by the knowledge that management could always replace them with other people—embodied in the corporeal presence of temporary workers—if they expressed too much discontent, disrespect, or anger to clients. Thus, the Reproco photocopy workers directed their efforts to acquiring and absorbing more of what the firm had to offer them, not to challenging clients or the decisions of their own managers who had placed them under stressful conditions and left them to resolve the daily problems that cropped up. Reproco workers saw the organizational resources made available to them as tools for crossing to the other side of the occupational/employment divide.

It is important not to overstate the positive aspects of the machine operators' situation. While they did learn how to negotiate and control their immediate situations to a greater degree, they weren't learning skills that would allow them to move up and out of the machine-operator niche in Reproco. Moreover, their employment fate was dependent on the robust economy. Should demand for these business services decline, quite likely the machine operators' positions would be vulnerable to the layoffs that top management had made in other divisions of Reproco. For these reasons, the machine operators' position can be considered no more than temporarily permanent.

Finally, there is a flip side to the production system in which machine operators felt enabled to voice their perspectives and affect change around them. They had internalized and identified with management's goals and actively monitored and controlled their own behavior, as well as the behavior of their coworkers. Acceptance of this process constitutes a defining feature of postbureaucratic control systems: the line between those who manage and those who are managed has become opaque, part of the slippery slope on which workers lose sight of who ultimately possesses and wields power.

WoodWorks exemplified another contradictory path taken through the flexibility terrain. The woodworkers' employment arguably was de jure stable—as union members, they could not be fired arbitrarily—but de facto highly uncertain, because of the possibility of plant closure, plant sale, or continued layoffs of work groups or units. As has happened in industry towns around the nation, plant closure didn't simply mean that workers lost their jobs; it meant that workers lost their identity, indeed, the core basis of the community.

These blue-collar workers were being asked to make concessions and throw themselves into the new participative model but to live with the possibility that they might lose their jobs. In limited ways, the model created some new opportunities for workers. They worked together more often in brainstorming groups; they were authorized and given modest resources to solve problems; and they learned new interactional and small-group-process skills that they deployed with coworkers, with customers, and with constituencies outside in the community. They gained a new language for involvement and empowerment, which in one case led workers to assert more-than-cosmetic demands for change and information from plant-level management.

The personal, individual-level risks for cooperating with the new model and for experimenting with new ways of working were minimal. Although there were some who resented the demands for greater engagement of the self and for new modes of communication, more often workers became absorbed in the participative management agenda and spoke enthusiastically of its benefits. Here, as in the Reproco case, workers were entering into the new terrain of control, in which they were identifying with goals that were consonant with plant management's goals. They willingly took on the task of managing both themselves and other workers.

For the woodworkers, the perception of opportunity was dampened by significant institutional uncertainty. Risk was structural and arose in *not* going along with participative management. In the perceptions of the workers, the very survival of the timber plant would be determined by their efforts to adjust to a new era in industrial relations. What I would call their global employment prospects were highly uncertain. The woodworkers hoped to move beyond the holding pattern I found them in, to trade in "risk without certainty of payoff" (engaging in PM when the fate of the plant was unclear) for "positive risk"—engaging, giving, and taking the plant toward more stable circumstances, whether under present or future ownership. These workers therefore directed their efforts toward keeping their plant open. Their perceptions of opportunity were fragile in that they could never forget the negative institutional context that was driving them to adopt a particular course of action within the unequal power relations of the plant. Even if they could carry the day and make sure their plant stayed open, their footing on the other side of the industrial divide would be tenuous.

The employment contract embodied risk and uncertainty for temporary assemblers and clerical workers at CompTech. CompTech vividly exemplified both the enabling and the worrisome sides of flexibility. Temporary workers shouldered tremendous risk due to the terms of their employment, both in their lives and in the lives of their families. Even for the long-term (permatemp) temporary at CompTech, every day had the potential to be the last, since technically a temporary could be "disemployed" with minimal explanation. The smallest behavioral misstep, personality conflict, or management decision to close an assembly line created experiential and structural uncertainty for these temporary workers. Temporary employees could not count on being able to pay the rent or mortgage, make their food money stretch to the end of a month, buy necessities for children, provide them health coverage, and the like. This was the daily, weekly, and monthly experience of the temporary.

But many of the temporary workers I interviewed and observed clung to the not unreasonable perception that opportunities were potentially accessible and abundant in this company. In a structural and organizational sense, certain aspects of even temporary employment at CompTech promised opportunities and rewards for risk taking. Like Reproco but unlike WoodWorks, CompTech was a reputable and enduring institution. No one entertained thoughts that CompTech's future was uncertain, and CompTech had managed to avoid layoffs of any workers across the company. Uncertainty derived from changes in product lines, changes in position (as when a person was rotated among different lines or different work units, much the same as in Reproco), and changes in employment policies (as in the decision to use or discard temporary workers) rather than from concerns about the enterprise itself.

Temporary workers put themselves on the line—they willingly learned new skills, took on responsibilities that appeared to be personally difficult and discouraging (such as training new permanent workers who had been offered a job that the temp applied and interviewed for, but didn't get), performed like a valued worker—precisely because they hoped to become a "permanent" member of a workforce where risk taking was expected and where workers were rewarded for it. In the eyes of temporary workers at CompTech, the personal risk incurred by consenting to a highly participative system as structurally marginalized temporary workers was low, and the potential payoff was huge. The trade that they set their sights on was similar to the trade the woodworkers sought: the temporaries hoped to trade in "risk without certainty of payoff" (being a temporary worker with an ambiguous future) for the rewards of "positive risk taking," which they saw as part and parcel of CompTech's culture. While the woodworkers' willingness to give PM a try was cemented by anxious questioning about institutional longevity and certainty, temporary workers' willingness was deepened by their belief in CompTech's longevity and institutional stability, and their desire to land a good, even if entry-level, job.

In sum, uncertainty and change were pervasive at CompTech. The temporaries believed that, were they to become a permanent member of the workforce, they would acquire and benefit from what recurring change and uncertainty could offer to more privileged workers: challenging jobs, developing personal and professional competencies, and nurturing for lateral and vertical mobility opportunities. Under such circumstances it becomes easier to talk optimistically about the benefits of uncertainty and unpredictability, of risk taking and experimentation with new ways of working. Toward that end, workers at CompTech, arguably the most tenuously positioned of the employed workers in this study, directed their efforts to developing a profile of a "valued worker" in order to maximize their chances of permanently joining CompTech's employment system.

The unemployed managerial and professional workers faced all these experiences of uncertainty and risk, multiplied, but lacked the institutional connections that led employed workers to believe there were immediate or substantive opportunities waiting in the wings. Products of traditional employment systems and work processes, these unemployed individuals were bogged down somewhere inside the industrial divide. Fervently wishing to inch up and onto the new industrial terrain, they actively sought to learn about it at Experience Unlimited: techniques for accessing it, new rules for succeeding in it, and new expectations and performance standards that would allow them to reach and stay on the twenty-first century side of the divide.

Risk and uncertainty were off-the-charts high for the unemployed; in substantive ways, their situations were more dire than those of the temporary workers. Long-term temporaries did, at least, earn a paycheck. They were developing relationships with a stable employment institution. They were learning new skills, developing work portfolios derived from hands-on experience, and demonstrating, to people who had the power to hire, that they were reliable, committed, and quality workers. Their status as temps was in many cases superior to their status in their previous tenuous jobs in the secondary labor market. Admittedly, all this hung in the balance: the potential in these jobs would be realized only if they were hired as a permanent worker at CompTech or another "good" firm.

Unemployed managers and professionals, in contrast, lacked the working relationship with and the social-relational connection to a stable business organization. They either lacked a job altogether or, if they had a temporary job, there was little basis for becoming attached to the employer or strategizing to develop a profile as a valuable worker. (As noted earlier, I uncovered no cases of professionals and managers working as long-term temps with one company, only short-term temps who were "job hoppers.") And to their best understanding any future job could well be a step down the mobility ladder from their previous positions.

Despite their professional experiences and identity, their location in the uncertainty, risk, and opportunity equation was the most compromised of all. While they viewed structural changes as inevitable—the "necessity" for maximizing profits in a highly competitive environment, corporate restructuring, and the expansion of a global economy—they also, to their detriment and disadvantage, saw the resolution of their problems as originating in their own initiative and efforts. The advice and information they learned at the job search club told them that they were individually responsible for turning around their employment fortunes. The job search and interview tactics they learned defied their own intuitions about the nature of the problem: the mandate to take control, repackage themselves, and erase their human capital and occupational history wore down their confidence, made them question and distrust their experiences, and confirmed their sense that they were very much not in control.

But positioned between structural change and personal transformation, these managers and professionals did not see an alternative to following the job club's advice about handling changes in the labor market and in economic institutions. Their circumstances and outlook paralleled that of the woodworkers, who saw no viable alternative to giving participative management a try in order to strengthen the marketability of the plant. The Experience Unlimited participants held dear ideologies about what it meant to be a middle-class professional, individualistic ideologies so entrenched that they even looked at other unemployed professionals and wondered what *their* individual dysfunction was.

Not to undertake these measures meant giving up the only remaining tools available to the professional unemployed, in the form of various job search tactics and personal self-management strategies. Indeed, herein lay the risk for these unemployed individuals: the risk of missing or losing out on an opportunity because the individual did not follow the advice of one of the only affordable organizations that was geared to the peculiarities of their position in the job market. Thus, the EU participants directed their efforts to rewrite, recombine, and re-present themselves in order to land reasonable employment.

From these four cases it is possible to cull the primary features of a system of control and consent in the postbureaucratic organization of work. The three cases of workplaces demonstrate the varied ways in which responsibility, authority, and accountability have devolved down to nonmanagerial workers, as well as ways in which control and power are exercised unobtrusively. In this, my research findings corroborate the findings in much of the critical literature on work reform. As I pointed out in Chapter 1, researchers have argued that under self-management schemes, monitoring, evaluation, and disciplinary action diffuses into the hands of workers (Sewell and Wilkinson 1992; Shaiken et al. 1986). Team-based systems of control have been termed "tyrannical" (Sinclair 1992), "concertive" (Barker 1993), and "unobtrusive" (Prechel 1994).

At Reproco, decentralized organizational arrangements and egalitarian rhetoric; at WoodWorks, an egalitarian cultural overlay; at CompTech, self-managing work units and a philosophy about worker involvement that wove even temporary workers into the tapestry of the participative system—all these systems appropriated organizational and cultural ingredients that gave workers meaningful degrees of freedom and opportunity at work. This space—what Burawoy (1979) might call a game field—in turn inspired workers to participate more to gain more. This cycle of participation and consent, at the same time, was predicated on a less visible cloak of control and discipline. In embracing work reform, workers in all three cases also became complicit in managing others and working in accordance with management's quest for profitability. All three groups struggled, using the organizational and programmatic resources available to them, to control the uneven types of uncertainty that had been created in the corporate design of restructured work systems.

The unemployed at Experience Unlimited, left out of this model, were nearly knocking down the doors to become participants in it, albeit it at a level consistent with their past work experiences. They actively sought access to this social organization of work and were priming themselves to adjust to it if they did enter it. Individuals in all four settings were tied together by one other conditioning factor: unlike protected workers in bureaucratically organized systems, they were not located inside internal labor markets and they were all just a hair away from the volatility of market forces. Specifically, all of them were exposed to rather than buffered from the appearance and disappearance of market niches, and most of the people I studied were extremely aware of their vulnerability. Indeed, it was their awareness of the larger market and their disadvantaged position in it that generated their commitment to work reform. They struggled to position themselves to benefit from that reform.

On the whole, the case studies documenting the nature of the great divide provide ample support for a critical perspective on work reform. Yet my research suggests that this perspective has missed some significant dimensions of restructured workplaces and labor markets, dimensions that explain the implementation and persistence of reform. In exploring these dimensions, I try to give workers credit for their role in facilitating reform, rather than seeing them as coerced or deceived or as losers for going along with it. Workers were neither passive nor hostile bystanders, but active agents in trying to turn work reform to their advantage. At one and the same time, I show that workers in diverse settings experienced multiple forms of insecurity, yet developed commitments and aspirations that drove them to gain control over and live with uncertainty. They did more on the job, took more risks, and stood accountable for a broader variety of outcomes, yet very often they believed that these new expectations constituted opportunities for personal and professional achievement.

As workers agreed to leave behind the hierarchical, bureaucratic model predicated on lines drawn between management and themselves, they often bought into a normative framework in which they scrutinized, regulated, and disciplined their coworkers in their everyday activities. Employee involvement programs, organizational arrangements that removed managers from the circuit of control, and egalitarian rhetoric created a decentralized and postbureaucratic apparatus that tightened its hold on workers and increasingly implicated them in the efficiency and profit goals of management. Given these conclusions, contrasts, and comparisons, what broader sociological generalizations can we draw from the four cases relative to concerns about stability, commitment, cost, and opportunity?

Risk. The four case studies analyzed in the preceding chapters highlight the fact that neither risk, uncertainty, nor opportunity can be discussed except in relation to one another. The three are intertwined and mutually reinforcing. Complicating matters, each category is multi- rather than one-dimensional and needs to be analyzed accordingly. As I mention in Chapter 1, Capelli et al. (1997) have asserted that U.S. workers are shouldering risk to a greater degree, especially as U.S. employers are sloughing off their role in protecting workers. But risk, and what it means for workers in a new economic era, must be subjected to closer scrutiny.

First, risk taking plays out in individual decision making and can have negative and positive meanings. Situations about which people calculate, and opportunities they refuse or accept, pose challenges at the level of the self—accommodation to an arrangement or an interaction that is an affront to dignity and self-esteem represent an instance of negative risk; experimentation with ideas or procedures that one may fear undertaking because of lack of previous experience, but for which one will be positively rewarded by the firm, offers an instance of positive risk. Individual-level risk ranges from mild to intense, and the depth and extent of risks taken by individuals are inextricably shaped by the *institutional context* within which they are taken. Reasons for undertaking and shouldering risk are similarly variegated: some people may choose to accept risk and shoulder great burdens because they feel they have no choice, others because they feel they have nothing to lose but quite possibly something to gain. Some are shouldering costs and risks because the corporation for which they work is no longer doing so; occasionally this brings them substantive and realizable payoffs.

Risk taking, often a product of instrumental calculations, is also deeply embedded within fields of meaning and identity. Thus, while much of what I discovered in this research supports a rational-actor perspective on employment and economic behavior, it also makes clear the degree to which instrumental action is undertaken within a complex of meanings, values, and personally constructed aspirations. This complicates a theory that postulates work and labor-market decisions as narrowly oriented to attaining the maximum wages or to attaining status and prestige as defined on an abstract prestige scale. As Hodson (2000) notes, workers care about citizenship in work organizations and about autonomy, respect, and relations with coworkers. Individuals' aspirations and goals, and the risks they take to reach them, reflect multiple factors, including economics but also including the quest for security, meaning, dignity, and personal biography.

Uncertainty. Personal risk taking or absorption is confounded by our second element, uncertainty. Multiple forms of uncertainty affect the way people do their jobs, the decisions they make, the direction and extent of their aspirations, and their willingness to comply with or consent to changes in workplaces and in the employment contract. Uncertainty plays out at the level of the organization and the employment contract (the *structural uncertainty* that is embodied in the temporary contract, that prevails when it is unclear whether a business will close or stay open, or that is incurred when one is unemployed) and at the level of organizational position (the *experiential uncertainty* that follows when a worker physically moves about from position to position or location to location). The type and the degree of uncertainty, especially relative to the other types of uncertainty that workers have experienced in the past, condition workers' willingness to participate in new work relations and arrangements.

Opportunity. Risk and uncertainty condition and are conditioned by perceptions of opportunity. Workers identified opportunities under unexpected and difficult conditions: when there was a threat of unemployment or loss of livelihood, when personal injuries were incurred in the course of interactions on the job, and when a job could be terminated on a dime. Their definitions of opportunity and success were quite varied and not limited to narrow criteria such as ongoing upward mobility, high wages, or "high prestige" jobs. In other words, perceptions of opportunity and of privilege are socially constructed within a matrix of variables, intrinsic and extrinsic to the workplace. Even mobility itself can have multiple meanings: getting an entry-level job with limited vertical opportunities but in a "good" company can feel subjectively and objectively rewarding to an individual who has been excluded from such companies, just as vertical movement on a career ladder signals mobility to a professional or manager.

What I am identifying, therefore, are a number of factors that need to be taken into consideration in decoding work reform, the rules of the new economy, and the ways in which different groups of workers agree to play by these rules. While all three elements prevail in restructured U.S. workplaces and in the labor market at large, their combined effect differs dramatically depending on organizational and institutional settings, personal biographies, and the prevailing stratification system. There is no simple way to predict how they will combine (that is, the import of each in any particular workplace), but there is a strong case to be made that these are central determinants of occupational dynamics, personal work experiences, and employment conditions in the United States at the turn of the century. They constitute the lens through which the employed and the unemployed view the nature of the great divide, the costs of not getting across it, and the payoffs to making it across. They will fundamentally shape how American workers will respond to the emergent rules of the new economy and to the implementation of workplace innovations.

The Fractured Workforce

I had hoped to conclude this book by summarizing evidence, however tentative, that unemployed or disadvantaged workers were mobilizing to fight the cruelty and degradation of arbitrary corporate power. However, my observations of and conversations with workers throughout the 1990s hold me back from making definitive claims about collective mobilization. Let me reemphasize how the arrangements I describe throughout this book undermined solidary stances toward major trends that seemed, on the whole, to disserve workers.

Throughout this book I identify fracturing forces—ideological, organizational, and structural in nature—that drive wedges between contemporary U.S. workers. These forces minimize the probability that workers will identify with other workers in ways that might lead to meaningful challenges or alternatives to the current configuration of corporate power and politics. Even when individuals spoke critically of economic trends and corporate behavior, their criticisms were detached from a political perspective capable of reversing those trends and behaviors. Rather than seizing this indeterminate moment in history, the economy, and the culture as a time for intervening in and shaping future trends in work and employment, many of the people profiled in this study were much more inclined—often because of their limited alternatives—to see and seize opportunity where possible, exploit it to personal advantage, and adjust to the rules of the new order.

In Reproco, the continual recombination of workers at different companies and into different work units at hiring companies individualized and separated white-collar service workers. They might belong to one group for a period from one to twelve months, but they always knew that their assignment and their workgroup would change. Even within a contracted facility that was stable for six months, there was a reasonable probability that any individual member would be taken out and reassigned to other newly constructed facilities. Thus, the photocopiers' everyday work experiences were defined by continual and unpredictable change. There was little opportunity to develop enduring relationships with coworkers. Furthermore, criticism or resentment of Reproco supervisors or managers was usually subsumed in photocopiers' relationships with clients, an instance of horizontal (organizational) rather than vertical (class) conflict (Burawoy 1979). Here, organizational practice and structure consistently eroded the likelihood that the workforce would coalesce into a body capable of redirecting, redefining, or resisting management's directives. And, of course, coming from the jobs and educational backgrounds that I identify in Chapter 2, photocopiers were already predisposed to look at the Reproco jobs in individualistic terms, as offering a path out of disadvantaged work histories and into individual career trajectories.

In CompTech there were numerous fracture lines defining temporary employment experiences. In Chapter 4 I discuss the ways temps' employment arrangements obscured the identity of their employer, with obvious consequences for their understanding of who their coworkers were and whose occupational situations and fates they shared. Not knowing whether they were employed by a temp agency, CompTech, or a vendor gave temporaries little basis on which to form solidarity with other temps. That destabilized sense of temporary identity was deepened by the defining fact of temporary employment: temporaries came and went; and if they didn't, they might.

The temporaries often identified with their managers more than with their coworkers because managers informally cultivated and mentored them, and often led them to desire permanent membership in the CompTech community. Even when temporary workers clearly understood who their temp comrades were, divisions developed around perceptions that "valued" temps held about "bad" temps, who conformed to stereotypes about dysfunctional individuals who couldn't hold down a real, permanent job. Finally, in much the same way as at Reproco, temporaries striving to land a permanent job at CompTech keenly desired mobility up and out of their previous alienating and poorly paid jobs. In their minds, the only way they would achieve this would be through persistent effort, developing strong one-on-one relationships with their supervisors and managers, and patiently demonstrating their ability to work like an attached worker. Fracture points began in the employment, organizational/cultural, and structural conditions of everyday life.

Experience Unlimited participants displayed the most puzzling yet graphic instance of division and fragmentation in my study. Because the job club participants had been thrown into a collective setting by shared circumstances of unemployment, I was inclined to predict that they, many of whom were unemployed because of impersonal corporate decisions, would easily identify with one another. It is in this organization, however, that we see, in ironic ways, divisions among the unemployed that inhibit them from doing anything more collective than training and socializing one another in job search workshops that are cruelly inadequate for remedying their circumstances. Even as they voiced a global critique of economic and industrial transformation and the way it banishes workers to the sidelines without regard for their individual competencies and experiences, it was difficult for some to refrain from interpreting others' unemployment as different, more dysfunctional than their own.

Here, a deeply held meritocratic ideology blinded unemployed professionals and managers to the possibilities of mobilizing with others like themselves. This ideology leads individuals to conclude that they are responsible for their own success or failure and is particularly strong among middle-class professionals (Newman 1988). Such an ideological orientation toward work and mobility was continually reinforced, day in and day out, through the rhetoric, the curriculum, the physical space, and the organizational structure of the job search club. The curriculum stressed that these people should cast aside a structural critique of the economy—in popular discourse, they should acknowledge and "get over it"—after all, a single individual or even fifty individuals could not put the brakes on capital and corporate restructuring. All the curriculum thus promoted individualistic tactics for repositioning oneself in the job market, for adapting to changing labor markets and institutions. These changes were inevitable and intractable, or so the expert advice and the narrative stories reiterated. Thus, meritocratic ideology and organizational structure and practice found sustenance in one another.

In these three cases, an individualistic approach to work and employment seemed to mute the turmoil, stress, or unpredictability of flexible workplaces. A meritocratic achievement ideology, then, partly explains why we find fracture lines within workplaces and across populations of workers that appear to be the targets of disadvantaging work conditions: the temporary, the unemployed, and those who are vulnerable because of race or ethnicity or because of the low status of their jobs. A culture of meritocracy played on the experiences of the people I studied and shaped their faith that if they continued to work hard and play by the (new) rules of the game, their efforts might pay off in achievement of an elusive American middle-class dream. This occurred even when the game and its outcomes were heavily skewed against them. Many of the people I discuss in this book hoped and to some extent truly believed that if they suspended their pessimism and toiled diligently they would be rewarded with a "good" job, defined in various ways but consisting of the key ingredients of security, protection, living wages and benefits, meaning, pride, and dignity, even challenge and satisfaction in one's jobs and relations with coworkers.

But autonomously formulated ideology is not sufficient to explain the deep and deepening divide among workers. I attempt to show how particular sets of organizational practices, structures, and employment relations powerfully reinforced personal ideologies about how to get jobs and keep them. The case studies reported here show what—with reference to employment and labor-market institutions, culture, and organizations—fed these beliefs and obscured the fact that only a modest number would finally be rewarded for their efforts. *Crossing the Great Divide*, then, documents the organizational and institutional conditions that enabled people to hold onto these deeply felt individualistic beliefs.

The woodworkers' case disrupts the pattern of atomization among workers. The woodworkers came closest to achieving consensus around the fate of their employment future and what they could do to preserve it. Aside from the isolated and highly resistant logyard workers, the majority of workers in the plant were experimenting with new methods of work, one-on-one interactional strategies for dealing with conflict and fixing production flaws, and small-group interactions. They hoped and wanted to believe that if they pumped up the value of their workforce by aligning themselves more with the techniques and philosophies of the new industrial era, they could save the plant. Their response was to keep themselves active at the local, shop-floor level, rather than direct their efforts to a larger political struggle such as mobilizing with other timber plants to stop the downsizing of the industry as a whole or design conversion plans for the plant. In comparison to the individualized viewpoints of the unemployed managers and professionals, the woodworkers drew on a tradition of collective action, forged in decades of collective bargaining and union organization.

Becoming more engaged in shop-floor production arrangements, relaxing the rules that historically had constricted their work tasks, and trying to solve problems collaboratively rather than heading for the union shop-floor representative, however, made it more and more difficult to exercise the institutional power available to the union and the labor movement. Here, individual-level empowerment, even in a limited form, caused institutional disempowerment, yet another element in the fracturing of the American workforce.

The issue of the fractured workforce and the difficulty of organizing workers from disparate industrial, temporally organized, and structurally unequal settings has been addressed by other researchers. They have shown how bases for collective political critique and action have been undermined, interrupted, and diminished by conditions that are endemic to the restructuring, postindustrial economy. Rogers and Barrett (N/D) and Carré, duRivage, and Tilly (1995), for example, have written about the structural and subjective impediments to organizing temporaries, considering issues such as the continual shift in and out of jobs that temps experience, the difficulty of organizing people on the basis of their temporary status when their goal is to *not* be a temporary worker at all, and the limited strategies that unions have for addressing the unique problems and situations of temporaries.

But my pessimism is tempered by examples of other labor struggles in which workers *do* contest the terms of the new contract and the new era. They *are* attempting to shape corporate power in a way that could put the brakes on the troubling aspects of the new economy. Over the last year unionized workers at Boeing, Kaiser Aluminum, and Reuters News Service have gone on strike over the issue of job security in relation to corporate restructuring, mandatory overtime, and wage concessions. Both Boeing and Kaiser workers are protesting their companies' increasing outsourcing practices and layoff policies. The workers are demanding job security in return for concessions in these areas. Auto workers at General Motors have done the same.[2]

Bronfenbrenner et al. (1998) discuss these problems in relation to the more general problem, for the labor movement, of organizing workers in a changing, flexible economy and have theorized new organizing strategies for unions, some of which certainly explain recent increases in the numbers of unionized workers in the United States. Osterman (1999) brainstorms about policy and institutional changes that would enable workers to adjust to turbulence. He recommends (as does Sabel 1991) intermediary labor-market institutions that can more flexibly handle the unique issues that temporary, part-time, displaced, and service workers face; changing the terms of unemployment insurance so that American workers in constant transition can protect themselves from such turbulence; and community-mobilization efforts, such as municipal living-wage campaigns that improve workers' economic standing and well-being and organizations that strike out for greater corporate responsibility. Policy analysts and theorists are thus actively searching for mechanisms to rectify the inequality and disadvantage that is being wreaked on many American workers under the unique conditions of postindustrial society.

The Quandary of the Contemporary Economy:
Connection and Uncertainty

Crossing the Great Divide underscores the profound importance of institutional connection, stability, and continuity. In the four cases examined in this book individuals were driven by feelings about and desire for attachment to a secure institution whether they were motivated to go along with the numerous, unpredictable demands made on them by management because they viewed their jobs as worth struggling to keep (Reproco), to work hard in the hope of establishing a connection to a good firm (CompTech), or motivated by fear and anxiety in an attempt to maintain or acquire formal connection to a secure institution (WoodWorks and people utilizing Experience Unlimited). Varying perceptions of risk, as well as decisions to take such risks—with consequences ranging from mild to the prospect of realizing no payoff whatsoever—were cemented, reinforced, or challenged by the stability and instability of the institutions in which people worked and those for which they wanted to work.

But workers' desire for secure, enduring employment was by no means an indication that they wished simply to do things in a rote and predictable way, climb until they reached a plateau where they could relax, or benefit from economic growth and prosperity without having to do much to create it. The cases strongly suggest that many workers were poised and willing to experiment, to undertake new responsibilities, to be held more accountable, and to identify their interests with those of their employers if they perceived that employers were committed to working *with* workers and not against them and to building quality work environments.

I drew much the same conclusion about corporate middle managers when I conducted research at the Bank of America in the mid-1980s (Smith 1990). Studying middle managers in the midst of corporate restructuring and downsizing processes, I criticized top management's agenda to exploit middle managers to do the dirty work of downsizing. Giving middle managers a new language of entrepreneurialism and a set of universal guidelines for managing people that ignored the complexities and conditions that middle managers faced, top management insisted that middle managers would "manage out" thousands of workers from the Bank of America's staff.

These middle managers were all too willing to learn and do what they needed to do to ride the upheavals of economic transformation that were shaking up corporate America, but they vigorously protested the use of such abstract, often useless, and patently cynical management methodologies. Middle managers carried on business in ways that were attentive to new pressures for profitability and were cognizant of the problems of efficiency and consent of those who worked under them. Yet they distrusted corporate management's ulterior agenda and long-term goals. They believed that new optimistic and entrepreneurial strategies glossed over very difficult problems and that top management's stated quest to "work with," not against bank workers was little more than lip service that would soon be revealed as the exploitative rhetoric it was.

Top management erroneously believed that middle managers would absorb the consequences of those practices without question. The former gave the latter tools to help the bank cross the divide into the new era of employment, but the tools were ineffective, built with flimsy materials appropriated from reigning corporate fads.

Now, as then, corporate-level managers expect their workforces to absorb the costs of doing business in a flexible, pressured, fast-paced, and global economy. It is a lopsided contract. Corporate leaders are, as I document throughout this book, asking workers to learn more, to take on more responsibilities, to collaborate, and to be held more accountable, but sometimes with low wages and usually without employment security. Even firms that espouse the importance of secure employment are wavering on this issue. Today, our historically trusted, core, stable institutions like Reproco and CompTech rarely guarantee employment security. Throughout the 1990s, the "good" companies have laid off workers by the tens of thousands. They have done so even when they are not facing a structural, market, or profit crisis.

Thus, in workplaces such as Reproco and CompTech, the reality is that institutional, structural insecurity is an unrelenting possibility. As many researchers have noted, U.S. labor relations are fragile. Companies that take the high road—the enabling form of the flexibility model that I have outlined—can, overnight, pull the plug on their workforces and lay off large percentages of their workers. U.S. firms have few legal or institutional limits on their power to lay off workers (Appelbaum and Batt 1994:159). What looks like a good contract for workers—participate, give extra effort and intensity to the job, sweat over production glitches and outcomes, all in return for being admitted into a partnership with management—is a contract betrayed when employment security is replaced with uncertainty or termination. Workers are reminded of this possibility every day by local, regional, and national news accounts.

Maximal managerial discretion, of course, fits all too well with the assumptions embedded in the free-agent model. *Crossing the Great Divide* and its defense of the importance of stable business institutions for workers is likely to disturb and irritate proponents of that model and to be brandished as evidence of the dysfunctional, lingering vestiges of an obsolete economy and employment model. This group's biases against the old social contract are not subtle. Tom Peters's assessment of the direction the U.S. economy, its free agents (aka, workers), and its institutions should take crystallizes developing normative ideologies about impermanence, the demise of attachment to particular employers or organizations, and ongoing work intensity. In the special issue of *The New York Times Magazine* (2000:83) discussed at the outset of this chapter, Peters orates on the new model of work in no uncertain terms:

> Loyalty is the glue that holds society together—including commercial society. That said, corporate loyalty is rubbish. If you apply for a job at the Tom Peters Company and imply that you'd like to make a life of it, I'll unceremoniously throw you out of the office...
>
> Here's my New Social Contract. I want my company to be so attractive, so laden with talent, so energetic it makes your head swim. I want to give you an exciting work environment, peerless teammates and a string of challenging projects with top clients you could not match anywhere else. In turn, I demand that you give your all to these hot projects. And I demand that you be loyal—to your teammates, to the client, to yourself. You must perform and grow as you've never performed and grown before.
>
> However, I also demand that you not be "loyal" to me or my company... Mindless corporate loyalty—the essence of 50's Babbittry—was always a rotten idea.

The necessity of having access to meaningful work opportunity and being *able* to develop commitments to the work we do and to the institutions where we carry it out is a given for sociologists and political theorists (Bernstein 1997; Hodson 2000; Kondo 1990; Newman 1999; Wallulis 1998; Wilson 1996). Yet this insight is erased from the free-agent model of work. Peters's vision includes continual mobility *out* of organizations—indeed, centralized organizations would be taboo given that everyone should be connected through *virtual* organization and should carry out *distributed* work in this digital society (Grantham 2000). Free agents should invest in developing fields of work rather than the pursuit of jobs and should assume exclusive, individual responsibility for their economic and social well-being. Gone is any sense of the importance of *corporate* responsibility or identity forged in connection to stable, productive, meaningful economic enterprises. And although some progressive business leaders and management theorists may disagree with the belief that companies should discourage workers from developing attachments and commitments, they are swimming against strong, hegemonic currents of the twenty-first century.

Conclusion

At the beginning of the twenty-first century, the U.S. economy feels like a bubble that could burst at any time. With every new announcement about sustained economic growth, record-low unemployment levels, and the skyrocketing stock market, there is a feeling of collective breath holding, a sense of wonderment over how much longer prosperity can last. When unemployment rates creep up by a couple of tenths of a percentage point, we come close to hyperventilating. During the period in which I did my research, employment relations were in a holding pattern, but it is a pattern over which the threatening potential inherent in the dark side of flexibility is hovering. So easily, an economic downturn could close the doors of tenuously positioned plants, mills, and offices around the country, lead to the termination of the contracts of millions of temporary workers, and forever leave mature, unemployed professionals and managers outside the labor market, spinning them into the ranks of discouraged workers who cease to search for employment. Even short of this drastic scenario, the trends I explore in this book have changed and shaped the terrain of the postindustrial, flexible economy irrevocably.

Richard Sennett, in *The Corrosion of Character: The Personal Consequences of Work in the New Capitalism* (1998), has noted the importance of secure institutions and stability for the very social fabric of American society. He reviews the different configurations of risk and uncertainty in the new era of industrial/corporate policies, concluding that when people lack sustained human relations with an employment institution, they also "lack durable purposes" (1998:98) and connection to society itself. Without romanticizing the past, he fears the loss of the work ethic that historically secured families, communities, and the nation, that fueled the growth of the U.S. economy and its prosperity. As he remarks, "it becomes absurd to work long and hard for an employer who thinks only about selling up and moving on" (1998:99).

Discussions of ways to assist workers whose jobs and careers are in continual turmoil and upheaval are necessary but are partial in terms of the diagnosis of the problem. Indeed, U.S. workers need organizations that can help them land on their feet (career counseling, job training) and policies to cushion them from repeated bouts of unemployment (extending unemployment benefits) and protect health coverage for individual and family (portable benefits packages) (Osterman 1999). But these are technical, policy, and administrative solutions to deep-seated moral and political problems that will remain unsolved if the larger question of corporations' responsibility for their workforces is not addressed. If deep desires for attachment and meaningful connection to our employment institutions and to the people with whom we work cannot be met, we will care little about sustaining the institutions that should play a positive role in shaping our social relations and identity or about the very social fabric supporting and benefiting from those institutions. If current trends serve to disadvantage a great many workers, they will have the power to make work and employment one of the most contentious and turbulent areas in American society.

Notes

Chapter One. At the Turn of the Century

1. I am concerned here with four sets of changes. The first is *progressive work reform*, in which new organizational and technological mechanisms have increased opportunities for worker participation, autonomy, exercise of discretion, and decentralization. Frequently grouped under the rubric of high-performance work systems, such mechanisms include employee involvement programs, participative management programs, quality circles, and just-in-time schemes. Appelbaum and Batt (1994), Appelbaum et al. (2000), Harrison (1994), Osterman (1994), Piore and Sabel (1984), and Smith (1997) summarize and analyze these innovations. The second is the spread of *flexible staffing arrangements*; notably, the growth of the temporary workforce (Barker and Christensen 1998; Callaghan and Hartmann 1991; Rogers 2000; Smith 1998), nonstandard work arrangements (Kalleberg, Reskin, and Hudson 2000), and the temporary help service industry (Gonos 1997; Gottfried 1991; Ofstead 1999).

The decline of career stability and job tenure and normative temporariness constitute the third set of changes (Baker and Aldrich 1996; Capelli et al. 1997; DiTomaso 1996; Hirsch and Shanley 1996; Mishel, Bernstein, and Schmitt 1999; Neumark 2000; Osterman 1996; Osterman 1999). Although the evidence is mixed, it appears that workers today experience shorter tenure on the job and that internal labor markets are eroding. Normative temporariness refers to the decline of expectations for "permanent" or lifelong jobs and the ascendance of beliefs that ongoing job change is an unavoidable reality of contemporary employment. Finally, *demographic shifts* in the composition of the workforce and in mobility patterns constitute the canvas on which the former changes are being mapped (Bernhardt, Morris, and Handcock 1995; Morris and Western 1999; Spalter-Roth and Deitch 1999). White women and men and women of color are entering occupations and professional settings to a degree that is thoroughly transforming workplaces. At the same time, white men have suffered significant declines in income and mobility opportunities (Mishel, Bernstein, and Schmitt 1999). The goal of this book is to ferret out the combined effect of these trends.

2. The gap between good and bad jobs has considerably widened the income gap in the United States (Mishel, Bernstein, and Schmitt 1999). Policy makers and economic analysts have documented the rising concentration of wealth at the top and the

growth of low-income earners at the bottom in relation to the simultaneous expansion of the professional, information, high-technology-based sector, alongside the spread of low-wage, entry-level, unskilled jobs (Mishel, Bernstein, and Schmitt 1999; Reich 1992, chaps. 14–19). The AFL-CIO's (AFL-CIO Special Report 1999) recent study of what young workers could expect when they enter the labor market and seek occupational mobility framed this as a problem of "rich economy, poor jobs."

3. Sabel (1991) has artfully sketched out the macro-level determinants of the dialectic of uncertainty and opportunity in his discussion of moebius-strip organizations in the flexible economy.

4. See Dudley 1994, Heckscher 1995, Newman 1988, Sennett 1998, Smith 1990, and Useem 1996.

5. Numerous public opinion polls provide evidence about the ambivalent insecurity felt by Americans. See Ginsberg 1997, Lohr 1996, and Reinemer 1995.

6. Milkman (1997:15) notes, for example, in her study of auto workers at the GM-Linden plant that some labor critics have vigorously opposed work reform because they believe that it adds up to little more than increased exploitation of workers, but that there actually has been very little research on how rank-and-file workers themselves feel about it.

7. See Smith 1994 for a review of these studies.

8. A word on my selection of occupational groups. First, my research design specified comparisons of worker involvement, employee participation, and flexibility across white-collar and blue-collar work settings. The overwhelming majority of studies of the high-performance model have focused on industrial, blue-collar settings, usually ones that are unionized.

Second, when I initiated this research project I deliberately chose not to focus on employed middle managers because I had seen work reform from their point of view when I conducted research at the Bank of America in the 1980s. In fact, in the concluding chapter of *Managing in the Corporate Interest* (1990, Chapter 7) I previewed the trends that are the subject of *Crossing the Great Divide* and argued that it was important to look in greater depth at the front line of work reform, in the hands and minds of workers for whom new, flexible practices were materializing. As I progressed through five years of research, the case of managers and professionals again had risen to the fore of my thinking about restructured workplaces, especially those who were *displaced* and *downwardly mobile* as a result of changes in the economy. As I carried out the workplace case studies I came to see that experiences of the unemployed constituted the related and severe downside of corporate change and decided to study Experience Unlimited. The EU job search club also gave me the opportunity to investigate the prescriptive rhetoric about the new rules of the economy.

9. Reproco, WoodWorks, and CompTech are all pseudonyms. My entry to these firms was strictly conditional on changing the names of the firms and of all study participants. The Sacramento Professional Network is the real name of the job search club, but all the names of individuals have been changed. I also conceal the exact dates of my research so that the staff person cannot be identified. One of the important facts about the club is that it is sponsored by the California Employment Development Department. As the only such organization of its kind it would have been difficult to disguise with a pseudonym.

10. Interviews ranged from thirty minutes to three hours. My interviews with temps at CompTech were the shortest. They were not chatty about their experiences and very often were hesitant when trying to articulate their thoughts about temporary work. I assumed that they felt awkward being interviewed by a sociologist more or less on the

shop floor. I know *I* felt awkward. Although I conducted these interviews in an enclosed cubicle, a stream of fellow temps and occasional supervisors would poke their heads over the partition, making good-natured fun of whichever interviewee was sitting there and demanding to know whether it was time yet for their own interview. It was a very stimulating environment, to say the least, and it took all my powers of concentration not to let it rattle me.

My interviews with managers at all the companies, and with the professional and managerial unemployed often ran two to three hours. It is illustrative to look at the transcripts from the latter set of interviews: not only did they run for a long time, but the text of each page is incredibly dense. My transcribers found these particular interviews extremely tedious to transcribe. I interviewed all the employed managers from the three companies in their offices or in company cafeterias; I interviewed the bulk of the unemployed professionals and managers at a busy downtown restaurant, which I would caution researchers to avoid if at all possible. The restaurant I chose, which was the most conveniently located for the interviewees (relative to the SPN facility), and where I didn't feel we had to rush off after eating, happened to be directly across the street from the University of California Medical Center in Sacramento. Our interviews were punctuated with sirens and with the sounds of med center helicopters delivering emergency patients from all over Northern California. One of my interviewees actually picked up my tape recorder during one of these episodes and started shouting his answers directly into the microphone, a moment on the tape that virtually blew away my transcriber. At these times it was hard for me to conceal how rattled and defeated I felt.

Chapter Two. Creating Flexibly Specialized Service Workers

1. The dynamism of Reproco's business services division parallels that of the business services sector in the U.S. economy. Business services, including computer and data processing, personnel supply, duplicating, mail and other office machine operators, advertising, building maintenance and security services, constituted the fastest growing industry between the mid-1970s and mid-1980s, growing more than four times as fast as all private nonagricultural industry (Howe 1986). This rapid growth rate has continued into the 1990s and is projected to continue into the beginning of the twenty-first century (Franklin 1997). Between 1988 and 1996 nearly 14.3 million jobs were added to the economy (Clinton 1997:3): more than 18 percent of them were in business services (Clinton 1997: Table 1, p. 4). In 1997 the business services industry produced more jobs than any other single industry (Ilg and Clinton 1998:49). Clinton (1997) argues that the growth of the business services industry is in large part explained by the fact that more firms are adopting various "market-mediated arrangements" in which "persons who formerly were hired directly are being replaced with purchases of services" (3), an arrangement that characterizes Reproco's market niche.

2. For the Reproco case study I conducted twenty-six semi-structured, in-depth interviews: ten with supervisors and managers and sixteen with nonmanagerial employees who were machine operators. Of the nonmanagerial employees eleven were women and five were men, six were white and ten were African American or Hispanic. I observed work processes and interactions in ten of forty work sites in the division, observing both the individuals I formally interviewed and numerous other machine operators. This enabled me to generalize about machine operators' labor process, their group procedures and dynamics, and their interactions with clients.

3. See Kimle and Damhorst (1997) for a delineation of the narrow range of fashion standards available to women dressing for work in the corporate and management world. Interestingly, Tannen (1994) argues that women can choose from a broader range of fashions, but that no matter what women wear, they are always "marked" and scrutinized for their choices in a way that men aren't. Even something as seemingly simple as not wearing makeup, which I didn't when I visited the law firm, is held against corporate women, used to mark and categorize them, even taken as a "hostile refusal" to buy into the power structure of corporate life (Tannen 1994:110–13).

4. In this facility there is a gendered division of labor: men work as couriers both in and outside the building; women perform the copy work. In the other facilities I observed, however, the distribution of tasks was not visibly divided by gender: I observed men and women doing copy work, women and men doing mailroom work. The more rigid division at Black, Moore, and MacIntire may be explained by the fact that courier work involves walking around the city and that these trips were perceived as potentially threatening to personal safety, therefore typed as work suitable for men and relegated to them.

5. Some of Reproco's accounts consisted exclusively of convenience copiers. An account at Boeing, for example, had 130 machines; the machine operator's job consisted of monitoring and maintaining them.

6. See Orr 1996 for a detailed account of the tech rep.

7. Nearly 40 percent of the machine operators in the division were African American and Hispanic. This aggregate figure covered up a much deeper *regional* stratification insofar as the urban facilities had an even higher representation of men and women of color.

8. Of the sixteen machine operators I formally interviewed, only one had a college degree. Many of the participants had attended college for short periods of time but had had to leave because of financial constraints or problems with academic performance. All the participants previously had had working-class jobs, often in the secondary labor market, that were transitory whether defined as a permanent or a temporary job. Interviews with managers and supervisors in the center confirmed that these characteristics were typical for workers in machine-operator jobs throughout the facilities.

9. In Chapter 4 I explore more fully how low-level workers, who previously have only been able to obtain unstable secondary-labor-market jobs and have lacked the privilege of entrance into core-sector employment, come to view even *temporary* jobs in good, core companies with paternalistic employment policies as very desirable.

10. In speaking of paternalism I'm referring to the bundle of practices and policies that core firms historically have implemented to gain the consent and loyalty of employees and to create high-performance work systems (Kalleberg and Moody 1996). They typically include generous wage and benefits packages, internal labor markets, opportunities for upward mobility, and human resource policies geared toward bringing workers' interests into alignment with those of firms'. Sociologists, economists, organizational, and industrial relations researchers have identified many variants or manifestations of paternalism and hegemonic control. For a definitive study of the way corporations purposely developed paternalistic employment relations over the course of the twentieth century, see Jacoby 1997. See also Heckscher 1995, chap. 1, and Smith 1990. For a full-blown theory that views this approach to control and coordination as a global strategy for ensuring worker cooperation under monopoly capitalism, see Burawoy's conceptualization of hegemonic regimes (1985, chap. 3). Bureaucratic control systems fall under this rubric (Edwards 1979; Marsden, Cook, and Kalleberg 1996),

closely associated with the expansion of internal labor markets as an orderly system for advancement and consent (Burawoy 1979; Doeringer and Piore 1971; Kalleberg et al. 1996; Osterman 1996). Other researchers have highlighted the importance of cultural systems as part and parcel of paternalistic and hegemonic systems (Barley and Kunda 1992; Kunda 1992; Trice and Beyer 1993; for a critique of corporate cultural control, see Smith 1990), cultural control being the successor of an earlier formulation, normative control (Etzioni 1961; Scott 1998:134). Finally, see Barley and Kunda 1992 for an important overview of shifts in ideologies and practices about different forms of control. What is noteworthy in the case of Reproco is that, while not paying low-level workers great wages, the company is extending other aspects of the paternalistic framework to workers in low-level positions.

11. Rogers (2000) explores these issues in her study of temporary workers, a population I analyze in Chapter 4. She, too, notes the continual regrouping and separation of workers from one another and the ways in which organizational arrangements and employment relations can individualize workers.

12. Machine operators worried, for example, that temps' work would not be of reasonable quality.

13. MacLeod (1995:227) and Bourgois (1995) make this very point with reference to the difficulties that urban African American men face in postindustrial service work settings.

14. Of course, if client dissatisfaction is widespread and persistent enough, the hiring company can terminate its contract with Reproco. I'm speaking here of unpredictable irritations and criticisms that crop up in any typical day.

15. A complicating factor here is that neither party has formal authority over the other, meaning that the parameters for trying to direct an interaction in your favor are very wide. Neither can easily rely on established rules or procedures, or a mediator, to resolve interactional conflicts.

Chapter Three. Reconstructing Endangered Workers

1. Because the population of timber plants in the Northwest is small, I use the pseudonym "Madison" to minimize the chances that any individuals will be identifiable.

2. It should be noted that the timber industry has experienced many boom-and-bust cycles throughout the twentieth century. For historical overviews of the industry and of regional dynamics as they have been shaped by the industry in the Northwest, see Carroll 1995, Hibbard and Elias 1993, Peterson 1987, and Robbins 1988.

3. Many labor leaders have been hostile to employee involvement and participative management programs. See Bluestone and Bluestone 1992 for an overview of the politics of worker involvement in the union movement, and Heckscher's (1988) argument about the necessity for organized labor to embrace a more involved stance. The involvement of the union in endorsing participative management at WoodWorks is instructive. When it was first introduced, the local union president was adamantly against the PM program, arguing that it just represented a cooptation of union workers. Other union leaders—the union vice-president, for one, as well as other vocal members—argued that the membership should give PM a try. One year after the introduction of the program, the local president stepped down from his position and a pro-PM candidate was voted in to replace him. Plant-level management tapped active and visible union members who had credibility and

trust in the eyes of the membership to come in and work as PM trainers. This degree of endorsement for PM most assuredly explains the willingness of many workers to give PM a chance.

4. For the WoodWorks case study I conducted sixteen in-depth, formal interviews, six with participative management trainers, ten with blue-collar workers. Seven of the ten worked in the plywood plant that is the focus of this chapter. One of the trainers was a woman, and the rest were men. Two of the blue-collar workers were women, and eight were men. (Finding a number of people to interview comparable to the number of interviews I conducted for my other case studies was difficult because workers had very little flexibility to leave the line.) I did, however, have extensive opportunities to observe. None of the people I interviewed formally was a person of color. The workforce was virtually all white. I saw two or three African Americans during my time at the plant but didn't have the opportunity to interview them. I interviewed seven other workers informally while conducting observations. I was able to observe work in four different production settings throughout the plant, as well as numerous workers on the job. I spent most of my observational time in the plywood plant, including a full day in the logyard, where I hung out with the log drivers and learned how to drive one of their log-toting vehicles. I also attended three different task force meetings and three of the weekly meetings that the plant manager held regularly with the participative management trainers.

5. The classic book on deindustrialization is Bluestone and Harrison's *The Deindustrialization of America* (1982). See also Bluestone and Bluestone 1992, Craypo and Nissen 1993, and Perrucci et al. 1988.

6. Varano's (1999) insightful study documents how these factors compelled workers at Weirton Steel to take part in an employee buyout plan.

7. For a more sympathetic treatment of worker participation, see Cole 1979, 1989.

8. There is also a large literature in the fields of administration, management, and human resources that can be termed the "organizational performance model," which investigates how worker participation and employee involvement programs contribute to efficiency, productivity, and other performance-related variables (Appelbaum et al. 2000; Batt 1999; Cooke 1989; Havlovic 1991; Margulies and Black 1987; Safizadeh 1991; Schwochau et al. 1997; Sillince, Sykes, and Singh 1996; Walton and Lawrence 1985).

9. For informative and rich studies of the demise of mills and factories, and the often-devastating consequences for occupational groups, communities, and regions, see Dudley 1994, Hoerr 1988, Lynd 1982, Moddell and Brodsky 1998, Newman 1988, Perrucci et al. 1988, Peterson 1987, and Serrin 1992.

10. See Carroll 1995 for a detailed description of the work and culture of log-bearing truck drivers, as well as the loggers themselves.

11. The ruminations of Madison citizens about the decline of logging and timber production are borne out in the findings of social science researchers. The explanation for the decline of the industry is multicausal. Technological innovation and automation of labor-intensive tasks have overwhelmingly shaped production processes and employment levels. Greber (1993) identified four types of technological change prevalent in the industry that displaced labor while increasing labor productivity: the introduction of labor-saving devices, especially automated materials-handling devices; raw-material-saving devices, such as thinner blade saws and machines for the retrieval and processing of waste; capital-saving technologies such as computer inventory control systems; and product-augmenting devices such as kiln dryers. There was a massive diffusion of these technologies into mills in the 1980s; many mills that didn't adopt

them and modernize closed down. Greber estimates that the bulk of the productivity increases was realized in the eighties, and that labor-saving technology effects have dramatically slowed down. Forest management decisions such as ineffective "sustained yield policies" that should have provided but failed to provide for the continuous growth of timber supply have had a negative effect on employment (Hibbard and Elias 1993). A lively and, in my view, inconclusive debate has taken place over the impact of environmental legislation on the industry and on employment levels, particularly over whether adding the spotted owl to the endangered species list in 1989 eliminated jobs by limiting access to timber supplies (Freudenburg, Wilson, and O'Leary 1998; Carroll et al. 1999; Freudenburg, O'Leary, and Wilson 1999). Finally, one more variable affecting the timber business and mill closure is the export of huge numbers of raw logs in recent years to Pacific Rim countries that pay about 40 percent more than domestic buyers (Satschell 1990).

12. During the summer months when I conducted my research, these seminars were not held. Information about the various sessions comes from in-depth interviews and by reading company documents.

13. These principles are taken from an evaluation report written by the PM trainers, a year after the initiation of the program.

14. There is a significant body of literature on *worker-owned* plywood cooperatives in the Pacific Northwest (Bellas 1972; Berman 1967; Bernstein 1976; Greenberg 1984; Gunn 1992). Berman (1967, chap. 4) provides an especially illuminating, step-by-step technical description of the general calculations (regarding quality, moisture, consistency, grading) used to produce plywood. Hartzell (1987) and Gunn (1984) analyze another type of cooperative and occupational group in the timber harvesting and production chain: Hoedads, a group of reforestation workers.

15. It is not self-evident that the spreader job would be categorized as high status. Two features set it off from other jobs, though: first, it is the only job in the plant in which workers receive bonuses for their work; second, individuals who work in this position are assumed to have significant stamina and focus.

16. Gottfried and Graham argue that under post-Fordist production arrangements, male workers "seek ways to reassert their sexuality by signifying masculinity in opposition to and through the negation of both femininity and subordinated masculinities" (1993:615). Although production arrangements in plywood conformed more to Fordist principles, it is quite possible that, by choosing virile names such as the stud runners, male plywood workers were "signifying masculinity" in opposition to the post-Fordist, interactive character of the task-force structure and the new ethos of involvement that I describe below. Because I did not conduct sustained observation in any one part of the plywood plant, I didn't have the chance to discover whether male WoodWorkers expressed their masculinity in the same anxious, dissociative ways that men did day-to-day in the auto assembly plant where Gottfried and Graham worked.

17. There was a task force in the stud mill whose scope went far beyond the micro-level of the work process. They were charged with designing a plan for a new stud mill with modernized equipment in which corporate management had publicly vowed to invest. The local newspaper and the employee newsletter carried multiple accounts of the task force, and the group's design was presented at a news conference.

18. Tannen (1994) analyzes the male style of communication in which maintaining the upper hand in conversation and performing one-upmanship in groups is a privileged style in white-collar professional settings.

Chapter Four. Temporary Work, Attachment, and Aspirations

1. These reasons are commonly cited in the burgeoning literature on the growth of temporary employment. See Barker and Christensen 1998, Henson 1996, Pfeffer and Baron 1988, and Smith 1997 for overviews.

2. As was the case at Reproco, many CompTech temps had had only low-level white- and blue-collar jobs, mainly in the secondary labor market, and had limited educational backgrounds. What was surprising about the temps in this case study was how diverse they were, including many white men, and how mature many of the workers were. As I note later in the chapter, I did observe a handful of youthful temps, but the majority of people I interviewed and observed seemed to be in their thirties and forties. It is impossible to discern precisely the demographic composition of the temporary labor force since CompTech management did not keep data on it; thus, I am forced to use my observations and interviews to generalize about the characteristics of the labor force. White men in my study had often had checkered employment histories (i.e., had moved through a series of impermanent, low-wage jobs); three of the older white men (all in their mid-to-late forties) once had had well-paying and/or union jobs that for various reasons they had had to leave (health factors were most commonly cited). The degree of whiteness of the temp labor force was surprising, given the fact that people of color tend to be disproportionately represented in the ranks of temporary workers in the United States.

3. For the CompTech case study I conducted forty-five interviews with company employees. This group included thirteen managers, supervisors, and staffing specialists who all had extensive involvement with either designing the temporary employment system or managing temporary employees; twenty-five entry-level assembly line, warehouse, distribution, and white-collar clerical workers (of whom fourteen were temporary workers; ten were "converts," my term for permanent workers who were first hired as temporary workers; and one was a permanent who had never worked as a temp); three high-level contract workers; and three representatives of a temporary-help service agency that recruited temps for the company. I also interviewed the director of personnel over a period of several months. Of the twenty-five entry-level workers I interviewed formally, twelve were women and thirteen were men; three were Hispanic and the rest were white. I extensively observed six of these individuals at their work sites. (The assembly workforce as a whole was fairly diverse; in the course of observing and informally interviewing others, I encountered significant numbers of Hispanics, Asian Americans, and African Americans. As noted elsewhere, one unanticipated finding was the number of white men working as temporary assemblers. The clericals that I interviewed and observed were all white women.) I informally interviewed ten additional temporary workers in various sites, closely observed twenty-one other workers while they were working, and observed, at more of a distance, hundreds of assembly workers.

4. See Schoch-Spana 1998 for a philosophical analysis of how company identification badges mark the boundaries between self and other.

5. See Kalleberg, Reskin, and Hudson 2000; Osterman 1999; and Polivka 1996 for extensive treatment of the different categories of temporary and contracted work.

6. See Chun forthcoming for a case study of temporary assemblers in a comparatively despotic work setting.

7. See Gonos 1997 for an incisive analysis of legal contestation over definitions of employer and employee, a contest played out in courts and formalized in policy and legislation, that gave employers the prerogative to deny temporary workers rights and advantages afforded to permanent workers. The ongoing legal battle between

Microsoft and contract programmers is one of the more visible examples of the problems companies face. DuRivage, Carré, and Tilly 1998 and Rogers 2000 discuss the complex problems related to organizing temps.

8. These are only a few dimensions along which the specific facts of the employment relationship are baffling to temps. Gonos (unpublished manuscript) notes that temps don't understand the calculations temp agencies make to determine their wages as a ratio of agencies' "mark-up" fees to companies that hire the temps; agencies also conceal the fees they're withholding in temps' paychecks by itemizing deductions "for transport, lunch, or safety equipment" (25–27). McAllister (1998:229) notes temps' confusion over whom they are supposed to report to on the shop or office floor.

9. When I interviewed higher-ranking managers and employees of one temporary agency that CompTech used, I frequently heard complaints that temps put CompTech as their place of employment and listed their CompTech supervisors' names for references when they applied for other jobs, for home mortgage loans, and auto loans. Obviously, having only a temporary job does not look well on a loan application.

10. Several temporaries with whom I spoke distinguished between good and bad temporary jobs as well.

11. As is typical of many organizations that use contingent workforces (Nollen and Axel 1998), CompTech did not keep data on the turnover or conversion rates of their temporary workers. My estimation is based on interviews with managers and converts.

12. As a general statement about the behavior of temporary workers anywhere, my claim is not especially surprising. If temporaries want a permanent job in a business, it is quite likely that they would display reliable, hard-working patterns of behavior to their employer. What is surprising, though, in the specific case of CompTech is that temps worked like valued workers for such long periods of time on a formally temporary basis.

Chapter Five. Structural Unemployment

1. For overviews of managerial/professional unemployment, displacement, and downsizing in the 1980s and 1990s, see Goffee and Scase 1992, Heckscher 1995, Newman 1988, and Osterman 1996. See my own book, *Managing in the Corporate Interest* (Smith 1990) for an account of managers' work when they are charged with initiating these changes.

2. Osterman's (1999) work on intermediary labor-market organizations is pertinent here. He calls for a new approach to addressing the problem of declining job tenure and increasing job mobility, with one pillar of his approach being to reorient organizations and agencies involved in career planning, job search and placement, and job retraining to enable American workers to make easier transitions in and out of jobs and in and out of unemployment.

3. For the case study of Experience Unlimited I collected four sets of data. First, I conducted formal, in-depth interviews with sixteen club members and two administrators. Second, I was a participant observer in the week-long training session that is mandatory for all new members. There, I informally spoke with many of the seventeen individuals who were my workshop mates. I attended three of the more specialized workshops: one on resume production, one on interviewing skills, and one on negotiating compensation. I attended six weekly general meetings. Finally, I made extensive use of the organization's educational, training, and promotional documents.

4. The major exception to the absence of sociological research on how people actively negotiate their entrance to jobs and labor markets is Granovetter's (1974/1995) study, *Getting a Job*. Granovetter examines the importance of networks in obtaining employment and looks at the dynamics of information flows: how individuals become aware of opportunities and how information that facilitates mobility is secured and disseminated. Because the subjects of his study were nearly all male, professional, and employed at the time of the study, and because they worked in professional settings with intact internal labor markets, his generalizations about looking for work are limited to one demographic population and one set of economic conditions.

Furthermore, Granovetter's work is more about behavior than action: that is, the monograph maps out what informants do—the methods they use, the contacts they take advantage of, the amount of time put into job searches—but doesn't explore in depth the meaning that informants give to their choices. Similarly, other social science and policy researchers who have examined the ways that people seek and enter jobs and occupational fields have focused primarily on *technique* rather than *process*—people's interpretation of how labor markets work and the series of activities through which individuals construct and reconstruct themselves, in which they actively appropriate certain organizational resources and even cultural themes, in order to prepare and qualify themselves for different locations in the formal employment system. The technical model of job search activities focuses, for example, on the *methods* of job search (i.e., the degree to which people are more likely to obtain jobs through personal networks, newspaper advertisements, agencies, or other impersonal means), the *frequency* with which people successfully use one method or another, the *intensity* of the search (measured by how actively the individual works to find a job) (Bradshaw 1973; Campbell and Rosenfeld 1985; Corcoran, Datcher, and Duncan 1980; Ports 1993), or the *optimality* of the job seeker's pursuit of employment (Lippman and McCall 1976).

The technical model describes how people obtain their jobs but doesn't touch on the circumstances under which individuals decide to pursue one method over another, or why it is that some methods work for some and not for others. This chapter examines action with reference to its meaning, to highlight ways in which strategies are strongly embedded in economic structures and cultural expectations.

5. There are other important cultural resources used by people who are un- or underemployed or seeking to make a career change. Widely read self-help books such as *What Color Is Your Parachute?* provide similar types of advice about and strategies for succeeding in the changing economy, as do proliferating web sites (see monster.com and aol.com/web centers/businesses and careers, for example).

6. Unless otherwise noted, all quotations from printed material are from documents prepared by EU participants, for the in-house use of members only. That is, they are original organizational artifacts. Much of the material was written several years before I appeared on the scene and was faithfully used as a set of guidelines for new members. I have assigned pseudonyms to all the members, including the one paid staff member, that I discuss and quote.

7. Of the seventeen people in my interview sample, nine were women and eight were men. Three were people of color (two African Americans and one Hispanic).

8. Because of time and logistical constraints I did not track down actual employment outcomes: whether people got a job, whether they got the job they wanted, and how they got it. This chapter concentrates on one organization's efforts to persuade the unemployed to adjust to the changing economy and the practices and discourses it used to do so.

9. The complicated realities that these unemployed face is revealed by news of a job fair held recently by the county of Sacramento. The larger Sacramento metropolitan area has experienced a prolonged economic boom in recent years. But, as is true around the nation, the boom conceals troubling labor-force trends such as patterns of multiple job holding, employment on a temporary and contingent basis, generalized job insecurity, and a proliferation of low-wage jobs that don't offer benefits. When Sacramento County sponsored its job fair, organizers were shocked when well over five thousand job seekers showed up. Fair organizers attributed the unanticipated turnout of people—ranging from "those wearing suits and ties (to) those wearing steel-toed construction boots," to accountants, nurses, janitors, forklift drivers, and computer technicians—to the appeal of secure, public-sector jobs in a context in which many people are underemployed, work odd jobs with low wages, or have limited benefits and deep concerns about job stability (Leavenworth 1999).

10. This language is mirrored at the Freeagent.com web site I mentioned in Chapter One. One topic that a site visitor can click is "Get Work: Xchange for free agents. A dynamic gig-matching tool finds you work with top companies."

11. There is a discrepancy between the eighty or so members at most meetings and the membership figure of two hundred, because on any given Monday morning, a certain number of members will be absent due to conflicting appointments, interviews, or illness. On top of that, there are always some members who simply don't attend on any given morning. Despite the mandate to attend meetings, some people don't. It is only when there is a persistent problem of nonattendance that members are warned about noncompliance.

12. I was granted permission to participate in one of the weeklong training sessions required of all new members. I attended the various workshops, chatted informally with fellow members of my cohort throughout that week, worked on my Thirty-Second Me along with everyone else, minimally participated in discussions about identification of career goals, the pitfalls of conducting job searches in one way rather than another, and dynamics of late twentieth-century jobs, careers, and labor markets. I declined the invitation to work on my "resume" with the group, both because my academic resume was so out of alignment with the resumes of my cohort members and because I felt uncomfortable taking up their valuable time with prolonged discussion of the peculiar dynamics of academic training, job searching, and employment. I also declined to be videotaped doing a mock job interview.

13. Karen and the workshop facilitators use mythical statistics as well. In the general meeting and in specialized workshops, for example, Dirk's story was told repeatedly. According to them, Dirk had successfully used the compensation negotiation skills he learned at EU. The first time I heard the story it was related by Dirk himself, at a general meeting. He reported, to the attending membership, that he had been able to increase his annual starting salary by $13,000 as a result of taking the compensation negotiation workshop. Dirk's success was reported in two other settings: first, in the introductory workshop I attended with my cohort at the beginning of my weeklong training, the facilitator reported that Dirk had managed to increase his starting package by $15,000, and in a workshop later in the week, we heard that Dirk had succeeded in raising his package by $20,000. Certain facts and stories obviously resonated strongly with people, and these were appropriated by participants as rallying points to mobilize others to find jobs.

14. In one of the workshops Anthony attended he had been advised to drop either the engineering or the business degree off his resume, depending on the job he was applying for.

15. This scenario or negative stereotype is comically depicted in the film *Mister Mom,* in which "Dad" is forced to become the full-time head of household after he is laid off by an auto firm in Detroit. Floundering because his professional identity has been devastated, Dad initially lets his beard grow out, gains weight, loses control over household appliances, develops an addiction for daytime soaps and beer drinking, and cares for his three children with rather unconventional methods, such as grilling cheese sandwiches with an iron, drying baby bottoms in public restrooms with the electric blow-dryer, and using a garden rake to "disappear" their clothes and toys under their beds to create an illusion of order and hygiene. When he snaps out of it, he shaves, pulls out his professional clothes to go job hunting, and discontinues daily poker games with other stay-at-home parents (all moms).

16. Arlie Hochschild (1983) and Robin Leidner (1993) have written two of the definitive studies of emotion work that employees are pushed to do on the job. Their thesis is that in contemporary service occupations, workers not only rationalize their physical tasks and interactions but are called on to reach inside themselves and rationalize their feelings and emotions. The goal of emotion work is to enable workers to adapt to unpredictable and often unpleasant service interactions, to give workers a way to align their feelings with external organizational circumstances. See also *Annals* 1999. "Positive Mental Attitude" training, as outlined by Leidner (1993), is based on the same philosophy as that imparted to EU participants.

17. Newman beautifully explores these contradictions in her pathbreaking book, *Falling from Grace* (1988), particularly in her analysis of displaced managers.

Chapter Six. Negotiating Uncertainty

1. *Microserfs* (1995), by Douglas Coupland, is a must read on the microserfs who toil and labor at Microsoft.

2. See the *New York Times*: July 5, 1999 (on Boeing); August 16, 1999 (on GM); December 26, 1999 (on Kaiser); and January 19, 2000 (on Reuters).

References

Acker, J. 1990. "Hierarchies, Jobs, Bodies: A Theory of Gendered Organizations." *Gender and Society* 4 (2):139–58.

AFL-CIO Special Report. 1999. *High Hopes, Little Trust: A Study of Young Workers and Their Ups and Downs in the New Economy.* Washington, D.C.: AFL-CIO.

Annals. 1999. *Annals of the American Academy of Political and Social Science.* Special editors: R. Steinberg, and D. Figart. Vol. 561 (January).

Appelbaum, E., T. Bailey, P. Berg, and A. Kalleberg. 2000. *Manufacturing Advantage: Why High-Performance Work Systems Pay Off.* Ithaca, N.Y.: Cornell University Press/ILR Press.

Appelbaum, E., and R. Batt. 1994. *The New American Workplace: Transforming Work Systems in the United States.* Ithaca, N.Y.: Cornell University Press/ILR Press.

Baker, T., and H. Aldrich. 1996. "Prometheus Stretches: Building Identity and Cumulative Knowledge in Multi-employer Careers." In *Boundaryless Careers: Employment in the New Organizational Era,* ed. M. Arthur, and D. Rousseau. New York: Oxford University Press:132–49.

Barker, J. 1993. "Tightening the Iron Cage: Concertive Control in Self-Managing Teams." *Administrative Science Quarterly* 38 (3):408–37.

Barker, K., and K. Christensen, eds. 1998. *Contingent Work: American Employment Relations in Transition.* Ithaca, N.Y.: Cornell University Press/ILR Press.

Barley, S., and G. Kunda. 1992. "Design and Devotion: Surges of Rational and Normative Ideologies of Control in Managerial Discourse." *Administrative Science Quarterly* 37 (3):363–99.

Batt, R. 1999. "Work Organization, Technology, and Performance in Customer Service and Sales." *Industrial and Labor Relations Review* 52 (4):539–64.

Bellas, C. 1972. *Industrial Democracy and the Worker-owned Firm: A Study of Twenty-one Plywood Companies in the Pacific Northwest.* New York: Praeger Press.

Berman, K. 1967. *Worker-owned Plywood Companies: An Economic Analysis.* Pullman: Washington State University Press.

Bernhardt, A., M. Morris, and M. Handcock. 1995. "Women's Gains or Men's Losses? A Closer Look at the Shrinking Gender Gap in Earnings." *American Journal of Sociology* 101 (2):302–28.

Bernstein, P. 1976. *Workplace Democratization: Its Internal Dynamics.* Comparative Administration Research Institute: Kent State University Press.

———. 1997. *American Work Values: Their Origin and Development.* New York: State University of New York Press.

Bluestone, B., and I. Bluestone. 1992. *Negotiating the Future: A Labor Perspective on American Business.* New York: Basic Books.

Bluestone, B., and B. Harrison. 1982. *The Deindustrialization of America: Plant Closings, Community Abandonment, and the Dismantling of Basic Industry.* New York: Basic Books.

Bourdieu, P. 1977a. "Cultural Reproduction and Social Reproduction." In *Power and Ideology in Education*, ed. J. Karabel, and A. Halsey. New York: Oxford University Press:487–511.

———. 1977b. *Outline of a Theory of Practice.* Cambridge: Cambridge University Press.

Bourgois, P. 1995. *In Search of Respect: Selling Crack in El Barrio.* Cambridge: Cambridge University Press.

Bradshaw, T. 1973. "Jobseeking Methods Used by Unemployed Workers." *Monthly Labor Review* 96 (2):35–40.

Brodsky, M. 1994. "Labor Market Flexibility: A Changing International Perspective." *Monthly Labor Review* 117 (11):53–60.

Bronfenbrenner, K., S. Friedman, R. Hurd, R. Oswald, and R. Seeber. 1998. *Organizing to Win: New Research on Union Strategies.* Ithaca, N.Y.: Cornell University Press/ILR Press.

Burawoy, M. 1979. *Manufacturing Consent: Changes in the Labor Process under Monopoly Capitalism.* Chicago: University of Chicago Press.

———. 1985. *The Politics of Production.* London: Verso Books.

Caldwell, D., and C. O'Reilly. 1982. "Boundary Spanning and Individual Performance: The Impact of Self-monitoring." *Journal of Applied Psychology* 67 (1):124–27.

Callaghan, P., and H. Hartmann. 1991. *Contingent Work: A Chart Book on Part-time and Temporary Employment.* Washington, D.C.: Institute for Women's Policy Research/Economic Policy Institute.

Campbell, K., and R. Rosenfeld. 1985. "Job Search and Job Mobility: Sex and Race Differences." *Research in the Sociology of Work* 3:147–74.

Capelli, P., L. Bassi, H. Katz, D. Knoke, P. Osterman, and M. Useem. 1997. *Change at Work.* New York: Oxford University Press.

Carnoy, M., M. Castells, and C. Benner. 1997. "Labour Markets and Employment Practices in the Age of Flexibility: A Case Study of Silicon Valley." *International Labour Review* 136 (1):27–48.

Carré, F., V. duRivage, and C. Tilly. 1995. "Piecing Together the Fragmented Workplace: Unions and Public Policy on Flexible Employment." In *Unions and Public Policy*, ed. L. Flood. Westport, Conn.: Greenwood Press:13–37.

Carroll, M. 1995. *Community and the Northwestern Logger: Continuities and Changes in the Era of the Spotted Owl.* Boulder, Colo.: Westview Press.

Carroll, M., C. McKetta, K. Blatner, and C. Schallau. 1999. "A Response to 'Forty Years of Spotted Owls.'" *Sociological Perspectives* 42 (2):325–33.

Chun, J. Forthcoming. "Flexible Despotisms: The Intensification of Uncertainty and Insecurity in the Lives of High-Tech Assembly Workers in the Silicon Valley." In *The Critical Study of Work: Labor, Technology, and Global Production*, ed. R. Baldoz, C. Koeber, and P. Kraft. Philadelphia: Temple University Press.

Clinton, A. 1997. "Flexible Labor: Restructuring the American Work Force." *Monthly Labor Review* 120 (8):3–17.

Cohen, Y., and Y. Haberfeld. 1993. "Temporary Help Service Workers: Employment Characteristics and Wage Determination." *Industrial Relations* 32 (2):272–87.

Cole, R. 1979. *Work, Mobility, and Participation: A Comparative Study of American and Japanese Industry.* Berkeley: University of California Press.

———. 1989. *Strategies for Learning: Small-Group Activities in American, Japanese, and Swedish Industry.* Berkeley: University of California Press.

Cooke, W. 1989. "Improving Productivity and Quality Through Collaboration." *Industrial Relations* 28 (2):299–319.

Corcoran, M., L. Datcher, and G. Duncan. 1980. "Most Workers Find Jobs Through Word of Mouth." *Monthly Labor Review* 103 (8):33–35.

Coupland, D. 1995. *Microserfs.* New York: Regan Books.

Craypo, C., and B. Nissen, eds. 1993. *Grand Designs: The Impact of Corporate Strategies on Workers, Unions, and Communities.* Ithaca, N.Y.: Cornell University Press/ILR Press.

Crouse, K. 1998. "Learning the New Rules of Work: Downsized Managers and the Breakdown of the Social Contract." Presented at the Annual Meetings of the American Sociological Association, San Francisco.

DiTomaso, N. 1996. "The Loose Coupling of Jobs: The Subcontracting of Everyone." Presented at the Annual Meetings of the American Sociological Association, New York.

Doeringer, P., K. Christensen, P. Flynn, D. Hall, and H. Katz, et al. 1991. *Turbulence in the American Workplace.* New York: Oxford University Press.

Doeringer, P., and M. Piore. 1971. *Internal Labor Markets and Manpower Analysis.* Lexington, Mass.: D. C. Heath.

Dudley, K. 1994. *The End of the Line: Lost Jobs, New Lives in Postindustrial America.* Chicago: University of Chicago Press.

DuRivage, V., F. Carré, and C. Tilly. 1998. "Making Labor Law Work for Part-time and Contingent Workers." In *Contingent Work: American Employment Relations in Transition,* ed. K. Barker, and K. Christensen. Ithaca, N.Y.: Cornell University Press/ILR Press:263–80.

Edwards, R. 1979. *Contested Terrain.* New York: Basic Books.

Etzioni, A. 1961. "Compliance Structures." In *A Sociological Reader on Complex Organizations,* ed. A. Etzioni, and E. Lehman. New York: Holt, Rinehart and Winston:87–100.

Faludi, S. 1999. *Stiffed: The Betrayal of the American Man.* New York: William Morris.

Fantasia, R., D. Clawson, and G. Graham. 1988. "A Critical View of Worker Participation in American Industry." *Work and Occupations* 15 (4):468–88.

Fine, M. 1991. *Framing Dropouts: Notes on the Politics of an Urban High School.* Albany: State University of New York Press.

Fine, M., L. Weis, J. Addelston, and J. Marusza. 1997. "(in)Secure Times: Constructing White Working-Class Masculinities in the Late Twentieth Century." *Gender and Society* 11 (1):52–68.

Ford, S. 1996. *Blacked Out: Dilemmas of Race, Identity, and Success at Capital High.* Chicago: University of Chicago Press.

Franklin, J. 1995. "Industry Output and Employment Projections to 2005." *Monthly Labor Review* 118 (11):45–59.

———. 1997. "Industry Output and Employment Projections to 2006." *Monthly Labor Review* 120 (11):39–57.

Frenkel, S., M. Korczynski, K. Shire, and M. Tam. 1999. *On the Front Line: Organization of Work in the Information Economy.* Ithaca, N.Y.: Cornell University Press/ILR Press.

Freudenburg, W., L. Wilson, and D. O'Leary. 1998. "Forty Years of Spotted Owls? A Longitudinal Analysis of Logging-Industry Job Losses." *Sociological Perspectives* 41 (1):1–16.

Freudenburg, W., D. O'Leary, and D. Wilson. 1999. "Spotting the Myths About Spotted Owls: Claims of Causality, Burdens of Proof, and the 'Cause' of Rain in Seattle." *Sociological Perspectives* 42 (2):335–54.

Fuller, L., and V. Smith. 1990. "Consumers' Reports: Management by Customers in a Changing Economy." *Work, Employment, and Society* 5:1–16.

Ginsberg, S. 1997. "Necessity, Uncertainty Drive Many to Take Multiple Jobs." *Washington Post,* November 9, p. H5.

Goffe, R., and R. Scase. 1992. "Organizational Change and the Corporate Career: The Restructuring of Managers' Job Aspirations." *Human Relations* 45 (4):363–85.

Gonos, G. 1997. "The Contest over 'Employer' Status in the Postwar United States: The Case of Temporary Help Firms." *Law and Society Review* 31 (1):81–110.

———. Unpublished manuscript. "No fees! The Miracle of the Postmodern Temporary Help and Staffing Agency." Potsdam: State University of New York-Potsdam, Department of Economics/Employment Relations.

Gottfried, H. 1991. "Mechanisms of Control in the Temporary Help Service Industry." *Sociological Forum* 6 (4):699–713.

Gottfried, H., and L. Graham. 1993. "Constructing Difference: The Making of Gendered Subcultures in a Japanese Automobile Assembly Plant." *Sociology* 27 (4):611–28.

Gouldner, A. 1954. *Patterns of Industrial Bureaucracy.* New York: Free Press.

Graham, L. 1995. *On the Line at Subaru-Isuzu: The Japanese Model and the American Worker.* Ithaca, N.Y.: Cornell University Press/ILR Press.

Granovetter, M. 1974/1995. *Getting a Job: A Study of Contacts and Careers.* Chicago: University of Chicago Press.

Grantham, C. 2000. *The Future of Work: The Promise of the New Digital Work Society.* New York: McGraw-Hill/Commerce Net Press.

Greber, B. 1993. "Impacts of Technological Change on Employment in the Timber Industries of the Pacific Northwest." *Western Journal of Applied Forestry* 8 (1):34-37.

Greenberg, E. 1984. "Producer Cooperatives and Democratic Theory: The Case of the Plywood Firms." In *Worker Cooperatives in America*, ed. R. Jackall, and H. Levin. Berkeley: University of California Press:171–214.

Grenier, G. 1988. *Inhuman Relations: Quality Circles and Anti-Unionism in American Industry*. Philadelphia: Temple University Press.

Gunn, C. 1984. "Hoedads Co-op: Democracy and Cooperation at Work." In *Worker Cooperatives in America*, ed. R. Jackall, and H. Levin. Berkeley: University of California Press:141–70.

———. 1992. "Plywood Cooperatives in the United States: An Endangered Species." *Economic and Industrial Democracy* 13 (4):525–34.

Halaby, C. 1988. "Action and Information in the Job Mobility Process: The Search Decision." *American Sociological Review* 53 (1):9–25.

Harrison, B. 1994. *Lean and Mean: The Changing Landscape of Corporate Power in the Age of Flexibility*. New York: Basic Books.

Harrison, B., and B. Bluestone. 1988. *The Great U-Turn: Corporate Restructuring and the Polarizing of America*. New York: Basic Books.

Hartzall, H. 1987. *Birth of a Cooperative: Hoedads, Inc., A Worker-Owned Forest Labor Cooperative*. Eugene, Ore.: Hulogos'i/Yes Press.

Havlovic, S. 1991. "Quality of Work Life and Human Resource Outcomes." *Industrial Relations* 30 (3):469–79.

Heckscher, C. 1988. *The New Unionism: Employee Involvement in the Changing Corporation*. New York: Basic Books.

———. 1995. *White-Collar Blues: Management Loyalties in an Age of Corporate Restructuring*. New York: Basic Books.

Henson, K. 1996. *Just a Temp*. Philadelphia: Temple University Press.

Herzenberg, S., J. Alic, and H. Wial. 1998. *New Rules for a New Economy: Employment and Opportunity in Postindustrial America*. Ithaca, N.Y.: Cornell University Press/ILR Press.

Hibbard, M., and J. Elias. 1993. "The Failure of Sustained-yield Forestry and the Decline of the Flannel-shirt Frontier." In *Forgotten Places: Uneven Development in Rural America*, ed. T. Lyson, and W. Falk. Kansas: University of Kansas Press:195–217.

Hirsch, P., and M. Shanley. 1996. "The Rhetoric of 'Boundaryless': How the Newly Empowered and Fully Networked Managerial Class of Professionals Bought into and Self-managed its Own Marginalization." In *Boundaryless Careers: Employment in the New*

Organizational Era, ed. M. Arthur, and D. Rousseau. New York: Oxford University Press:218–33.

Hochschild, A. 1983. *The Managed Heart*. Berkeley: University of California Press.

——. 1989. *The Second Shift.* New York: Viking Press.

Hodson, R. 1991. "The Active Worker: Compliance and Autonomy at the Workplace." *Journal of Contemporary Ethnography* 20 (1):47–78.

——. 1996. "Dignity in the Workplace under Participative Management: Alienation and Freedom Revisited." *American Sociological Review* 61 (5):719–38.

——. 2000. *Working with Dignity*. Cambridge University Press.

Hoerr, J. 1988. *And the Wolf Finally Came: The Decline of the American Steel Industry*. Pittsburgh: University of Pittsburgh Press.

Holzer, H. 1998. "Employer Skill Demands and Labor Market Outcomes of Blacks and Women." *Industrial and Labor Relations Review* 52 (1):82–98.

Howe, W. 1986. "The Business Services Industry Sets Pace in Employment Growth." *Monthly Labor Review* 109 (4):29–36.

Ilg, R., and A. Clinton. 1998. "Strong Job Growth Continues, Unemployment Declines in 1997." *Monthly Labor Review* 121 (2):48–68.

Indergaard, M. 1999. "Retrainers as Labor Market Brokers: Constructing Networks and Narratives in the Detroit Area." *Social Problems* 46 (1):67–87.

Jackall, R. 1988. *Moral Mazes*. Berkeley: University of California Press.

Jacoby, S. 1997. *Modern Manors: Welfare Capitalism since the New Deal*. Princeton: Princeton University Press.

Juravich, T. 1985. *Chaos on the Shopfloor*. Philadelphia: Temple University Press.

Kalleberg, A., D. Knoke, P. Marsden, and J. Spaeth, eds. 1996. *Organizations in America: Analyzing Their Structures and Human Resource Practices*. Thousand Oaks, Calif.: Sage Publications.

Kalleberg, A., P. Marsden, D. Knoke, and J. Spaeth. 1996. "Formalizing the Employment Relation: Internal Labor Markets and Dispute Resolution Procedures." In *Organizations in America*, ed. A. Kalleberg, D. Knoke, P. Marsden, and J. Spaeth. Thousand Oaks, Calif.: Sage Publications:87–112.

Kalleberg, A., and J. Moody. 1996. "Human Resource Management and Organizational Performance." In *Organizations in America*, ed. A. Kalleberg, D. Knoke, P. Marsden, and J. Spaeth. Thousand Oaks, Calif.: Sage Publications:113–29.

Kalleberg, A., B. Reskin, and K. Hudson. 2000. "Bad Jobs in America: Standard and Nonstandard Employment Relations and Job Quality in the United States." *American Sociological Review* 65 (2):256–78.

Kanter, R. M. 1977/1993. *Men and Women of the Corporation*. New York: Basic Books.

Kennelly, I. 1999. " 'That Single-Mother Element': How White Employers Typify Black Women." *Gender and Society* 13 (2):168–92.

Kimle, P., and M. Damhorst. 1997. "A Grounded Theory Model of the Ideal Business Image for Women." *Symbolic Interaction* 20 (1):45–68.

Kochan, T., H. Katz, and N. Mower. 1984. *Worker Participation and American Unions*. Kalamazoo, Mich.: W. E. Upjohn Institute for Employment Research.

Kondo, D. 1990. *Crafting Selves: Power, Gender, and Discourses of Identity in a Japanese Workplace*. Chicago: University of Chicago Press.

Kunda, G. 1992. *Engineering Culture: Control and Commitment in a High-Tech Corporation*. Philadelphia: Temple University Press.

Lamont, M., and A. Lareau. 1988. "Cultural Capital: Allusions, Gaps, and Glissandos in Recent Theoretical Developments." *Sociological Theory* 6:153–68.

Lamphere, L., and G. Grenier. 1994. "Women, Unions, and Participative Management: Organizing in the Sunbelt." In *Critical Studies in Organization and Bureaucracy*, ed. F. Fischer, and C. Sirianni. Philadelphia: Temple University Press:144–74.

Lareau, A., and E. Horvat. 1999. "Moments of Social Inclusion and Exclusion: Race, Class, and Cultural Capital in Family-School Relationships." *Sociology of Education* 72:37–53.

Leavenworth, S. 1999. "County Job Fair Draws Throng: Excitement over 2,400 Vacancies." *Sacramento Bee*, October 3:B1, B5.

Leidner, R. 1993. *Fast Food/Fast Talk: Service Work and the Routinization of Everyday Life*. Berkeley: University of California Press.

———. 1999. "Emotional Labor in Service Work." *Annals* 561, ed. R. Steinberg, and D. Figart:81–95.

Lippmann, S., and J. McCall. 1976. "The Economics of Job Search: A Survey: Part I." *Economic Inquiry* 14:155–89.

Lohr, S. 1996. "Though Upbeat on Economy, People Still Fear for Their Jobs." *New York Times*, December 29: A1.

Lynd, S. 1982. *The Fight against Shutdowns: Youngstown's Steel Mill Closings*. San Pedro, Calif.: Singlejack Books.

Macdonald, C., and C. Sirianni, eds. 1996. *Working in the Service Society.* Philadelphia: Temple University Press.

MacLeod, J. 1995. *Ain't No Makin' It: Aspirations and Attainment in a Low-Income Neighborhood.* Boulder, Colo.: Westview Press.

Margulies, N., and S. Black. 1987. "Perspectives on the Implementation of Participative Approaches." *Human Resource Management* 26 (3):385–412.

Marsden, P., C. Cook, and A. Kalleberg. 1996. "Bureaucratic Structures for Coordination and Control." In *Organizations in America*, ed. A. Kalleberg, D. Knoke, P. Marsden, and J. Spaeth. Thousand Oaks, Calif.: Sage Publications:69–86.

McAllister, J. 1998. "Sisyphus at Work in the Warehouse: Temporary Employment in Greenville, South Carolina." In *Contingent Work: American Employment Relations in Transition*, ed. K. Barker, and K. Christensen. Ithaca, N.Y.: Cornell University Press/ILR Press:221–42.

Milkman, R. 1997. *Farewell to the Factory: Auto Workers in the Late Twentieth Century.* Berkeley: University of California Press.

Mishel, L., J. Bernstein, and J. Schmitt. 1999. *The State of Working America: 1998–99.* Ithaca, N.Y.: Cornell University Press/ILR Press.

Moddell, J., and C. Brodsky. 1998. *A Town Without Steel: Envisioning Homestead.* Pittsburgh: University of Pittsburgh Press.

Morris, M., and B. Western. 1999. "Inequality in Earnings at the Close of the Twentieth Century." *Annual Review of Sociology* 25:623–57.

Moss, P., and C. Tilly. 1996. " 'Soft' Skills and Race: An Investigation of Black Men's Employment Problems." *Work and Occupations* 23 (3):252–76.

Neckerman, K., and J. Kirschenman. 1991. "Hiring Strategies, Racial Bias, and Inner-City Workers." *Social Problems* 38 (4):801–15.

Neumark, D., ed. 2000. *On the Job: Is Long-Term Employment a Thing of the Past?* New York: Russell Sage Foundation.

Newman, K. 1988. *Falling from Grace: The Experience of Downward Mobility in the American Middle Class.* New York: Vintage Books.

———. 1999. *No Shame in My Game: The Working Poor in the Inner City.* New York: Alfred Knopf and Russell Sage Foundation.

New York Times, 7/5/99. "Boeing's Unions Are Worried about Job Security." 30, News, Analysis and Commentary.

New York Times, 8/16/99. "G.M. Expects Tough Stance in Union Talks." C2, column 4.

New York Times, 12/26/99. "A 15-month Labor Dispute Turns into a War of Attrition." A26, column 1.

New York Times, 1/19/00. "Metro Business: Sickout Hits Reuters as Talks Drag On." B8, column 5.

New York Times. 2000. Special Issue of *The New York Times Magazine.* "The Liberated, Exploited, Pampered, Frazzled, Uneasy New American Worker." March 5.

Nollen, A., and H. Axel. 1998. "Benefits and Costs to Employers." In *Contingent Work: American Employment Relations,* ed. K. Barker, and K. Christensen. Ithaca, N.Y.: Cornell University Press/ILR Press: 126–43.

Ofstead, C. 1999. "Temporary Help Firms as Entrepreneurial Actors." *Sociological Forum* 14 (2):273–94.

O'Reilly, J. 1994. *Banking on Flexibility.* Brookfield, Vt.: Avebury Press.

Orr, J. 1996. *Talking about Machines.* Ithaca, N.Y.: Cornell University Press/ILR Press.

Osterman, P. 1994. "How Common Is Workplace Transformation and Who Adopts it?" *Industrial Labor Relations Review* 47 (2):173–88.

———, ed. 1996. *Broken Ladders: Managerial Careers in the New Economy.* New York: Oxford University Press.

———. 1999. *Securing Prosperity.* Princeton: Princeton University Press.

Parker, M., and J. Slaughter. 1988. *Choosing Sides: Unions and the Team Concept.* Boston: South End Press.

Parker, R. 1994. *Flesh Peddlers and Warm Bodies: The Temporary Help Industry and Its Workers.* New Brunswick, N.J.: Rutgers University Press.

Perrucci, C., R. Perrucci, D. Targ, and H. Targ. 1988. *Plant Closings: International Context and Social Costs.* New York: Aldine de Gruyter.

Peterson, K. 1987. *Company Town: Potlatch, Idaho and the Potlatch Lumber Company.* Pullman: Washington State University Press.

Pfeffer, J., and J. Baron. 1988. "Taking the Workers Back Out: Recent Trends in the Structuring of Employment." *Research in Organizational Behavior* 10:257–303.

Pierce, J. 1995. *Gender Trials.* Berkeley: University of California Press.

Piore, M., and C. Sabel. 1984. *The Second Industrial Divide: Possibilities for Prosperity.* New York: Basic Books.

Polivka, A. 1996. "Contingent and Alternative Work Arrangements, Defined." *Monthly Labor Review* 119 (10):3–21.

Pollert, A. 1988. "The 'Flexible Firm': Fixation or Fact?" *Work, Employment, and Society* 2 (3):281–316.

Ports, M. 1993. "Trends in Job Search Method, 1970–1992." *Monthly Labor Review* 116 (10):63–67.

Powers, B. Forthcoming. *Academic Hoop Dreams: The Making of Marginality in an Urban High School.* New Haven, Conn.: Yale University Press.

Prechel, H. 1994. "Economic Crisis and the Centralization of Control over the Managerial Process." *American Sociological Review* 59 (5): 723–45.

Reich, R. 1992. *The Work of Nations.* New York: Vintage Books.

Reinemer, M. 1995. "Work Happy (Many American Workers Like Their Job)." *American Demographics* 17 (7):26–45.

Reskin, B., and P. Roos. 1990. *Job Queues, Gender Queues.* Philadelphia: Temple University Press.

Robbins, W. 1988. *Hard Times in Paradise: Coos Bay, Oregon, 1850–1986.* Seattle: University of Washington Press.

Rogers, J. K. 2000. *Temps: The Many Faces of the Changing Workplace.* Ithaca, N.Y.: Cornell University Press/ILR Press.

Rogers, J. K., and M. Barrett. N/D. "Barriers and Building Blocks: Organizing Temporary Workers in a Contingent Economy." State College: Department of Industrial and Labor Relations, Pennsylvania State University.

Sabel, C. 1991. "Moebius-strip Organizations and Open Labor Markets: Some Consequences of the Reintegration of Conception and Execution in a Volatile Economy." In *Social Theory for a Changing Society,* ed. P. Bourdieu, and J. Coleman. Boulder, Colo.: Westview Press: 23–54.

Safizadeh, M. 1991. "The Case of Workgroups in Manufacturing Operations." *California Management Review* 33 (4):61–82.

Satschell, M. 1990. "The Endangered Logger: Big Business and a Little Bird Threaten a Northwest Way of Life." *U.S. News and World Report* 108 (25):27–29.

Schoch-Spana, M. 1998. "National Security and Radiological Control: Worker Discipline in the Nuclear Weapons Complex." In *More Than Class: Studying Power in U.S. Workplaces,* ed. A. Kingsolver. Albany: State University of New York Press:21–53.

Schwochau, S., J. Delaney, P. Jarley, and J. Fiorito. 1997. "Employee Participation and Assessments of Support for Organizational Policy Changes." *Journal of Labor Research* 18 (3):379–400.

Scott, W. 1998. *Organizations: Rational, Natural, and Open.* Upper Saddle River, New Jersey: Prentice-Hall/Simon and Schuster.

Sennett, R. 1998. *The Corrosion of Character: The Personal Consequences of Work in the New Capitalism.* New York: W. W. Norton and Co.

Serrin, W. 1992. *Homestead: The Glory and Tragedy of an American Steel Town.* New York: Times Books/Random House.

Sewell, G., and B. Wilkinson. 1992. "Someone to Watch over Me: Surveillance, Discipline, and the Just-in-Time Labor Process." *Sociology* 26 (2): 271–89.

Shaiken, H., S. Herzenberg, and S. Kuhn. 1986. "The Work Process under More Flexible Production." *Industrial Relations* 25 (2):167–83.

Sillince, J., G. Sykes, and D. Singh. 1996. "Implementation, Problems, Success, and Longevity of Quality Circle Programmes: A Study of 95 UK Organizations." *International Journal of Operations and Production Management* 16 (4):88–111.

Sinclair, A. 1992. "The Tyranny of a Team Ideology." *Organization Studies* 13 (4):611–26.

Smith, V. 1990. *Managing in the Corporate Interest: Control and Resistance in an American Bank.* Berkeley: University of California Press.

———. 1993. "Flexibility in Work and Employment: The Impact on Women." *Research in the Sociology of Organizations* 11:195–216.

———. 1994. "Institutionalizing Flexibility in a Service Firm: Multiple Contingencies and Hidden Hierarchies." *Work and Occupations* 21 (3):284–307.

———. 1994. "Braverman's Legacy: The Labor Process Tradition at 20." *Work and Occupations* 21 (4):403–21.

———. 1997. "New Forms of Work Organization." *Annual Review of Sociology* 23:315–39.

———. 1998. "The Fractured World of the Temporary Worker." *Social Problems* 45 (4):411-30.

———. Forthcoming A. "Ethnographies of Work and the Work of Ethnographers." *Handbook of Ethnography*, ed. P. Atkinson, A. Coffey, S. Delamont, L. Lofland, and J. Lofland. London: Sage Publications.

———. Forthcoming B. "Teamwork vs. Tempwork: Managers and the Dualisms of Workplace Restructuring." In *Working in Restructured Workplaces: New Directions for the Sociology of Work*, ed. K. Campbell, D. Cornfield, and H. McCammon. Thousand Oaks, Calif.: Sage Publications.

Spalter-Roth, R., and C. Deitch. 1999. "I Don't Feel Right Sized: I Feel Out-of-Work Sized: Gender, Race, and Ethnicity and the Unequal Costs of Displacement." *Gender and Society* 26 (4):446–82.

Stacey, J. 1990. *Brave New Families.* New York: Basic Books.

Strohschein, L. 1998. "It's the Little Things That Get You: Strategies of Coping in a Self-Help Group for Unemployed Professionals." Presented at the 1998 Annual Meetings of the Society for the Study of Social Problems, San Francisco.

Swidler, A. 1986. "Culture in Action: Symbols and Strategies." *American Sociological Review* 51 (2):273–86.

Tannen, D. 1994. *Talking from 9–5: Women and Men in the Workplace, Language, Sex and Power.* New York: Avon Books.

Thomas, R. 1994. *What Machines Can't Do: Politics and Technology in the Industrial Enterprise.* Berkeley: University of California Press.

Tilly, C. 1991. "Reasons for the Continuing Growth of Part-time Employment." *Monthly Labor Review* 114 (3):10–18.

Torres, L. 1996. "When Weak Ties Fail: Shame, Reciprocity, and Unemployed Professionals." Presented at the 1996 Annual Meetings of the Pacific Sociological Association, Seattle.

Trice, H., and J. Beyer. 1993. *The Cultures of Work Organizations.* Englewood Cliffs, N.J.: Prentice Hall.

Useem, M. 1996. *Investor Capitalism: How Money Managers are Changing the Face of Corporate America.* New York: Basic Books.

Vallas, S. 1999. "Rethinking Post-Fordism: The Meaning of Workplace Flexibility." *Sociological Theory* 17 (1):68–101.

Vallas, S., and J. Beck. 1996. "The Transformation of Work Revisited: The Limits of Flexibility in American Manufacturing." *Social Problems* 43 (3):339–61.

Varano, C. 1999. *Forced Choices: Class, Community, and Worker Ownership.* New York: State University of New York Press.

Wallulis, J. 1998. *The New Insecurity: The End of the Standard Job and Family.* New York: State University of New York Press.

Walton, R., and P. Lawrence. 1985. *Human Resources Management: Trends and Challenges.* Boston: Harvard Business School Press.

Weber, M. 1904/1958. *The Protestant Ethic and the Spirit of Capitalism.* New York: Charles Scribner's Sons.

Wells, Donald. 1987. *Empty Promises: Quality of Working Life Programs and the Labor Movement.* New York: Monthly Review Press.

Wharton, A., and R. Erickson. 1993. "Managing Emotions on the Job and at Home: Understanding the Consequences of Multiple Emotional Roles." *Academy of Management Review* 18 (3):457–86.

Willis, P. 1977. *Learning to Labor.* Aldershot: Gower.

Wilson, W. J. 1996. *When Work Disappears: The World of the New Urban Poor.* New York: New Vintage Books.

Zuboff, S. 1988. *In the Age of the Smart Machine: The Future of Work and Power.* New York: Basic Books.

Index